RUDIMENTS OF MUSIC

Robert W. Ottman / Frank Mainous
School of Music
North Texas State University

PRENTICE-HALL, INC., Englewood Cliffs, New Jersey

© 1970 by PRENTICE-HALL, INC.
Englewood Cliffs, New Jersey

All rights reserved. No part of this book may be reproduced in any form or by any means without permission in writing from the publisher.

Printed in the United States of America

13-783662-7

Library of Congress Catalog Card No.: 71-79834

Current printing (last digit):

17   16   15   14   13

PRENTICE-HALL INTERNATIONAL, INC., London
PRENTICE-HALL OF AUSTRALIA, PTY. LTD., Sydney
PRENTICE-HALL OF CANADA, LTD., Toronto
PRENTICE-HALL OF INDIA PRIVATE LTD., New Delhi
PRENTICE-HALL OF JAPAN, INC., Tokyo

PREFACE

Almost everybody can hum, whistle, or sing a good tune after hearing it a few times. In this sense, almost every person has at least a minimum of musical talent. A smaller number of fortunate people can actually go to an instrument, such as the piano or clarinet or violin, and "play by ear" with various degrees of success, even with no formal music instruction.

These activities are the simplest accomplishments in musical performance. Most of you who are reading this have found musical performance so enjoyable that you have enlisted the aid of some one more experienced than yourself in the expectation of heightening your enjoyment even more.

If you are one of these, you have seen that your teacher helps you learn a new piece of music in one or more ways. In the simplest way, your teacher sings, or plays on an instrument, the piece you are to learn, and you simply imitate him. If you play an instrument, your teacher has probably provided you with a list of fingerings or a chart so that when you look at a note on the staff, you will know what key to depress, or the approximate location of the finger on a string, or the position of the trombone slide, and so forth.

Finally, your instructor will begin to teach you some of the *theory* of music even if only such simple theory as note values, how to count time, the names of lines and spaces, etc.; he may also suggest that you take a course in *music theory*. He does this in order that you can become literate in the art of music, thereby increasing your skill in reading and performing music and ultimately enhancing your enjoyment of music to the fullest extent.

Music theory is a study of the materials composers use when they write music. We might say that music theory covers the technical aspects of music. But don't let the word "technical" alarm you. A recipe for chocolate cake is one of the technical aspects of baking, and quite necessary if a delicious product is to be expected. We can carry the analogy further: many people cook adequately without written recipes, just as many people play music by ear with pleasant results. But the cook who studies food materials and their combinations (the "theory" of the culinary arts) will ultimately become a better cook and provide many more and varied culinary treats than when he started his study. Likewise, the musician, no matter what his native untutored performance abilities, will find greater accomplishments available to him as he expands his knowledge of materials and devices used to create a musical composition.

This book is for beginners in music theory; the material covered in this volume is often known under such titles as "Elements of Music," "Rudiments of Music," or "Basic Principles of Music," and precedes more advanced theoretical studies such as Harmony, Counterpoint, and Orchestration. In this book, we will study the most elementary aspects of music notation: pitch, scales, intervals, keys and key signatures, note values, meter, time signatures, and rhythm.

The basic principle behind each technical factor listed above is easy enough to understand. If that were all that is necessary, this book would be much smaller than it is. In fact, you can look up these topics in a music dictionary if you need only to know the principles involved. If, however, a study of these principles is to aid you in better performing ability, it is necessary that you be able to apply these principles quickly and accurately in a given musical situation. To this end, this text provides you with enough practice in each lesson that not only will you be able to say, "Yes, I've got the general idea," but more important, you can say, "I can actually do these things quickly and accurately." Then you will receive your dividends in terms of better understanding of the music you perform and in terms of quicker learning and more accurate performance of your music. In addition, you will have laid the groundwork for more advanced theoretical courses and perhaps even for original composition.

To get the maximum value from these lessons, do all parts of all exercises until you can do each quickly and accurately. It may seem that we have used the phrase "quickly and accurately" redundantly, but this aspect of your study cannot be overemphasized. And just as important, examine and analyze the music you are performing to find examples of the theoretical materials you are studying, and if this should elude you, be sure to discuss this either with your performance teacher or your theory teacher.

R. W. O.
F. M.

TABLE OF CONTENTS

CHAPTER ONE

PITCH   *1*

Pitch. The Staff. The Musical Alphabet. Clefs, Treble and Bass. Ledger Lines. The Great Staff.

CHAPTER TWO

THE KEYBOARD   *19*

The Keyboard. Names of White Keys. Intervals. Half-Steps and Whole-Steps. Accidentals. Names of Black Keys. Enharmonic.

CHAPTER THREE

PITCH   *39*

Octave. Octave Registers. 8va.

CHAPTER FOUR

TIME   *47*

Beats. Tempo. Grouping of Beats.

CHAPTER FIVE

TIME (continued)   *53*

Division of Beats. Simple Beat. Compound Beat. Meter.

CHAPTER SIX

TIME (continued)   63

The Construction of Notes. The Relationship of Notes to Each Other. Notation of Rests.

CHAPTER SEVEN

TIME (continued)   75

Notation of the Simple Beat. Simple Meter (Time) Signatures. Notation of the Compound Beat. Compound Meter Signatures. Bar-lines. Measure.

CHAPTER EIGHT

TIME (continued)   93

Conductor's Beats.

CHAPTER NINE

TIME (continued)   101

Rhythm. Anacrusis. Repeat Signs. Rhythmic Reading.

CHAPTER TEN

TIME (continued)   113

Beams in Notation. Rests in Notation. Rhythmic Dictation. Rhythmic Transcription.

CHAPTER ELEVEN

MAJOR SCALES   137

CHAPTER TWELVE

MAJOR SCALES (continued)   149

Names of Scale Degrees.

CHAPTER THIRTEEN

MAJOR SCALES (continued)   157

Playing Scales at the Keyboard.

CHAPTER FOURTEEN

MAJOR SCALES (continued)   167

Singing Major Scales

CHAPTER FIFTEEN

MAJOR KEY SIGNATURES   171

Key. Key Signature. Circle of Fifths. Order of Sharps and Flats on the Staff.

CHAPTER SIXTEEN

MINOR SCALES   187

Accidentals, continued. Minor Scales: Natural (Pure), Harmonic and Melodic Forms. Historical Derivation of Major and Minor Scales.

CHAPTER SEVENTEEN

MINOR SCALES (continued)   213

Names of Scale Degrees in Minor.

CHAPTER EIGHTEEN

MINOR SCALES (continued)   219

Playing Minor Scales at the Keyboard.

CHAPTER NINETEEN

MINOR SCALES (continued)   231

Singing Minor Scales.

CHAPTER TWENTY

MINOR KEY SIGNATURES   235

Minor Key Signatures. Circle of Fifths for Minor Keys. Minor Key Signatures on the Staff.

CHAPTER TWENTY-ONE

MAJOR AND MINOR KEY RELATIONSHIPS   249

The Circle of Fifths for Major and Minor Keys Together. Relative Keys. Parallel Keys. Solmization in Relative Major and Minor Keys.

CHAPTER TWENTY-TWO

INTERVALS: MAJOR AND PERFECT   261

Interval. Major and Perfect Intervals in the Major Scale. Naming the Interval. Simple and Compound Intervals. Analysis of Major and Perfect Intervals in the Major Scale.

CHAPTER TWENTY-THREE

INTERVALS (continued)   275

Minor Intervals. Diminished Intervals. Augmented Intervals. Modification of Intervals. Intervals above Tonic Notes other than C. Intervals above Notes Which Cannot Be Tonics of Major Scales. Analysis of All Types of Intervals.

APPENDIX 1

KEYBOARD SCALE FINGERINGS   299

APPENDIX 2

THE CHROMATIC SCALE AND SYLLABLES   301

APPENDIX 3

FOREIGN WORDS AND MUSICAL TERMS   303

INDEX   309

CHAPTER ONE

PITCH

Pitch
The Staff
The Musical Alphabet
Clefs, Treble and Bass
Ledger Lines
The Great Staff

Obviously the most important aspect of music is its *sound,* and all study of music should have as its primary goal the production of correct and beautiful sound. One important approach to this goal is the study of the symbols used to notate sound on paper. Notation of sound, even in its most elementary aspect, involves several factors, as you have already discovered in reading the "Preface." We will begin our study with one of these factors: *pitch*.

Pitch

When we hear two different sounds produced by a musical instrument such as the piano, we hear one of the sounds as being higher or lower than the other. Actually, sounds are not "high" or "low" in the sense that they are different heights above ground level, but sounds do give a feeling of highness and lowness in relation to each other. This property of sound, its seeming highness or lowness, is called *pitch*. To indicate on paper the difference in pitch in musical sound, we use a device called the *staff*.

The Staff

The music *staff* (plural, *staves*) consists of five parallel horizontal lines and four resultant spaces. These lines and spaces represent successively higher pitches when progressing from the lowest to the highest line.

FIGURE 1.1. *The Staff*.

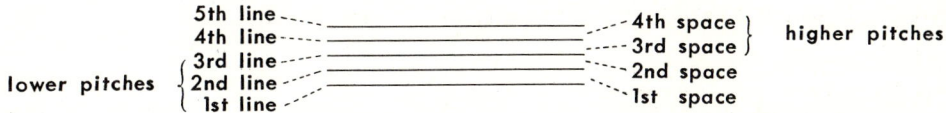

The lines are numbered from the bottom to the top, 1 through 5. Spaces are similarly numbered from the bottom, 1 through 4. The pitches represented by lines and spaces are identified by letters of the *musical alphabet*.

The Musical Alphabet

The first seven letters of the alphabet, *a b c d e f g*, comprise the musical alphabet. These letters are used to name the lines and spaces of the staff, but what letter is assigned to a specific line or space is determined by a symbol appearing at the beginning of the staff called a *clef*.

Clefs

The two clefs most commonly used in music are (1) 𝄞 , the G clef, in which the lower loop encircles a line of the staff to be designated as *g;* and (2) 𝄢 , the F clef, in which the two dots are found on either side of a line of the staff to be designated as *f*. When the G clef is placed on the staff in a certain position, it is called the *treble clef*.

Treble Clef

When the G clef is placed on the staff with the lower loop encircling the second line it is known as the *treble clef*. Thus the second line of the staff receives the designation *g*. By fixing *g* on the staff, names of other lines and the spaces are also determined. Letters of the musical alphabet are employed in order on ascending adjacent lines and spaces (staff degrees). After *g*, *a* follows on the next higher staff degree, which is the second space.

FIGURE 1.2.   *Treble Clef and Names of the Lines and Spaces.*

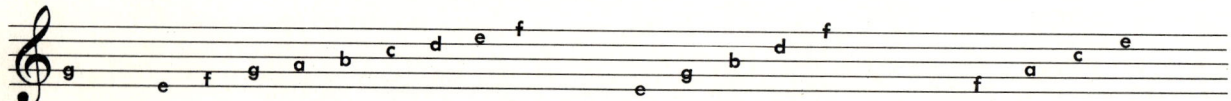

Lines and spaces receive different designations when the F clef is placed on the staff in a certain position and called the *bass clef*.

Bass Clef

When the F clef is placed on the staff with the two dots on either side of the fourth line, it is known as the *bass clef*. Thus the fourth line of the staff receives the designation *f*. By fixing *f* on the staff, names of other lines and the spaces are also determined. After *f*, *g* follows on the next higher staff degree, which is the fourth space.

FIGURE 1.3.   *Bass Clef and Names of the Lines and Spaces.*

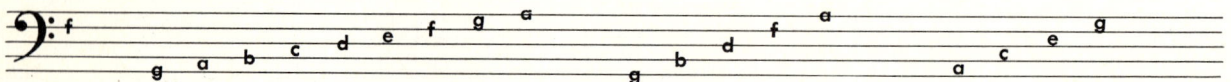

At times a musical sound may be either higher or lower than those pitches represented by lines and spaces of the staff. Means of writing such pitches are provided by *ledger lines*.

Ledger Lines

Short lines added above and below the staff are called *ledger (leger) lines*. By extending the staff, ledger lines provide means for indicating pitches either higher or lower than the limits of the five-line staff. Added ledger lines and resultant ledger spaces are drawn *equidistant* to lines and spaces of the staff. In Figure 1.4, notes [1] are used to show specific pitches more clearly.

FIGURE 1.4. *Ledger Lines.*

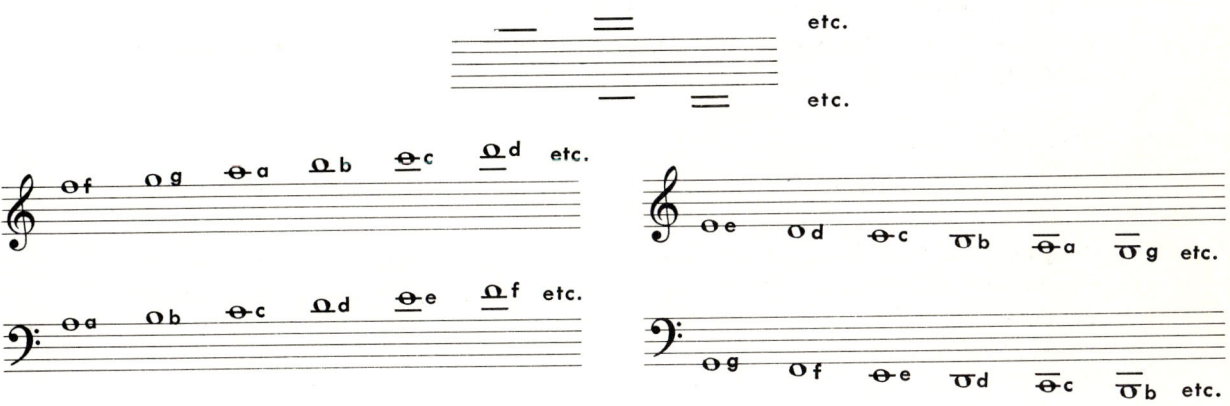

Observe that a note on the space above or the space below the staff does *not* require a ledger line:

Players of instruments producing relatively high pitches, such as flute, violin, and clarinet, read music written in the treble clef; players of instruments producing relatively low pitches, such as trombone, tuba, and string bass, read music written in the bass clef. Soprano and alto voices use the treble clef; the bass voice uses the bass clef. The tenor voice uses the "transposing treble clef"; the actual pitch produced is one octave (eight staff degrees) [2] lower than written:

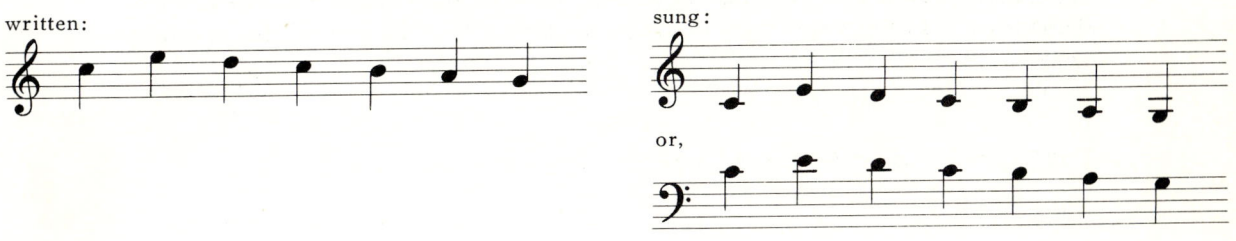

---

[1] A note is a symbol based on an oval shape called *note-head* (𝅗𝅥 , ●) to which may be added stems (e.g., ♩) and flags (e.g., ♪) in varying combinations to express pitch and duration of sound. The varieties of notes will be studied in Chapter 6.

Actually, only notes, which are named, should represent pitches; lines and spaces are merely numbered. However, in the absence of notes as in Figures 1.2 and 1.3, lines and spaces may be named just as though notes were present.

[2] Explanation of *octave* will be found in Chapter 3.

The transposing treble clef is also written as 𝄞 or 𝄞𝄞 . Use of this clef eliminates the need for large numbers of ledger lines, as shown in the illustration above.

Music for the piano, which encompasses a wide range of pitches from low to high, requires two staves in a combination called the *great staff*.

The Great Staff

When two staves are used together and are joined by a vertical line and a bracket, called a *brace,* this combination is known as the *great staff,* or *grand staff,* or *piano staff*.

In theory, the great staff is like one large staff of eleven lines (Fig. 1.5a) but with the middle line omitted (Fig. 1.5b) to create a separation which permits quick visual discrimination of the upper and lower staff degrees.

FIGURE 1.5. *Eleven-line Staff.*

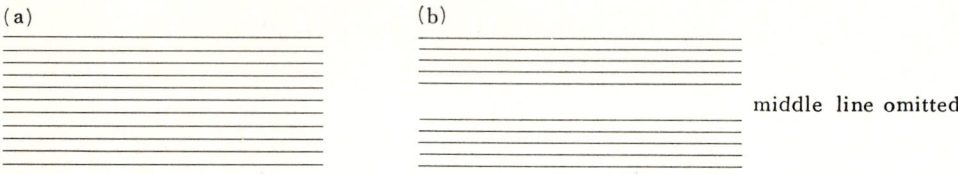

With the brace added, the great staff is normally found with the treble clef in position on the upper five lines and the bass clef in position on the lower five lines.

FIGURE 1.6. *The Great Staff.*

If a ledger line were placed between the staves, like the omitted middle line in the eleven-line staff, then this single ledger line would be considered either the first ledger line above the bass or the first ledger line below treble. See Figure 1.7 in which the pitch found on this ledger line centered between the staves is called *middle c.*

Notice that the space formed between the fifth bass line and the ledger line for middle *c* is occupied by the pitch *b;* continuing upward, notice that the space formed between the ledger line for middle *c* and the first treble line is occupied by the pitch *d.* Observe the alphabetical order of pitches throughout on successive lines and spaces from the bass upward through middle C and into treble.

Figure 1.7, with the staves placed closely together to show relation of bass to

FIGURE 1.7. *Pitches on the Great Staff.*

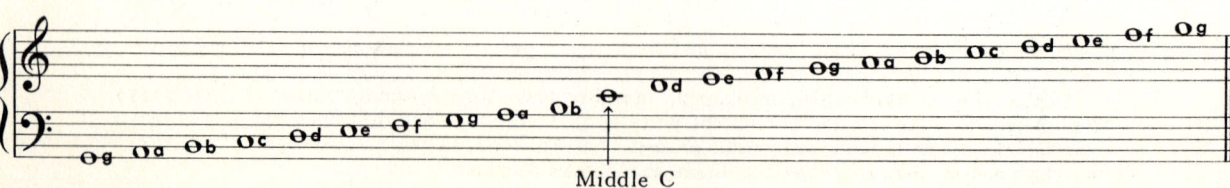

treble, is purposefully a theoretical illustration. Actually, in printed music the distance between the two staves of the great staff is increased sufficiently to provide room for several added ledger lines both above the bass and below the treble. Figure 1.8 shows such a great staff. The series of pitches in the treble clef is identical in sound to the series in the bass clef; this is easily seen by comparing *middle c* in each clef.

FIGURE 1.8. *The Great Staff with Ledger Lines Above Bass and Below Treble.*

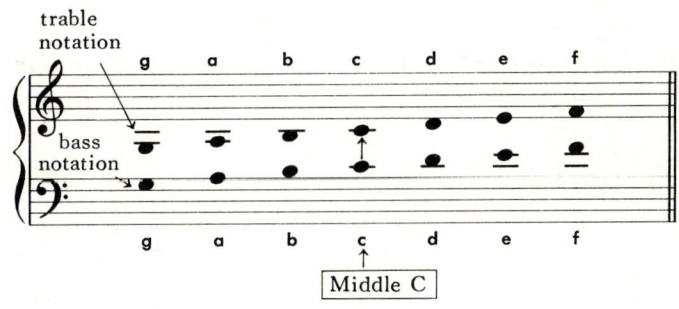

Remember that in printed music, or when you draw the great staff, the two staves are not close together but are well separated as in Figure 1.8 and as in the following music excerpts.

FIGURE 1.9. *The Great Staff: Usual Form.*

Beethoven, Sonata for Piano, Op. 2 No. 1[3]

When necessary, each staff of the great staff may carry: (1) a treble clef (Fig. 1.10), (2) a bass clef (Fig. 1.11), or (3) a change from bass to treble, or vice versa (Fig. 1.12).

FIGURE 1.10. *Great Staff: Two Treble Clefs.*

Mozart, Sonata for Piano, K. 279[4]

[3] Opus (Latin, work), abbreviated op., together with a number identifies a composition, and is usually supplied by the composer.

[4] K., abbreviation for Ludwig von Köchel, who in 1862 made a chronological listing of Mozart's works. Mozart did not give his works opus numbers.

FIGURE 1.11. *Great Staff: Two Bass Clefs.*

FIGURE 1.12. *Great Staff with Change of Clef.*

_____ NAME

EXERCISE 1.12

Reading Notes by Letter Names

Read aloud the letter names of notes in the following melodies. This oral reading is to be done in a normal speaking voice with no attempt to produce highness or lowness of the actual sounds of pitches. You are merely to recite names of the pitches and not sing them. Read as quickly as possible. Through additional practice try to increase your speed.

Note to the Instructor: In this exercise the student should ignore rhythm and any key signature and simply recite the alphabetical names. For example, *America* will be read *ccdbcdeefedcdcbeggggfeffffedefedcefgafedc*. The objective of this reading practice is to develop the ability for instant recognition of lines and spaces and response by pitch names.

(1) America

(2) Auld Lang Syne

(3) MSS 34

_____ NAME

Reminder to the Instructor: In these exercises the student should ignore rhythm and any key signature and simply recite the alphabetical names (without accidentals).

EXERCISE 1.13

Reading Notes by Letter Names

For additional practice, continue the procedure of Exercise 1.12 by reading letter names of notes in any melodies in Chapters 1 and 2 of *Music for Sight Singing,* second edition, by Robert W. Ottman, Prentice-Hall, Inc., 1967.

CHAPTER TWO

THE KEYBOARD

**The Keyboard
Names of White Keys
Intervals
Half-Steps and Whole-Steps
Accidentals
Names of Black Keys
Enharmonic**

The Keyboard

The standard piano keyboard has 88 keys consisting of 52 white keys and 36 black keys. Black keys are found in alternate groups of two and three. This can easily be seen on the keyboard because one group of black keys is always separated from another by a pair of white keys.

FIGURE 2.1. *Keyboard Groups of Two and Three Black Keys.*

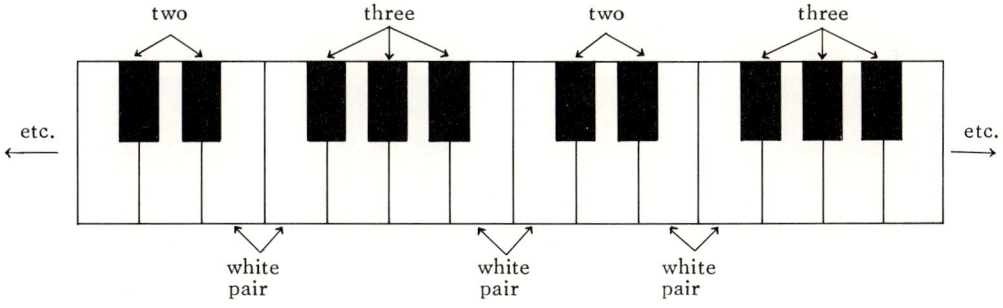

FIGURE 2.2. *The Standard Piano Keyboard.*

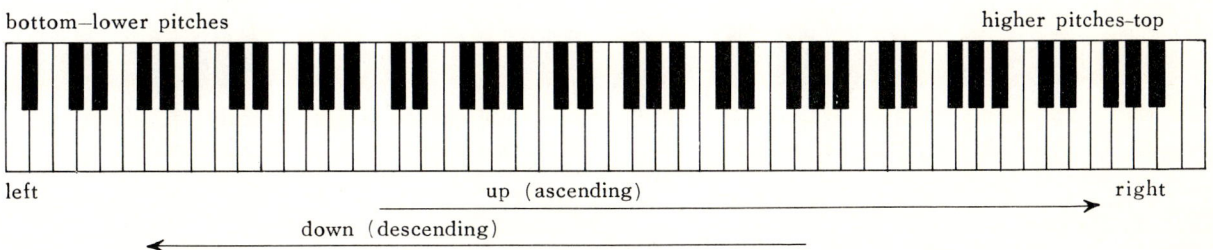

19

Keys at the left of the keyboard sound the lower pitches while keys at the right sound higher pitches. Pitches at the extreme left are said to be at the *bottom* of the keyboard; pitches at the extreme right are said to be at the *top* of the keyboard. Accordingly, when looking from right to left, you look *down* the keyboard; when looking from left to right, you look *up* the keyboard.

Each white and black key of the keyboard is identified by name. First, we shall learn the *names of white keys*.

Names of White Keys

White keys are named with the seven letters of the musical alphabet. The key at the far left side, at the bottom of the keyboard, is a white key and it is named *a*. The next white key to the right of *a* is named with the next letter of the alphabet, *b*. This application of the alphabet in naming white keys continues in order up the keyboard. After *g*, which is the seventh and last letter of the musical alphabet, *a* occurs again and this process is repeated through all succeeding white keys ending with the highest pitch *c* at the top of the keyboard.

FIGURE 2.3. *Names of the White Keys on the Piano.*

Observe that any *c* is located at the immediate left of any group of two black keys. When studying the keyboard in more detail, we will often use the pitch *c* as a point of orientation, or as a starting point when playing at the keyboard.

FIGURE 2.4. *Location of* C *at Left of Two Black Keys.*

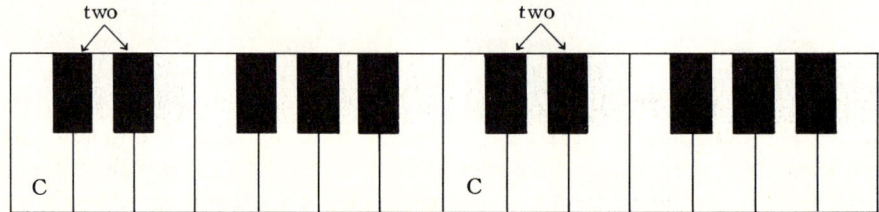

The *c* nearest the middle of the keyboard is called *middle c*. Middle *c* on the piano corresponds to middle *c* on the great staff (also see Figs. 1.7 and 1.8 of Chapter 1).

FIGURE 2.5. *Middle* C *on the Keyboard and Great Staff.*

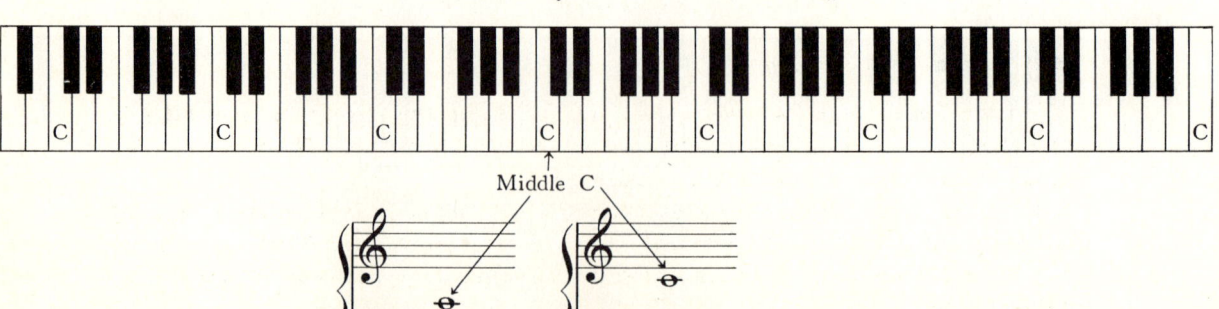

In Figure 2.6 pitches of white keys to the right of (above) middle *c* are represented as notes in ascending order on lines and spaces of the staff.

FIGURE 2.6. *White Keys above Middle C and Notation on the Staff.*

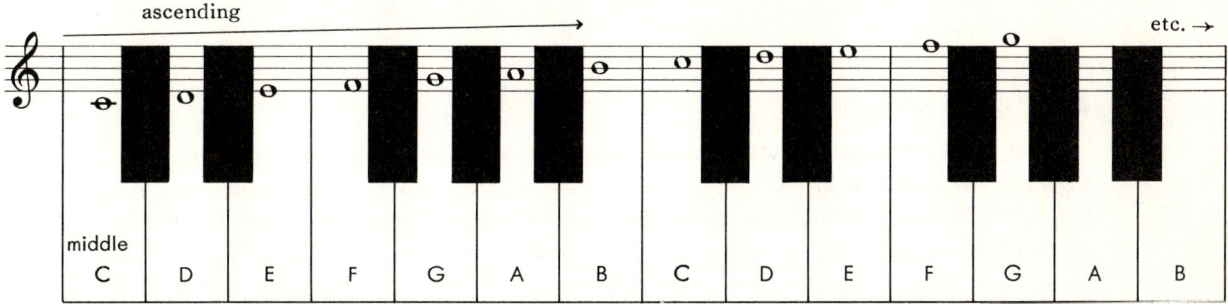

In Figure 2.7 pitches of white keys to the left of (below) middle *c* are represented as notes in descending order on lines and spaces of the staff.

FIGURE 2.7. *White Keys below Middle C and Notation on the Staff.*

We have now named all the *white keys* of the keyboard with special attention given to the location of *c*'s and, in particular, to the location of middle *c*. And we have found how white-key pitches are notated on the staff. *Black keys* are also to be named but not until we have gained certain knowledge of *intervals* and *accidentals*.

Intervals

An *interval* is the distance between two different pitches, or between two different notes on the staff, or between two different keys on the piano. For the present, we shall study two intervals, the *half-step* and *whole-step*.

Half-Steps and Whole-Steps

On the keyboard, a *half-step* is the interval from *any key to its adjacent key,* whether that key be white or black. See Figure 2.8. From *c,* a white key, to the next higher pitch, a black key, is a half-step.

From this black key to the adjacent white key above is a half-step. From any black key to the adjacent white key is a half-step. Notice that there is no black key between *e* and *f* or between *b* and *c;* therefore, these adjacent white keys are half-steps apart.

21

FIGURE 2.8. *Half-Steps on the Keyboard.*

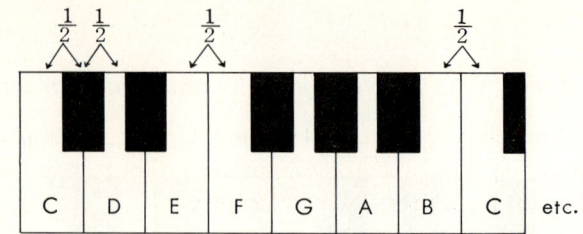

Two half-steps in succession equal *one step,* usually called a *whole-step.* See Figure 2.9. C to d is a whole-step, the black key in between producing the two half-steps. Because of the irregularity of the keyboard with its black keys in groups of two and three, whole-steps on the keyboard are found in three different combinations of white keys and black keys. Whole-steps exist (1) from one key to the next white key, (2) between a white and black key or (3) between a black and another black key.

FIGURE 2.9. *Whole-Steps on the Keyboard.*

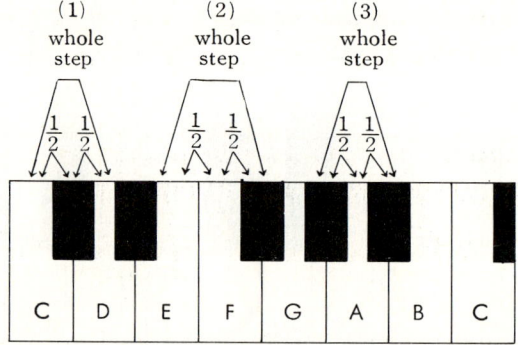

(1) A whole-step between a white key and another white key.
(2) A whole-step between a white key and a black key.
(3) A whole-step between a black key and another black key.

In Chapter Eleven, half-steps and whole-steps will be studied further.

Accidentals

An accidental is a symbol (sign) which alters the pitch of a note. There are five different accidentals.

(1) The *sharp,* ♯ , raises the pitch of a note one half-step.
(2) The *flat,* ♭ , lowers the pitch of a note one half-step.
(3) The *natural,* ♮ , cancels a preceding accidental.
(4) The *double sharp,* 𝄪 , raises the pitch of a note two half-steps or one whole-step.
(5) The *double flat,* ♭♭ , lowers the pitch of a note two half-steps or one whole-step.

In music writing, the accidental is placed immediately to the left of the note to be altered and precisely on the same line or space of the staff occupied by the note.

FIGURE 2.10. *Accidentals.*

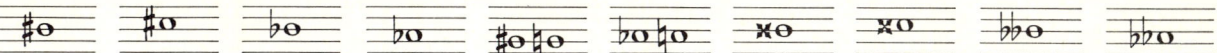

When an accidental is to be written in notation, it is, without exception, placed *before* the note as in Figure 2.10. But, in speaking the name of an altered note the accidental comes *after* the letter name. Therefore,

is spoken "c sharp."

At first, we shall study only sharps and flats. Later, the remaining accidentals will be studied. We are now ready to employ sharps and flats to determine the *names of black keys* of the keyboard.

Names of Black Keys

On the piano keyboard, black keys are named in relationship to the white keys. The black key one half-step above *c* is named *c sharp*. The black key one half-step below *d* is named *d flat*. Observe that the same black key is named both *c♯* and *d♭*.

FIGURE 2.11. *Naming the Black Key C♯ and D♭.*

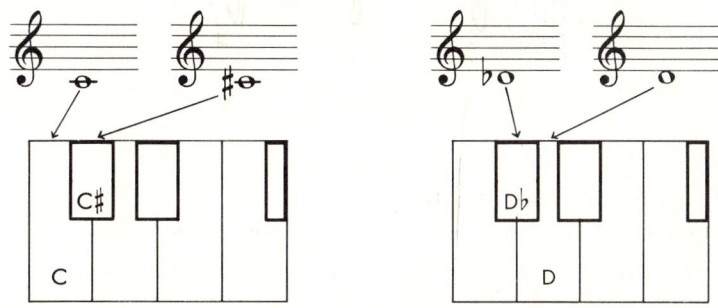

The other black keys are named in a similar manner. For example, the black key one half-step above *d* is *d♯*; the black (same) key a half-step below *e is e♭*. Figure 2.12 shows names of black and white keys and their representation on the staff.

FIGURE 2.12a. *The Keyboard and Treble Notes on the Staff.*

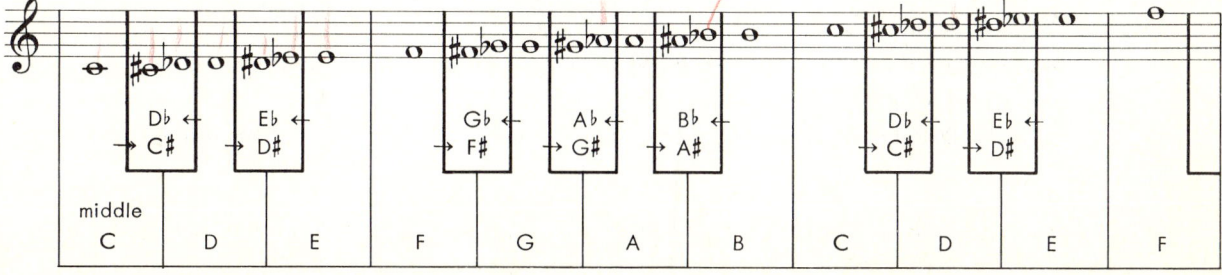

23

FIGURE 2.12b. *The Keyboard and Bass Notes on the Staff.*

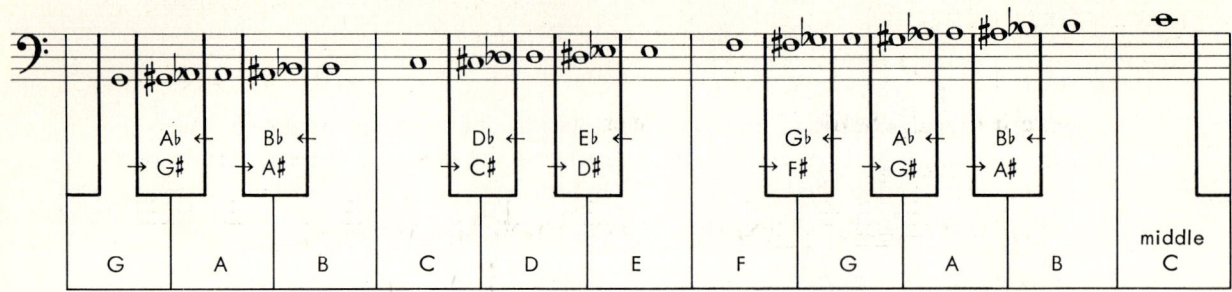

You have noticed that each black key has two different names. To describe this and similar situations we use the term *enharmonic*.

Enharmonic

Enharmonic is an adjective describing one and the same pitch as having different spellings. For example, c♯ and d♭ are enharmonic (see Fig. 2.11); they are played on the piano by the same black key. White keys may also have enharmonic spellings, either by the use of ♯ or ♭, or ✕ or ♭♭. These will be studied later in Chapter 13.

Playing Exercises at the Keyboard

The following exercises will be played at the keyboard. They are planned so that you can practice without the presence of a teacher.[1]

EXERCISE 2.12

Playing White Keys

Play on the keyboard each written note. Follow this procedure:

1. Name the written note.
2. Place finger on piano key having the same name and pitch as the written note.
3. Play key.

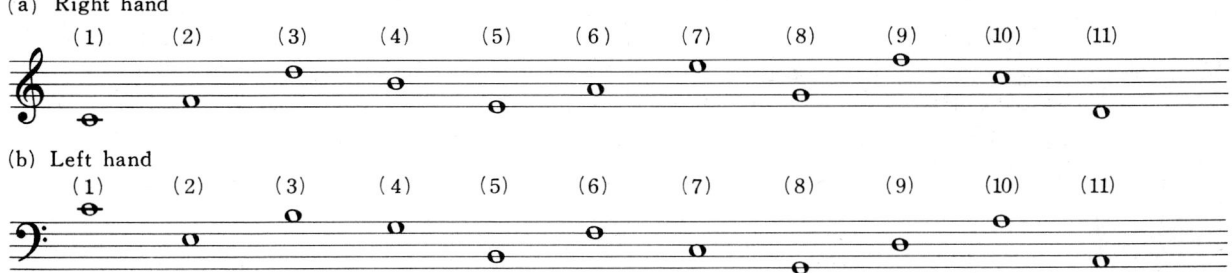

EXERCISE 2.13

Playing Half-Steps

Find the white key for the first note of each pair by following the procedure outlined in Exercise 2.12. Then play the half-step above or below according to the notation.

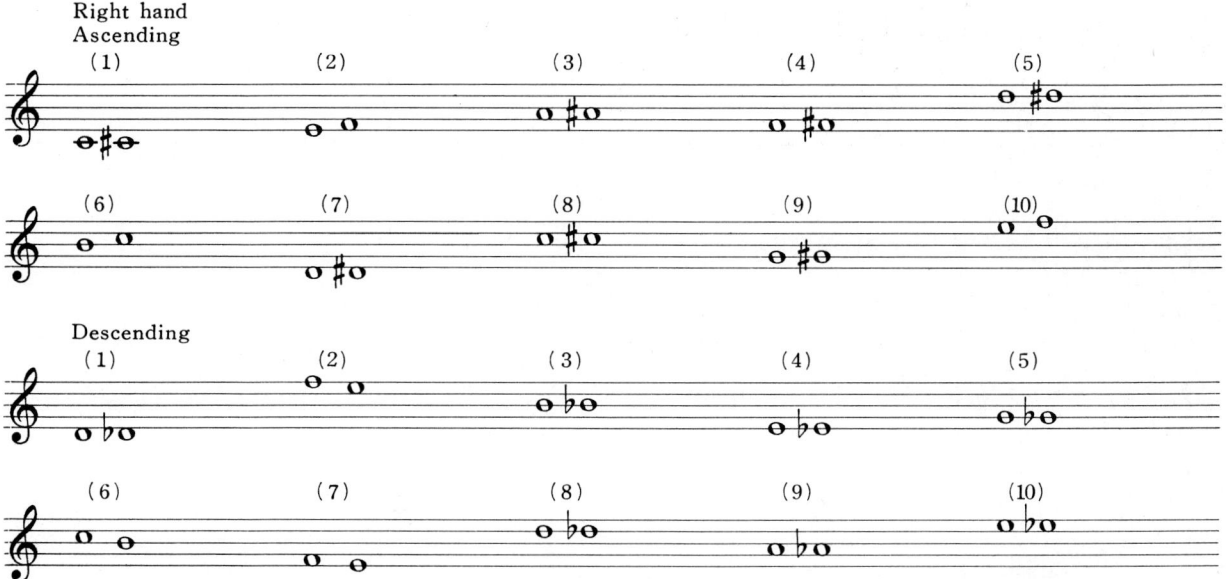

[1] To aid in familiarity with the keyboard, the authors suggest that the student purchase a cardboard facsimile keyboard available in most music stores. Place the card behind the black keys. Make sure that *middle c* of the cardboard is directly in line with *middle c* on the keyboard. Seated at the keyboard, facing *middle c,* you will find it convenient to play treble notes with the right hand and bass notes with the left hand.

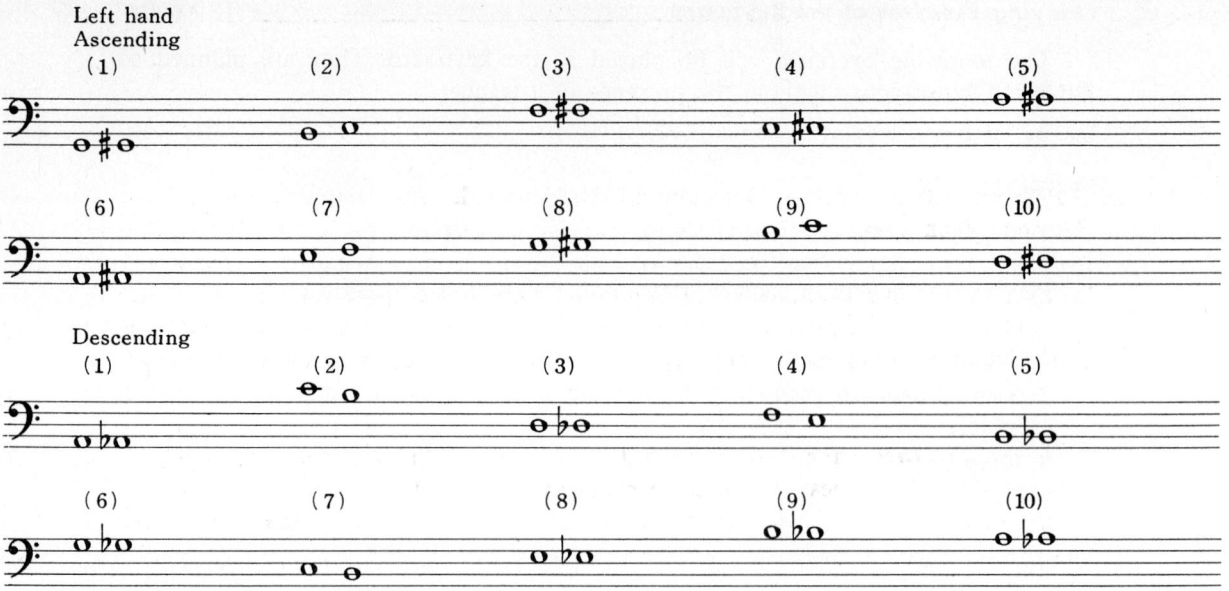

EXERCISE 2.14
Playing Any White or Black Key from Written Notes on the Staff

Play on the keyboard each written note. Each accidental refers only to the note immediately following it.

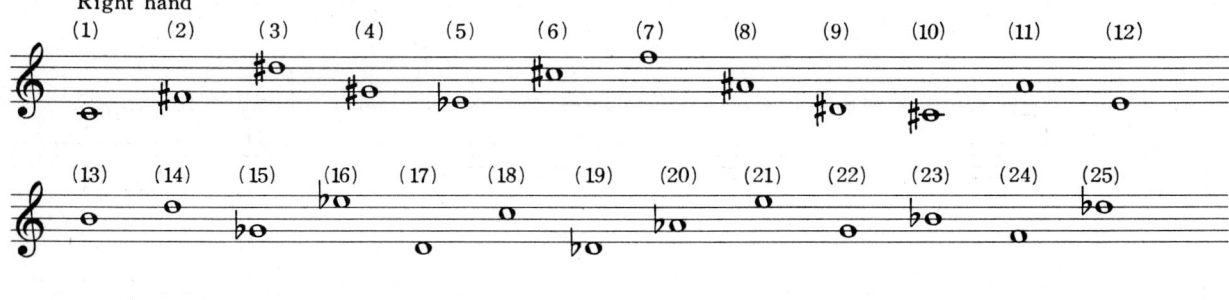

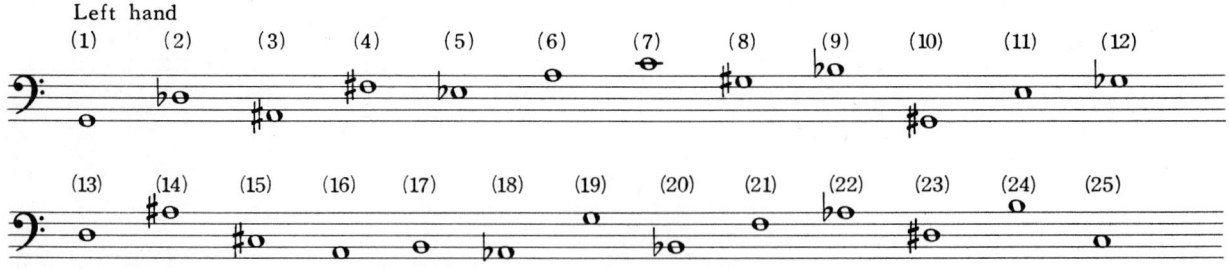

EXERCISE 2.15

Ear Training and Singing: Matching Tones

Play individually each written note on the keyboard. After you play a note, sing the same pitch using the neutral syllable *la*. Listen carefully to determine that the pitch you sing is identical to the one played. This is called *matching the tone*. Women should match the tones of the treble clef pitches; men should match the tones of the bass clef pitches. If at first you find that you are hesitant or unsure in matching tones, continue to practice this exercise in order to acquire the ability for instant and sure response.

Note to the Instructor: Listen carefully to determine that the matched tones are unisons. Matching tones one or more octaves distant will be practiced in the following chapter. If full class participation with both women and men is desired, (a) and (b) can be sung at the same time. In this case, play each pitch in both treble and bass before class response.

CHAPTER THREE

PITCH

Octave
Octave Registers
8va

Octave

The word *octave* is derived from the Latin *octo* meaning eight. Look at the piano keyboard. Considering *middle c* as 1 and counting consecutively up the white keys to 8, we find we have arrived at another *c*. 1 and 8 are the same letter name. This interval of eight degrees from *c* to *c* is called an octave. In similar fashion it can be shown that the interval from any pitch to the next pitch of the same letter name, either up or down, is an octave. For example, from *a* up to the next *a* is an octave. Or, from *a* down to the next *a* is an octave.

FIGURE 3.1. *Octaves.*

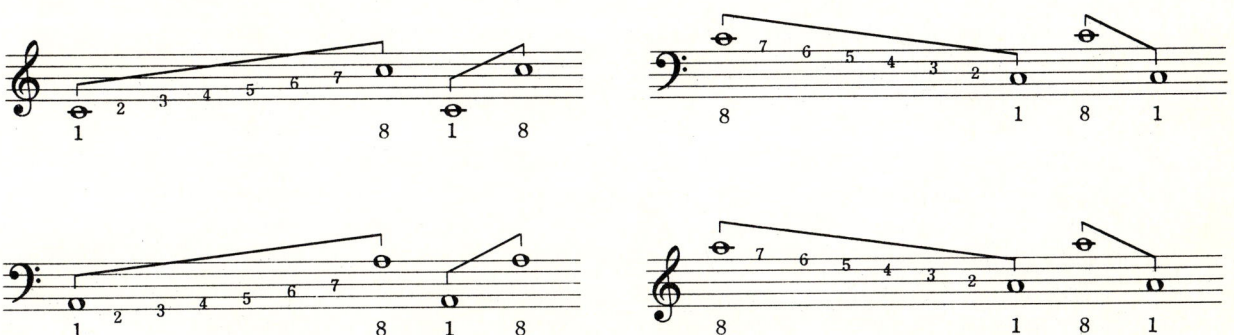

In studying the keyboard you have noticed that each letter name is used more than once in naming keys. In fact, there are eight *a*'s, eight *b*'s, and eight *c*'s, plus seven each of the remaining letters of the musical alphabet. Therefore, there is needed a system whereby any one pitch can be designated distinctly from any other pitch of the same letter name. Such a system is provided through the location and naming of octaves or *octave registers*.[1]

Octave Registers

The term *octave register* refers to a system in which pitches are grouped into differently designated octaves. The system provides for individual identification of

---

[1] The word *register* in music ordinarily means range, compass, or placement of pitches.

any particular pitch and its specific notation on the staff and is shown complete in Figure 3.2.

Here is how the system works: [2]

General Principle

1. Each *c* is given a designation different from any other *c*.
2. All letter names immediately above a given *c* and up to the next *c* are designated in a manner similar to the given *c*.

Pitches Above Middle c

3. Middle *c* is designated c^1, called "one-line c," or "c-one."
4. Working up from c^1 (middle *c*), each successive *c* is designated:

c^2	two-line c	c-two
c^3	three-line c	c-three
c^4	four-line c	c-four
c^5	five-line c	c-five

5. All pitches above c^1 but below c^2 are designated as one-line, such as d^1, e^1, f^1. All pitches above c^2 but below c^3 are designated as two-line, such as d^2, e^2, f^2. This process applies in a similar manner to pitches above c^3 and c^4. c^5 is the highest pitch on the piano.

Pitches Below Middle C

6. Working down from middle *c*, each successive *c* is designated:

c	small c
C	great c
CC	contra c

7. As before, any pitch is designated the same as the nearest *c* below it.
8. The lowest remaining pitches below CC are located in the sub-contra range. The lowest pitch on the piano is AAA, "sub-contra a."

In Figure 3.2, more notes appear above and below the two staves than are actually located on the staff lines and spaces. In fact, of the 52 white notes of the piano keyboard, only 18 appear on the lines and spaces of the treble and bass clefs (five lines and four spaces in each clef). In most music compositions, a very large percentage of pitches can be represented in these two clefs and with one or two ledger lines above or below. On the other hand, there are compositions that utilize many pitches far above or below the staff. Such music containing many ledger lines in the notation can be quite difficult to read. To ease this difficulty, a special sign is used, *8va*.

8va

The sign *8va* (or *8*), an abbreviation for the Italian, *all' ottava* (at the octave), is used to indicate that notes are to be performed an octave higher or lower than written. When this sign is used with the treble clef, notes so high as to be difficult to read are written an octave (eight notes) lower; for example, c^3, d^3, e^3, f^3, g^3 are written on the staff in the location for c^2, d^2, e^2, f^2, g^2. Over these notes is placed

---

[2] The word *line* as used in item 3 below has nothing to do with the lines of the staff. Rather, *line* should be thought of in the sense of a division, limitation, or boundary. Some theorists use, instead of superscript numerals, simply a vertical line following the letter. Instead of c^1 or c^2, such would appear c' or c'' and therefore coincide with the terminology c, *one-line*, or c, *two-line*.

FIGURE 3.2. *Octave Registers.*

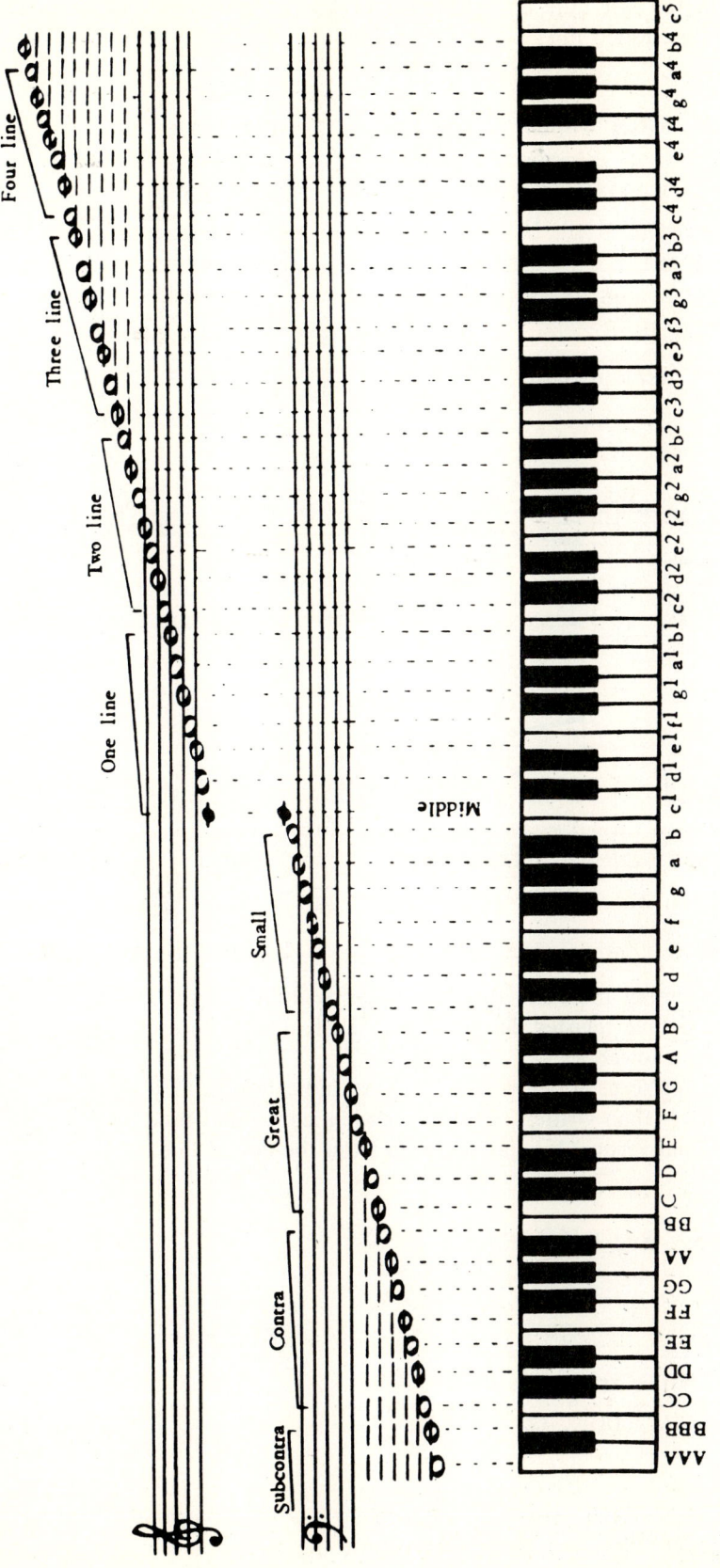

Courtesy of Raymond Elliott, *Fundamentals of Music*, 2nd edition (Englewood Cliffs, N.J., Prentice-Hall, Inc., 1965).

the sign 8⌐ ⌐; the "8" is placed over the first note affected, the dotted line continues to the last note affected and the sign is concluded with a vertical line down from the dotted line.

FIGURE 3.3. *8va Above Treble Clef.*

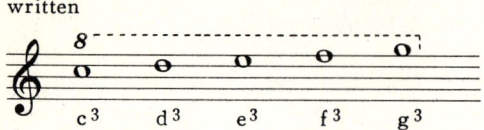
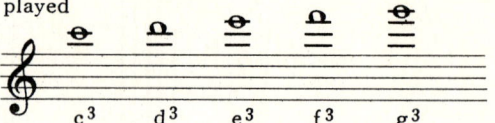

FIGURE 3.4. *Use of 8va.*

The sign simply indicates that the notes written are to be played one octave higher. The octave register designation of each pitch is not changed by its placement an octave lower.

This sign is also used below bass notes to indicate that they are to be performed an octave lower than written. The sign is identical to that used with the treble clef, except that final vertical line proceeds up from the dotted line: 8┈┈┘

FIGURE 3.5. *8va Below Bass Clef.*

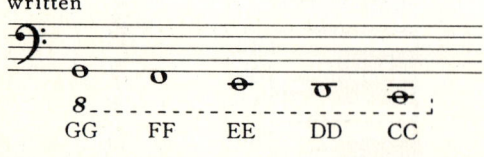

Following the same principle, the 8va sign is sometimes used above the bass clef, but rarely below the treble clef. While the sign is most frequently found in connection with a series of pitches as in the preceding illustrations, 8va may also be used with but a solitary note. An "8" at the last note of a composition may be used without the horizontal line.

In the exercise numbers following, and throughout this book, the letter T indicates that drill will be most efficient in the presence of a teacher or an instructor. When students are working together, one can assume the role of instructor.

EXERCISE 3.3T
Keyboard: Playing Pitches by Octave Register Designations

The instructor will designate any pitch using octave register terminology. Play the pitch on the piano.

EXERCISE 3.4T
Ear Training and Singing: Matching Tones

Play any pitch on the piano selected from the great, small, one- or two-line octaves. Using the neutral syllable *la,* sing (match) the pitch. If the pitch is too high or too low, sing some octave of the pitch in a range comfortable for your voice.

EXERCISE 3.5T
Ear Training and Singing: Matching Tones (continued)

Continue exercises in matching tones and include pitches played from the extreme lower and upper piano registers. Play any pitch on the piano from AAA to c^5. Using the neutral syllable *la,* sing (match) the pitch; when it is beyond your vocal range, sing some octave of the pitch.

EXERCISE 3.6T
Ear Training: Octave Registers

(1) The instructor designates a pitch by octave register.
(2) The instructor plays this pitch and then a pitch of the same letter name one or more octaves removed.
(3) Using the ear as a guide, the student identifies the second pitch by octave register.

EXERCISE 3.7T
Ear Training: Octave Registers (continued)

The instructor plays a pitch on the piano and calls it by letter name but without octave register identification. The student identifies the pitch by octave register.

CHAPTER FOUR

TIME

Beats
Tempo
Grouping of Beats

In the first three chapters, we studied one of the primary characteristics of music, the sensation of highness or lowness of sound, called *pitch,* and we learned methods of notating pitch on paper. Another primary characteristic of music is the sensation of duration of a sound, that is, how long or how short a length of time it is held. Our next study is to learn how durations are measured through beats (pulsations) and ways to put these measurements on paper so they can be read by a performer.

Music when committed to paper is merely a representation of its sound; music as an art exists only through performance of the written symbols. When we attempt to measure performed sounds, we find that these sounds exist in time, making it necessary to measure short or long periods of time. This is unlike the comparable problem in the visual arts: a painting uses a two-dimensional surface such as a canvas; a sculpture uses a three-dimensional surface such as a block of wood or stone. The painting or sculpture, existing in space, can easily be measured by a common device for measuring space, the ruler. An art that exists in time, such as music, can be measured only by a measuring device existing in time. Such a device cannot be put in solid form, like a ruler, but can exist only as a physical or mental reaction on the part of the performer or listener. Such measuring devices are common in your everyday experience. The normal heart beats with a regular pulsation, marking off regular units of time. When you walk, each step usually takes the same amount of time as the preceding and following steps, at least until you consciously change your rate of speed. These two physical sensations, among many others, mark off units of time of equal length. For purposes of measuring equal lengths of time in music, these regularly recurring pulsations are called *beats*.

Beats

Beats are regularly recurring physical pulsations which divide time into units of equal length. In your ordinary experiences in music, you have already felt this sensation and expressed yourself by regular tapping with your fingers or your feet, or you have danced or marched in conformity with the beats of the music. We will begin our study of time by experiencing again the sensation of beats. The instructor will play several melodies. Your reaction is simply to tap naturally with the right hand. The melodies you will hear are shown in Figure 4.1. The vertical lines below the staff represent the taps or beats.

FIGURE 4.1. *Tapping Beats.*

AULD LANG SYNE

You may have noticed that you tapped at a different rate of speed for different melodies. This phenomenon is explained by the term *tempo*.

Tempo

Tempo (pl. tempos, or tempi) is the rate of speed of the beats. The faster the succession of beats, the faster is the tempo; the slower the succession of beats, the slower is the tempo. In a fast tempo the beats measure relatively short durations of time; in a slow tempo the beats measure relatively long durations of time. The varying durations of the beat depend on the kind of music and the intent of the composer.

The length of the beat can be precisely measured by a mechanical device known as the metronome, which produces a regular recurring ticking sound. The metronome can be regulated to produce the ticking sound from very fast successions to very slow successions. It is calibrated so that when set on "60" it produces one tick per second; at "120," two ticks per second, etc. Composers often indicate tempo by placing the abbreviation M.M.[1] plus the desired number at the beginning of a piece (for example, M.M. 60).

While listening to music, certain beats are felt as being stronger than others. There are heavy beats and light beats; the succession of combinations of heavy and light beats produces *grouping of beats*.

Grouping of Beats

Beats tend to group themselves into regular recurring patterns. Three patterns are commonly found in music: (1) a heavy beat followed by a light beat (duple); (2) a heavy beat followed by two light beats (triple); and (3) a heavy beat followed by three lighter beats with the third beat slightly stronger than the second and fourth (quadruple). See Figure 4.2. As the instructor plays, you will experi-

FIGURE 4.2. *Beat Patterns.*

```
Duple Beats        Triple Beats        Quadruple Beats
|   |              |   |   |           |   |   |   |
1   2              1   2   3           1   2   3   4
```

ence these groupings as shown in Figure 4.3. As in Figure 4.2, the vertical lines below the staff represent beats. A long line represents a heavy beat, a short line

---

[1] M.M. stands for Mälzel's metronome. Johann N. Mälzel invented the instrument in 1816. It was first used to indicate tempi by Beethoven.

a light beat. When listening to each melody, tap the beats as before with the right hand, but make a stronger tap at the place of each long vertical line and a weaker tap at each short vertical line in accordance with the sensation of heavy and light beats in the music.

FIGURE 4.3. *Grouping of Beats.*

It is sometimes difficult in listening to distinguish between groupings of two and groupings of four because the semi-heavy beat on "3" in quadruple can easily be mistaken for the heavy beat "1" in a group of two beats. For a comparison see Figure 4.4.

FIGURE 4.4. *Comparison of Duple and Quadruple Groups of Beats.*

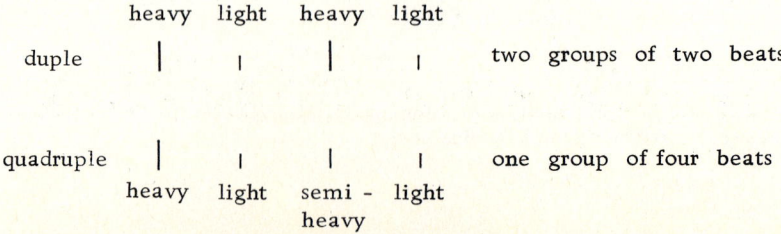

EXERCISE 4.1T
Tapping Beats and Groupings

Listen to a melody played by the instructor. On the second hearing, tap the beats, making a heavy tap where you hear the heavy beat in the music. Determine whether the beats are in groups of two, three, or four and be prepared to identify the grouping for the piece as "duple," "triple," or "quadruple." For this exercise, use music found in Figure 4.5 at the end of the chapter.

EXERCISE 4.2T
Aural Identification of Groupings of Beats

Listen to a melody played by the instructor. On the second hearing, try to recognize the beats without tapping. Identify the grouping of beats as before. For this exercise also, use music found in Figure 4.5 at the end of the chapter.

FIGURE 4.5. *Melodies for Exercises in Groupings of Beats.*

LONG, LONG AGO

Thomas H. Bayly

DANISH FOLKSONG

FRENCH FOLKSONG

HARK! THE HERALD ANGELS SING

Felix Mendelssohn

COME, THOU ALMIGHTY KING

Felice de Giardini

WHEN JOHNNY COMES MARCHING HOME

Louis Lambert

EXERCISE 4.3T

Aural Identification of Groupings of Beats

For additional drill, continue Exercises 4.1T and 4.2T using the following melodies from *Music for Sight Singing* (second edition). Observe the recommended metronome indications.

melody
number

(1) 18 M.M. 108   (7)   93 M.M. 116
(2) 28 M.M. 116   (8) 113 M.M. 120
(3) 61 M.M. 76   (9) 118 M.M. 104
(4) 81 M.M. 100 (10) 128 M.M. 63
(5) 87 M.M. 138 (11) 137 M.M. 80
(6) 88 M.M. 108 (12) 179 M.M. 142

CHAPTER FIVE

TIME
(continued)

Divisions of Beats
Simple Beat
Compound Beat
Meter

In the preceding chapter you were asked to listen to a number of musical examples. One characteristic common to all the melodies was the sensation of a regular recurring beat. Readily noticeable, however, was the fact that in different melodies the beats grouped themselves in different combinations of two, three, or four. Now we will consider another characteristic quality of the beat, the sensation of *divisions of beats*.

Divisions of Beats

There are two varieties of the beat, each identified by the way the beat duration can be divided. You can demonstrate this when listening to a melody by making either two or three taps with the left hand to each tap in the right hand. Whether you tap two or three in the left hand will be sensed from the sound of the melody itself, as will be shown in the following discussion of *simple* and *compound beats*.

Simple Beat

A beat which can be divided into two parts is called a *simple beat*. Listen to the melody in Figure 5.1. On the second hearing tap the beats in the right hand as done previously and as shown in Step 1. On the third hearing tap twice with the left hand for each tap in the right hand as shown in Step 2.

FIGURE 5.1. *Tapping Simple Division.*

MSS 4

In Figure 5.1 the taps in the right hand determine the duration of each beat. The taps in the left hand divide each of these durations into two equal parts. This division is called *simple division of the beat* or *simple background of the beat*.

Compound Beat

A beat that can be divided into three parts is called a *compound beat*. Listen to the melody in Figure 5.2. On the second hearing tap the beats in the right hand as done previously and as shown in Step 1. On the third hearing tap three times with the left hand for each tap in the right hand as shown in Step 2. The left hand is *dividing the beat* into three parts; this division is called the *compound division of the beat* or the *compound background of the beat*.

FIGURE 5.2. *Tapping Compound Division.*

MSS 194

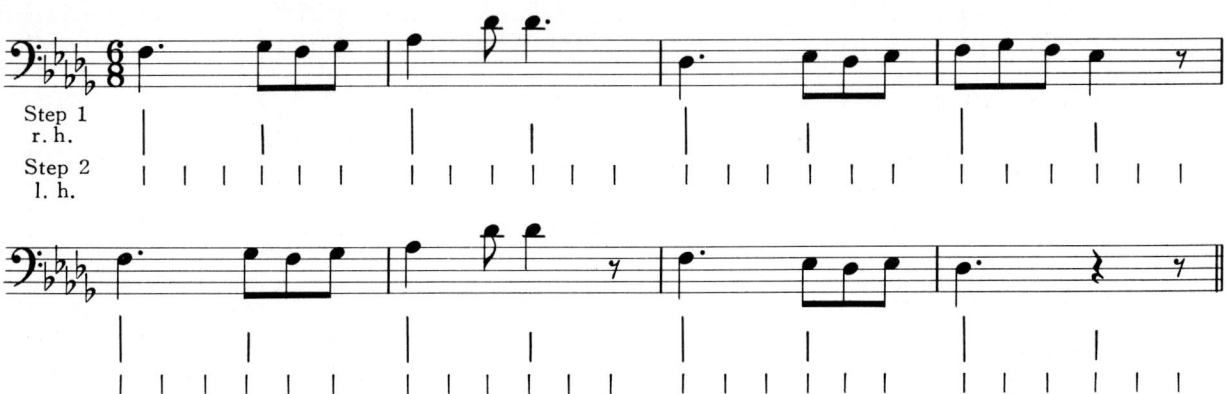

In the preceding chapter we recognized groupings of beats in patterns of two, three, or four; in this chapter we have examined the two varieties of beats. We have now found three different groupings of beats, and two different divisions for each beat, making a total of six possible combinations for groupings of beats and their backgrounds. The terminology for identifying these various combinations comes under the general term *meter*.

Meter

In music, *meter* is the systematic grouping of beats and their divisions in regularly recurring patterns of pulsations. Meter is described as being *duple, triple,* or *quadruple* according to the grouping of beats, and *simple* or *compound* according to the division of each beat. Therefore, the six possible meter designations are:

FIGURE 5.3. *Meter Designations.*[1]

1. duple simple   4. duple compound
2. triple simple   5. triple compound
3. quadruple simple   6. quadruple compound

The sensations for these six meter designations can be manifested by tapping: the right hand taps the particular grouping of beats, as practiced in Chapter 4,

---

[1] Some theoreticians prefer to reverse these designations, e.g., simple duple, compound triple, etc.

while simultaneously the left hand taps the particular division of each beat. Figure 5.4 shows diagrams for tapping the various combinations.

FIGURE 5.4. *Diagrams for Tapping Meter.*

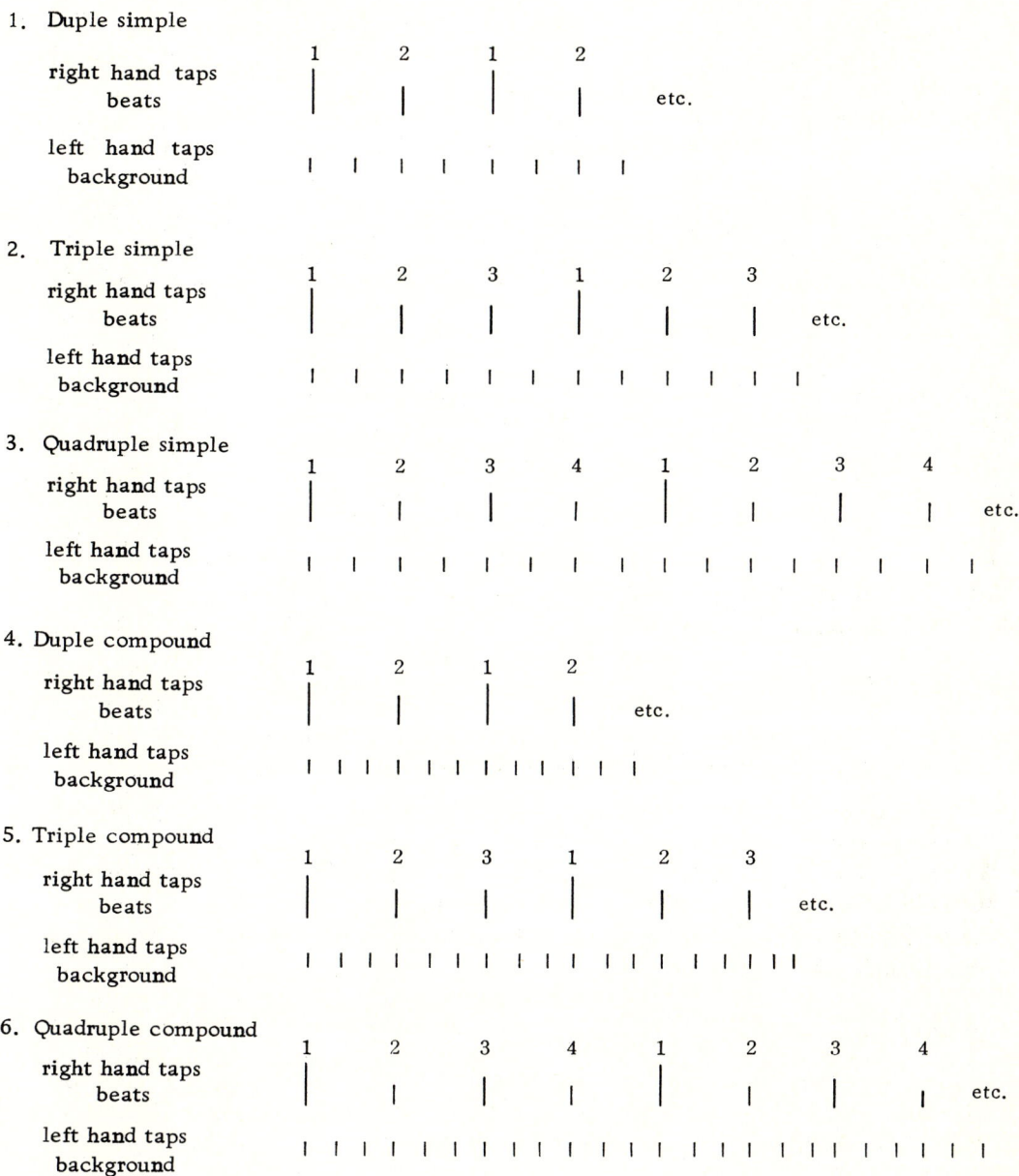

EXERCISE 5.1T
Tapping Simple Meters

The instructor will announce a meter designation as duple simple, or triple simple, or quadruple simple. The student taps the beats and background as shown in Figure 5.4. Using the metronome, the tempo for the beats should not be slower than M.M. 52 nor faster than M.M. 116.

EXERCISE 5.2T
Tapping Compound Meters

The instructor will announce a meter designation as duple compound, or triple compound, or quadruple compound. The student taps the beats and background as shown in Figure 5.4. Using the metronome, the tempo for the beats should be neither slower than M.M. 46 nor faster than M.M. 96.

EXERCISE 5.3T
Tapping Simple Meters with Music

Listen to a melody played by the instructor. On the second hearing tap the groupings of beats with the right hand. On the third playing add the background of two with the left hand. Be prepared to identify the meter by one of the three simple meter designations.

FRENCH FOLKSONG

(a) M.M. 84

BRITISH FOLKSONG

(b) M.M. 92

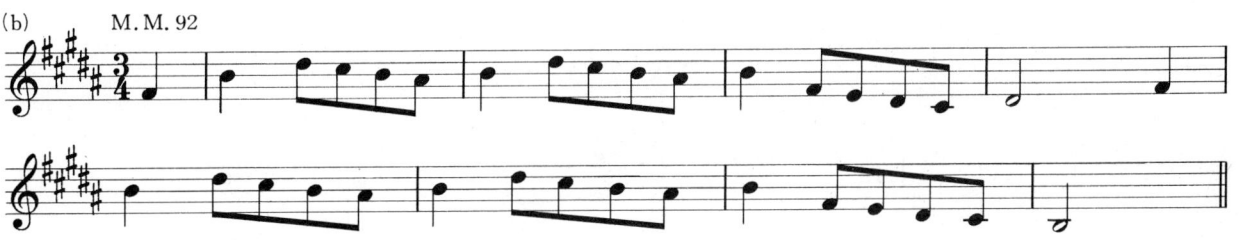

UKRANIAN FOLKSONG

(c) M.M. 100

SWEDISH FOLKSONG

FRENCH FOLKSONG

RUSSIAN FOLKSONG

EXERCISE 5.4T

Tapping Compound Meters with Music

Listen to a melody played by the instructor. On the second hearing tap the groupings of beats with the right hand. On the third playing add the background of three with the left hand. Be prepared to identify as either duple compound or triple compound. (Quadruple compound time is not frequently used in music composition since one quadruple unit usually sounds like two duple units. For this reason, no quadruple compound meter is included in this exercise.)

SWEET AND LOW

Joseph Barnby

GREETING AT MORN

Felix Mendelssohn

DRINK TO ME ONLY WITH THINE EYES

(c) M.M. 52

IT CAME UPON A MIDNIGHT CLEAR

Richard S. Willis

(d) M.M. 54

DOWN IN THE VALLEY

(e) M.M. 60

EXERCISE 5.5T
Tapping Simple or Compound Meters with Music

Listen to a melody played by the instructor. It may be in either a simple or compound meter as selected by the instructor. On the second hearing tap both the groupings of beats and the background, and identify as before. (There will be no quadruple compound meter included in this exercise.)

DANISH FOLKSONG

(a) M.M. 72

BRITISH FOLKSONG

(b) M.M. 100

BEAUTIFUL DREAMER

Stephen Foster

(c)   M.M. 60

CZECH FOLKSONG

(d)   M.M. 92

TYROLEAN FOLKSONG

(e)   M.M. 108

EXERCISE 5.6T
Tapping Simple or Compound Meters with Music

For additional drill, continue Exercise 5.5T using the following melodies from *Music for Sight Singing*. Observe the recommended metronome indications.

(1)	5 M.M. 92		(9)	199 M.M. 60
(2)	59 M.M. 84		(10)	341 M.M. 80
(3)	15 M.M. 108		(11)	212 M.M. 86
(4)	27 M.M. 116		(12)	95 M.M. 92
(5)	116 M.M. 80		(13)	66 M.M. 92
(6)	68 M.M. 69		(14)	83 M.M. 100
(7)	176 M.M. 112		(15)	201 M.M. 69
(8)	182 M.M. 100		(16)	113 M.M. 112

_____ NAME

EXERCISE 5.7
Identification of Meter Diagrams

Identify by name (duple simple, etc.) the following arrangements of beats:

(a)
beat | |
background | | | | duple
                                                    _____
                                                       simple
                                                    _____

(b)
beat | | |
background | | | | | | | | | triple compound

(c)
beat | |
background | | | | | | duple compound

(d)
beat | | | |
background | | | | | | | | quadruple simple

(e)
beat | | |
background | | | | | | triple simple

(f)
beat | | | |
background | | | | | | | | | | | | quadruple compound

61

EXERCISE 5.8
Drawing Meter Diagrams

Make diagrams as shown in Figure 5.4 and Exercise 5.7 for the following:

Triple simple:

Duple compound:

Quadruple compound:

Duple simple:

Triple compound:

Quadruple simple:

CHAPTER SIX

TIME
(continued)

The Construction of Notes
The Relationship of Notes to Each Other
Notation of Rests

In our study to this point, we have found that a common element of time in music is the sensation of the beat, a regularly recurring duration of time easily recognized in the sound of the music. In addition, we have found that we hear durations longer or shorter than the beat. All durations of time can be represented by written symbols called notes (first described in the footnote on page 3). The functions of a note are to indicate the duration of a musical sound, and when placed on a staff, the pitch of a sound. In Chapters 1–3, one type of note (o) was used on the staff to indicate pitch, but no attempt was made to describe its use in measuring duration. Continuing the study of notation we shall consider how notes can indicate durations. This includes (1) the construction of notes, (2) the relationship of notes to each other, and (3) [1] relationship of notation to the sensation of the beat. We will consider the first two points in this chapter, beginning with *the construction of notes*.

The Construction of Notes

The note is made up of one, two, or three elements: (1) the note head; (2) the stem; (3) the flag.

1. The *note head* is a tilted ellipse, white (open) or black.

FIGURE 6.1. *Note Heads.*

2. The *stem* is a vertical line connected to a note head. When a single note head is placed on the staff below the third line, the stem points up; when the note head is above the third line, the stem points down; when the note head is on the third line, the stem may point either up or down. Pointing up, the stem is connected to the right side of the note head; pointing down, the stem appears on the left side of the note head. The length of the stem is approximately equal to a distance of three spaces of the staff.

[1] To be studied in the following chapter.

FIGURE 6.2. *Stems.*

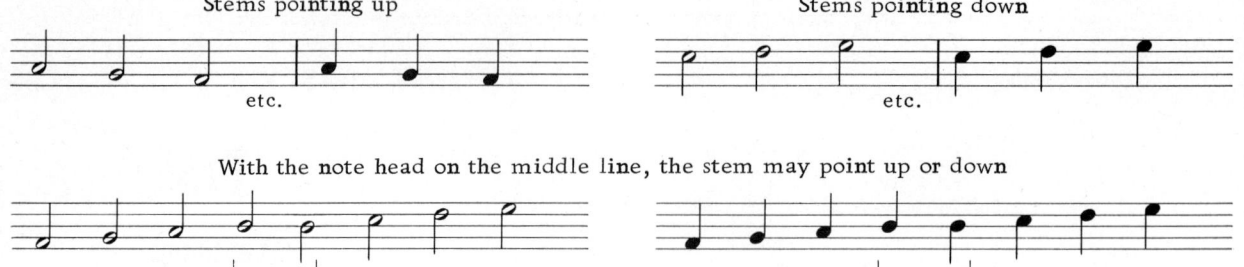

3. The *flag* (*hook*) is placed at the end of the stem. One to three flags are commonly used; four and five flags are infrequently used. Flags always appear to the right of the stems. Only black notes can have flags.

FIGURE 6.3. *Flags.*

One flag   Two flags   Three flags

Groups of two or more similar notes requiring flags are written two different ways: (1) as separate notes with stems and flags, 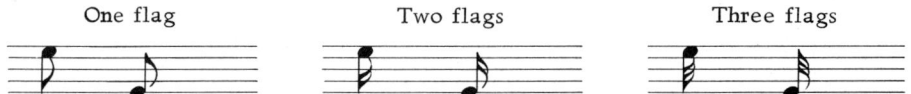 , or, in place of flags, (2) with the stems of the notes connected by a heavy line called *beam* or *ligature*, . One beam serves the same function as one flag; two beams serve as two flags, or , etc.

If several notes of different pitch are beamed together, use a stem direction which is correct for a majority of the notes in the group.

FIGURE 6.4. *Beamed Notes on the Staff.*

The Relationship of Notes to Each Other

Notes are named according to mathematical relationships to the number 1 (one whole). The open ellipse is called a *whole note* and assigned the value "1." Other notes are named and evaluated in relationship to the whole note. Figure 6.5 shows the names of commonly used notes, their symbols and values.

FIGURE 6.5. *Note Values.*

Name	Note	Value
Whole note	𝐨	1
Half note	♩ or ♩	$\frac{1}{2}$
Quarter note	♩ or ♩	$\frac{1}{4}$
Eighth note	♪ or ♪	$\frac{1}{8}$
Sixteenth note	♬ or ♬	$\frac{1}{16}$
Thirty-second note	♬ or ♬	$\frac{1}{32}$
Sixty-fourth note etc.	♬ or ♬	$\frac{1}{64}$

Infrequently used in modern notation:

| Double whole note | |o| or ‖o‖ or ⊟ | 2 |

The relationship of notes to each other is further illustrated in Figure 6.6. Each mathematical value is divided into the next smaller fraction.

FIGURE 6.6. *Note Divisions.*

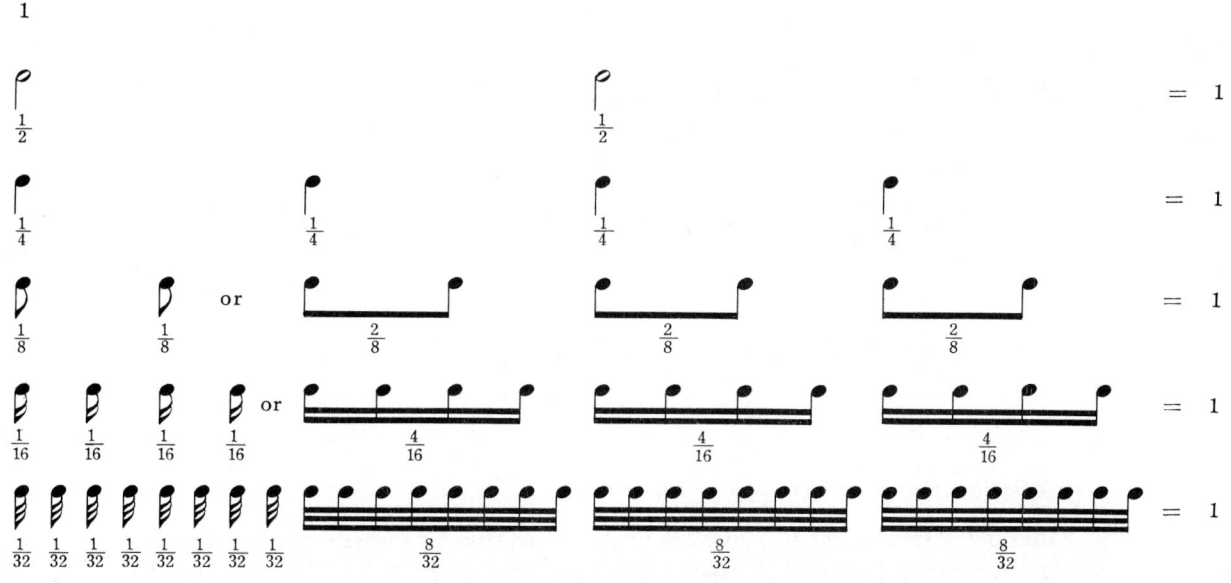

Just as a musical sound has duration, so does silence in music have duration. Symbols representing silence are called *rests*.

Notation of Rests

Silence in music is represented by symbols called *rests*. For each note value representing sound, there is a corresponding rest value for silence. Figure 6.7 shows names and symbols for commonly used rests.

FIGURE 6.7. *Rests.*

Name	Rest
Whole rest	▬ (beneath 4th line)
Half rest	▬ (upon 3rd line)
Quarter rest	𝄽 or ⌐[2]
Eighth rest	𝄾
Sixteenth rest	𝄿
Thirty-second rest	𝅀
Sixty-fourth rest	𝅁

Also, corresponding to the double whole note:

Double whole rest	▮

Observe that while the symbols for the whole and half rests are similar in being a black, oblong shape, they are distinguished in that the whole rest is found *beneath* (suspended from) the fourth staff line while the half rest is *upon* the third line. Notice also in Figure 6.7 that the stems of the eighth rests and following rests are slanted, and that the flags, or hooks, are pointed to the left.

Figure 6.8 shows different note values and corresponding rests. While notes may be placed on any line or space of the staff, rests are ordinarily found on the staff as shown in this figure.

---

[2] This quarter rest symbol, ⌐, may be found particularly in foreign editions of music. Because of possible confusion with the eighth rest, 𝄾, its use is not recommended.

FIGURE 6.8. *Notes of Different Values and Corresponding Rests.*

| whole | half | quarter | 8th | 16th | 32nd | 64th | double whole |

Whether treble or bass clef is used, the position of a rest on the staff is not affected.

Notes and rests presented above are commonly used in music compositions. Many of these are shown in the following short excerpt from Haydn (Figure 6.9).

FIGURE 6.9. *Music Excerpt Showing Many Note Values.*

Haydn, Sonata for Piano in E♭ Major

* *Tremolo*, played as sixteen 32nd notes, alternating contra F and great F.

_____ NAME

EXERCISE 6.1
Drawing Notes on the Staff

After each note, draw others as indicated. Write the name of the given note below the staff.

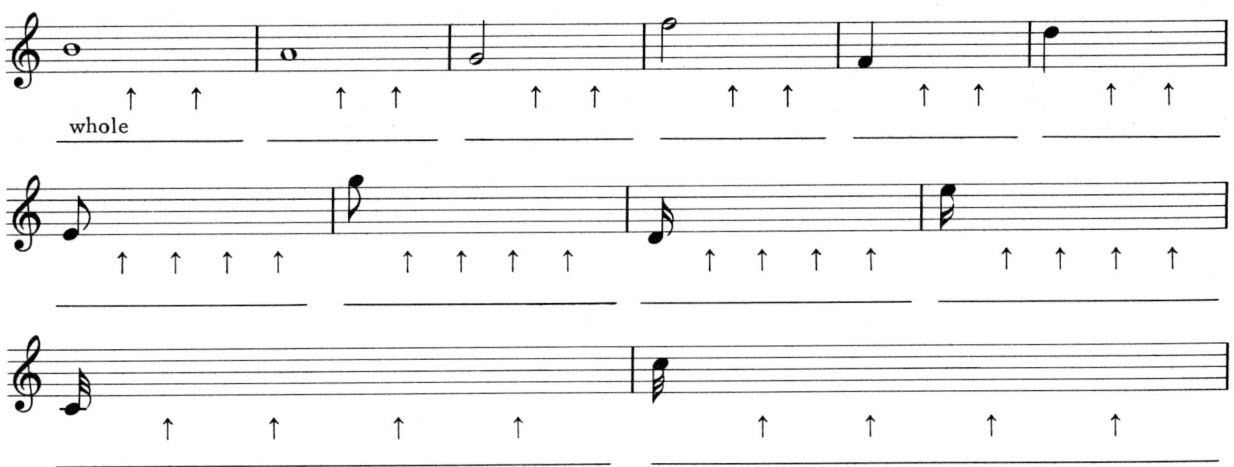

EXERCISE 6.2
Writing Various Note Values

On the middle line, write the note value designated.

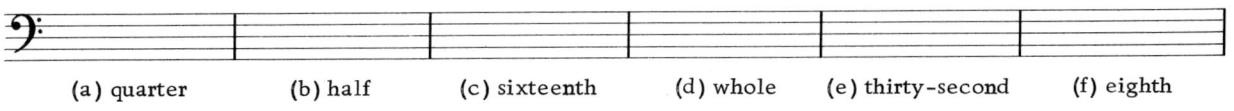

(a) quarter   (b) half   (c) sixteenth   (d) whole   (e) thirty-second   (f) eighth

EXERCISE 6.3
Writing Various Notes in Treble and Bass Clefs

Write the note value at the pitch designated. Make sure that stems point the correct way.

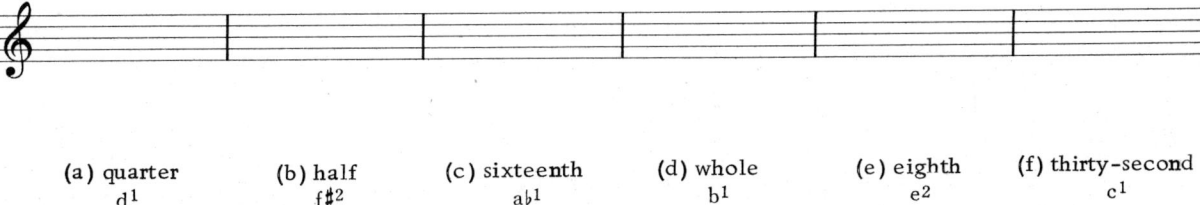

(a) quarter   (b) half   (c) sixteenth   (d) whole   (e) eighth   (f) thirty-second
d^1 $f\sharp^2$ $a\flat^1$ b^1 e^2 c^1

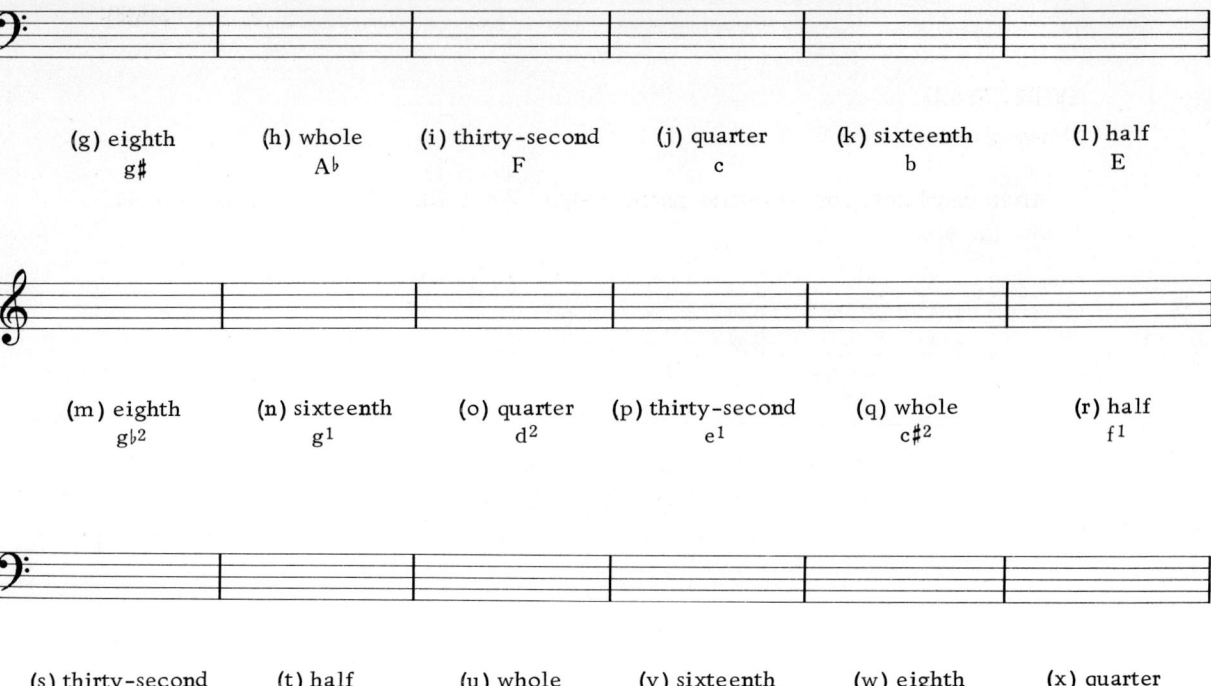

_____ NAME

EXERCISE 6.4
Note Divisions

Indicate the division of each given note.

𝅝 = 𝅗𝅥 𝅗𝅥

𝅗𝅥 =

♩ =

♪ =

𝅘𝅥𝅯 =

𝅘𝅥𝅯 =

EXERCISE 6.5
Relationship of Notes

Fill in the blanks using words only, for example, *two quarter* notes; *eighth* note. Write your answers in the blanks at the right side of the page.

(a) A quarter note equals two _____ notes.

_____

(b) An _____ note equals two sixteenth notes.

_____

(c) A thirty-second note equals two _____ notes.

_____

(d) A whole note equals two _____ notes.

_____

(e) A _____ note equals two quarter notes.

_____

(f) A _____ note equals two eighth notes.

_____

(g) A sixteenth note equals two _____ notes.

_____

(h) A _____ note equals two half notes.

(i) An eighth note equals two _____ notes.

(j) A _____ note equals two thirty-second notes.

EXERCISE 6.6
Writing Divisions of Various Notes on the Staff

Write on the staff the division of the given note at the designated pitch. In this exercise, use beams whenever possible.

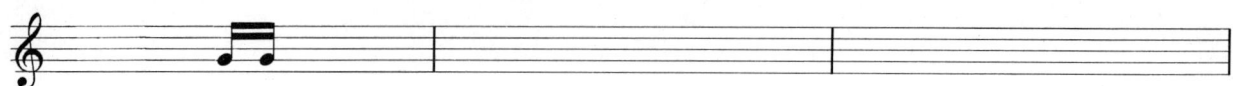

(a) g^1, eighth note   (b) c^2, half note   (c) d^1, sixteenth note

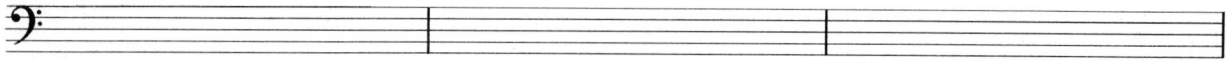

(d) f, quarter note   (e) A, thirty-second note   (f) B, whole note

EXERCISE 6.7
Drawing Rests on the Staff

After each rest, draw others as indicated. Write the name of the given rest below the staff.

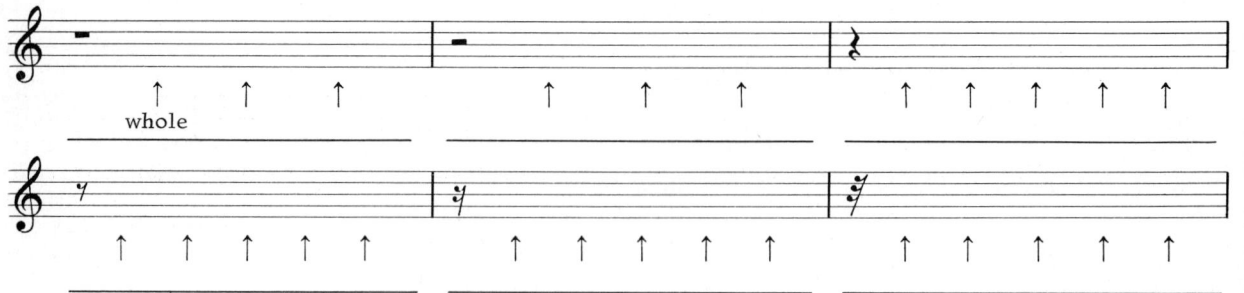

whole

NAME _____

EXERCISE 6.8
Drawing Rests Corresponding to Notes

For each note value, draw and name the corresponding rest.

EXERCISE 6.9
Writing Various Rest Values

Write on the staff the rest value designated.

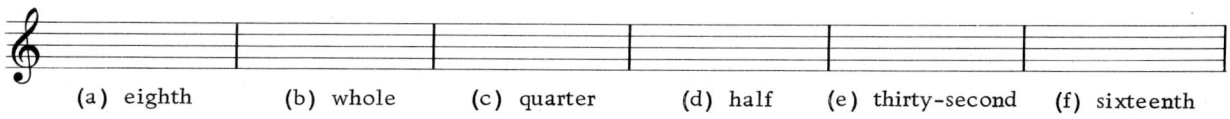

(a) eighth   (b) whole   (c) quarter   (d) half   (e) thirty-second   (f) sixteenth

CHAPTER SEVEN

TIME
(continued)

**Notation of the Simple Beat
Simple Meter (Time) Signatures
Notation of the Compound Beat
Compound Meter Signatures
Bar-lines
Measure**

We have found that beats in music can be grouped in two's, three's, or four's, and that they also can be divided into backgrounds of two or three. We have experienced these sensations and depicted them on paper with six meter designations and diagrams, previously shown in Figures 5.3 and 5.4. Most music is written in these six metrical patterns, but each can be represented on paper only when a note value is assigned to the beat. We shall first study how a note value may be assigned to represent the simple beat, or *notation of the simple beat*, followed by a similar study of the *notation of the compound beat*.

Notation of the Simple Beat

A simple beat divides into a background of two equal parts. Therefore, a note assigned to represent a simple beat must have a value divisible into two equal parts. The value most often used by composers to represent the simple beat is the quarter note.[1]

FIGURE 7.1. *Note Values Assigned to Represent the Simple Beat.*

The quarter note may represent the simple beat:

beat

♩ = 1/4 value

♫ = simple division

---

[1] Theoretically, any note value divisible by two could represent a simple beat. For the present, we shall study three different note values, the quarter, the eighth and the half, which are commonly used to represent the simple beat.

The eighth note also may represent the simple beat:

beat
♪ = 1/8 value

♫ = simple division

The half note may represent the simple beat:

beat
𝅗𝅥 = 1/2 value

♩ ♩ = simple division

When we know the number of beats in a group and the assigned value of a beat, we can derive a *meter signature*.

Simple Meter (Time) Signatures

A meter signature is a pair of numbers aligned vertically, such as $\frac{2}{4}$, $\frac{4}{8}$, etc., and placed at the beginning of a composition. It may be compared to a mathematical fraction placed on the staff with the numerator above and denominator below the third line. Its function is to indicate to the performer which metrical pattern is to be used in the piece of music, and, in addition, what note values will be used to represent the metrical pattern. Simple meter signature is derived according to the beat value and the beat grouping as shown in Figure 7.2.

FIGURE 7.2. *Derivation of Simple Meter (Time) Signatures.*

Beat Value	Beat Grouping	Meter (Time) Signature	Meter Name
♪ $\frac{1}{8}$	one ♪ $\frac{1}{8}$ + two ♪ $\frac{1}{8}$ =	$\frac{2}{8}$	
♩ $\frac{1}{4}$	one ♩ $\frac{1}{4}$ + two ♩ $\frac{1}{4}$ =	$\frac{2}{4}$	DUPLE SIMPLE
♩ $\frac{1}{2}$	one ♩ $\frac{1}{2}$ + two ♩ $\frac{1}{2}$ =	$\frac{2}{2}$ or ¢*	
♪ $\frac{1}{8}$	one ♪ $\frac{1}{8}$ + two ♪ $\frac{1}{8}$ + three ♪ $\frac{1}{8}$ =	$\frac{3}{8}$	
♩ $\frac{1}{4}$	one ♩ $\frac{1}{4}$ + two ♩ $\frac{1}{4}$ + three ♩ $\frac{1}{4}$ =	$\frac{3}{4}$	TRIPLE SIMPLE
♩ $\frac{1}{2}$	one ♩ $\frac{1}{2}$ + two ♩ $\frac{1}{2}$ + three ♩ $\frac{1}{2}$ =	$\frac{3}{2}$	
♪ $\frac{1}{8}$	one ♪ $\frac{1}{8}$ + two ♪ $\frac{1}{8}$ + three ♪ $\frac{1}{8}$ + four ♪ $\frac{1}{8}$ =	$\frac{4}{8}$	
♩ $\frac{1}{4}$	one ♩ $\frac{1}{4}$ + two ♩ $\frac{1}{4}$ + three ♩ $\frac{1}{4}$ + four ♩ $\frac{1}{4}$ =	$\frac{4}{4}$ or C**	QUADRUPLE SIMPLE
♩ $\frac{1}{2}$	one ♩ $\frac{1}{2}$ + two ♩ $\frac{1}{2}$ + three ♩ $\frac{1}{2}$ + four ♩ $\frac{1}{2}$ =	$\frac{4}{2}$	

Observe in Figure 7.2 that all meter signatures with the numerator of 2 indicate duple simple meter; all with the numerator of 3 indicate triple simple meter; and all with the numerator 4 indicate quadruple meter. The denominator 8 means that the eighth note value (♪) represents one beat; the denominator 4 means that the quarter note value (♩) represents one beat; the denominator 2 means that the

* called *cut time:* ¢ is a symbol substituting for 2/2.
** called *common time;* C is a symbol substituting for 4/4.

half note value (𝅗𝅥) represents the beat; etc. Figure 7.3 shows the meaning of different simple meter signatures by the notation of their metrical patterns.

FIGURE 7.3. *Meaning of Simple Meter Signatures.*

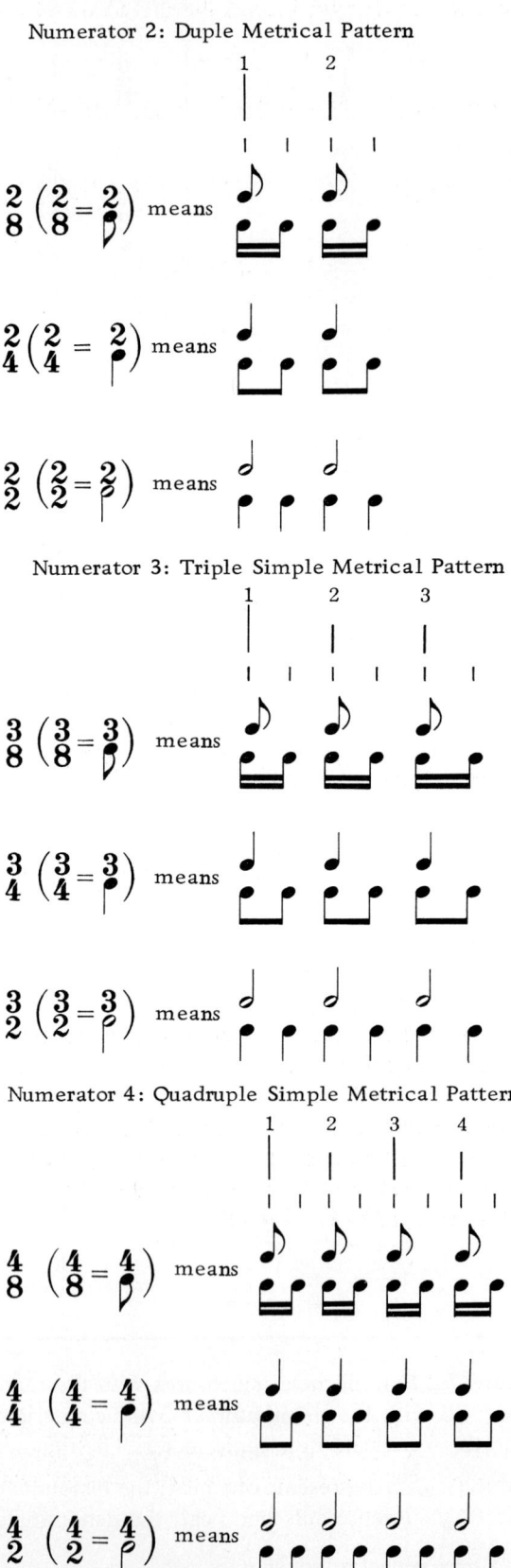

Notation of the Compound Beat

A compound beat divides into a background of three equal parts. Therefore a note representing a compound beat must have a value divisible into three parts. Such a value requires a *dotted note*. A dot placed after a note (♩.) increases the duration by one half the value of the note. The value most often used by composers to represent the compound beat is the dotted quarter note.[2]

FIGURE 7.4. *Note Values Assigned to Represent the Compound Beat.*

The dotted quarter note may represent the compound beat:

beat

♩. = ♩ + ♪   therefore ♩. = 3/8 value

$\frac{1}{4} + \frac{1}{8}$ ♫♪ = compound division

$\left(\frac{2}{8} + \frac{1}{8} = \frac{3}{8}\right)$

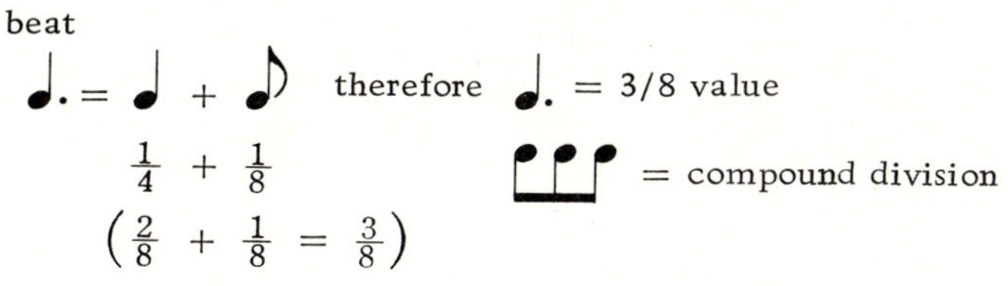

The dotted eighth note also may be used to represent the compound beat:

beat

♪. = ♪ + ♬   therefore ♪. = 3/16 value

$\frac{1}{8} + \frac{1}{16}$ ♬♬ = compound division

$\left(\frac{2}{16} + \frac{1}{16} = \frac{3}{16}\right)$

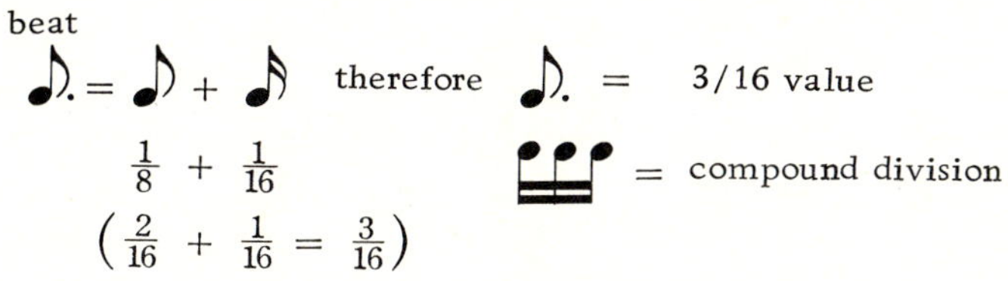

The dotted half note may be used to represent the compound beat:

beat

𝅗𝅥. = 𝅗𝅥 + ♩   therefore 𝅗𝅥. = 3/4 value

$\frac{1}{2} + \frac{1}{4}$ ♩♩♩ = compound division

$\left(\frac{2}{4} + \frac{1}{4} = \frac{3}{4}\right)$

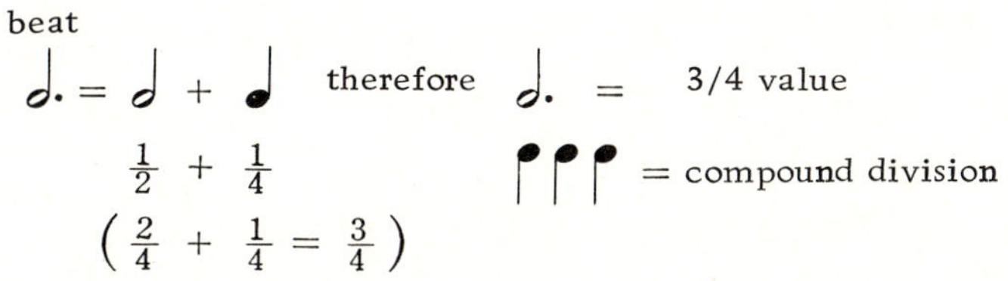

Notice that a dotted quarter can be represented mathematically only by the fraction $\frac{3}{8}$; the dotted eighth is represented by the fraction $\frac{3}{16}$; and the dotted half note is represented by the fraction $\frac{3}{4}$. Some theorists prefer to call a dotted quarter a *three-eighths note;* a dotted eighth a *three-sixteenths note;* and a dotted half a *three-quarters note.* However, this terminology is not generally used.

According to the number of beats in a group and the assigned value of a beat, we can derive the *compound meter signatures.*

---

[2] Theoretically, any note value divisible by three could represent a compound beat. For the present, we shall study three values, the dotted quarter, the dotted eighth, and the dotted half, which are note values commonly used to represent the compound beat.

Compound Meter Signatures

The compound meter signature is derived from the beat value and the beat grouping as shown in Figure 7.5.

FIGURE 7.5. *Derivation of Compound Meter Signatures.*

Beat Value	Best Grouping	Meter (Time) Signature	Meter Name
♪. $\frac{3}{16}$	one ♪. $\frac{3}{16}$ + two ♪. $\frac{3}{16}$ =	$\frac{6}{16}$	DUPLE COMPOUND
♩. $\frac{3}{8}$	one ♩. $\frac{3}{8}$ + two ♩. $\frac{3}{8}$ =	$\frac{6}{8}$	
♩. $\frac{3}{4}$	one ♩. $\frac{3}{4}$ + two ♩. $\frac{3}{4}$ =	$\frac{6}{4}$	
♪. $\frac{3}{16}$	one ♪. $\frac{3}{16}$ + two ♪. $\frac{3}{16}$ + three ♪. $\frac{3}{16}$ =	$\frac{9}{16}$	TRIPLE COMPOUND
♩. $\frac{3}{8}$	one ♩. $\frac{3}{8}$ + two ♩. $\frac{3}{8}$ + three ♩. $\frac{3}{8}$ =	$\frac{9}{8}$	
♩. $\frac{3}{4}$	one ♩. $\frac{3}{4}$ + two ♩. $\frac{3}{4}$ + three ♩. $\frac{3}{4}$ =	$\frac{9}{4}$	
♪. $\frac{3}{16}$	one ♪. $\frac{3}{16}$ + two ♪. $\frac{3}{16}$ + three ♪. $\frac{3}{16}$ + four ♪. $\frac{3}{16}$ =	$\frac{12}{16}$	QUADRUPLE COMPOUND
♩. $\frac{3}{8}$	one ♩. $\frac{3}{8}$ + two ♩. $\frac{3}{8}$ + three ♩. $\frac{3}{8}$ + four ♩. $\frac{3}{8}$ =	$\frac{12}{8}$	
♩. $\frac{3}{4}$	one ♩. $\frac{3}{4}$ + two ♩. $\frac{3}{4}$ + three ♩. $\frac{3}{4}$ + four ♩. $\frac{3}{4}$ =	$\frac{12}{4}$	

Observe in Figure 7.5 that all meter signatures with the numerator of 6 indicate duple compound meter; all with the numerator of 9 indicate triple compound meter; and all with the numerator 12 indicate quadruple compound meter. Unlike the simple meter signature where the numerator is identical with the number of beats in a group, in a compound meter signature the numerator is identical with the number of divisions of the beats. The denominator shows the assigned value to each division of the compound beat, three of which equal one beat. Figure 7.6 shows the meaning of different compound meter signatures by the notation of their metrical patterns.

FIGURE 7.6. *Meaning of Compound Meter Signatures.*

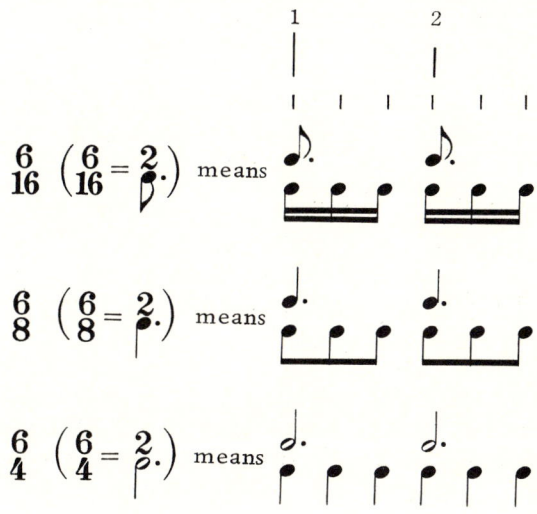

FIGURE 7.6. *continued.*

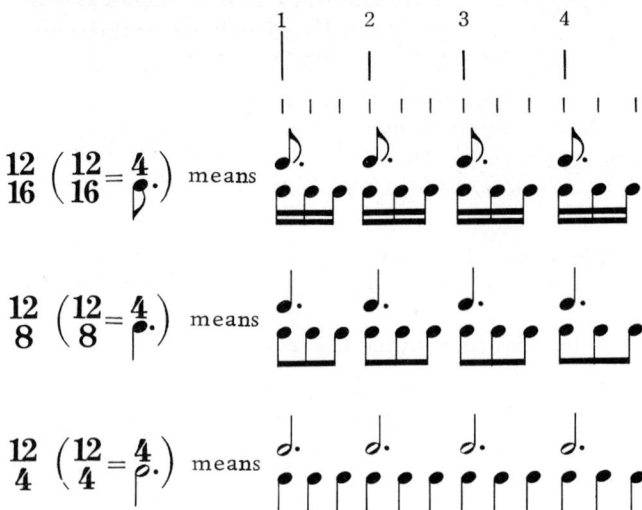

In listening to music, we have established the fact that beats recur consistently in duple, triple, or quadruple meter. In notation, as a visual aid in recognizing this organization of meter, we use a device known as the *bar-line* with resulting *measure*.

Bar-lines

A single *bar-line* serves to separate one group of beats from the next. It is a vertical line placed across the staff extending from the bottom to the top lines. A *double bar-line* is used at the end of a composition or at the end of a section of a composition.[3]

FIGURE 7.7. *Bar-lines.*

Single bar-line   Double bar-line

Measure

A measure as seen on the staff is the distance between bar-lines. Each measure is heard as a group of beats; each measure contains the number of beats indicated by the meter signature.

---

[3] Other uses of bar-lines will be discussed in a later chapter.

FIGURE 7.8. *Measures.*

The heavy beat of a group is the first beat of a measure. The heavy beat, therefore, always occurs immediately following the bar-line.

FIGURE 7.9. *Location of the Heavy Beat at the Beginning of Measures.*

_____ NAME

EXERCISE 7.1
Notating the Metrical Grouping in Simple Time

Using the beat note given, convert the given metrical pattern to notation. Place a meter signature before the beat grouping and name the meter in the blanks provided.

Example: ♩ = 1 beat

Answer: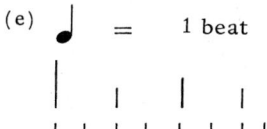
duple simple

(a) ♪ = 1 beat

| |
| | | |

_____

(b) ♩ = 1 beat

| | |
| | | | | |

_____

(c) ♪ = 1 beat

| | | |
| | | | | | |

_____

(d) 𝅗𝅥 = 1 beat

| | |
| | | | | |

_____

(e) ♩ = 1 beat

| | | |
| | | | | | | |

_____

(f) 𝅗𝅥 = 1 beat

| |
| | | |

_____

(g) ♪ = 1 beat

| | |
| | | | | |

_____

(h) 𝅗𝅥 = 1 beat

| | | |
| | | | | | |

_____

EXERCISE 7.2
Notating the Metrical Grouping in Compound Time

Follow the directions given in Exercise 7.1.

(a) 𝅘𝅥𝅮. = 1 beat

(b) ♪. = 1 beat

(c) 𝅗𝅥. = 1 beat

(d) 𝅗𝅥. = 1 beat

(e) 𝅗𝅥. = 1 beat

(f) ♪. = 1 beat

(g) 𝅗𝅥. = 1 beat

(h) 𝅗𝅥. = 1 beat

(i) ♪. = 1 beat

_____ NAME

EXERCISE 7.3

Supplying Metrical Patterns for Given Simple Time Signatures

After the given time signature, write the metrical pattern with correct notation and name the meter.

Example: given 2/4   answer 2/4 ♩ ♩
                                        duple simple

(a) 3/4

(e) 4/2

(b) 2/8

(f) 3/8

(c) 4/4

(g) 4/8

(d) 2/2

(h) 3/2

87

EXERCISE 7.4
Supplying Metrical Patterns for Given Compound Time Signatures

Follow directions given in Exercise 7.3.

(a) $\frac{6}{8}$

_____ _____

(b) $\frac{12}{4}$

_____ _____

(c) $\frac{9}{8}$

_____ _____

(d) $\frac{9}{4}$

_____ _____

(e) $\frac{9}{16}$

_____ _____

(f) $\frac{6}{4}$

_____ _____

(g) $\frac{12}{8}$

_____ _____

(h) $\frac{6}{16}$

_____ _____

(i) $\frac{12}{16}$

_____ _____

EXERCISE 7.5

Identifying the Meter Designation

Write the meter signature and notate the metrical pattern when the meter designation and the beat value are given.

Example: Duple simple, ♩ = 1 beat

$\frac{2}{4}$ ♩ ♩ (with subdivided eighth notes)

(a) Triple simple, ♩ = 1 beat

(b) Duple compound, ♩. = 1 beat

(c) Quadruple simple, ♩ = 1 beat

(d) Triple compound, ♪. = 1 beat

(e) Quadruple compound, ♩. = 1 beat

(f) Duple simple, ♪ = 1 beat

89

(g) Quadruple simple, ♩ = 1 beat

(h) Triple compound, ♩. = 1 beat

(i) Duple compound, 𝅗𝅥. = 1 beat

(j) Triple simple, ♪ = 1 beat

(k) Duple simple, 𝅗𝅥 = 1 beat

(l) Quadruple compound, ♩. = 1 beat

(m) Duple compound, ♪. = 1 beat

(n) Triple simple, 𝅗𝅥 = 1 beat

(o) Quadruple compound, ♪. = 1 beat

(p) Quadruple simple, ♪ = 1 beat

(q) Triple compound, ♩. = 1 beat

EXERCISE 7.6
Explaining the Meaning of Simple Meter Signatures

Example: Explain the meaning of $\frac{2}{4}$. Answer: The "2" indicates that the music is in duple simple meter, meaning that there are two beats in the measure, each beat divisible into two parts. The "4" indicates that a quarter note is used to represent the beat, and it is divisible into two eighth notes.

Explain each of the following in a similar manner.

$$\frac{3}{4} \qquad \frac{4}{4} \qquad \frac{2}{8} \qquad \frac{3}{2} \qquad \frac{3}{8} \qquad \frac{4}{2} \qquad \frac{4}{8}$$

EXERCISE 7.7
Explaining the Meaning of Compound Meter Signatures

Example: Explain the meaning of $\frac{6}{8}$. Answer: The "6" indicates that the music is in duple compound meter, meaning that there are two beats in the measure, each beat divisible into three parts. The "8" indicates that an eighth note is used to represent the division (background) of the beat, and three eighth notes equal one beat, a dotted quarter note.

Explain each of the following in a similar manner.

$$\frac{6}{4} \qquad \frac{9}{8} \qquad \frac{12}{8} \qquad \frac{6}{16} \qquad \frac{12}{4} \qquad \frac{9}{4} \qquad \frac{9}{16} \qquad \frac{12}{16}$$

CHAPTER EIGHT

TIME
(continued)

Conductor's Beats

With the knowledge gained thus far concerning notation and meter, it becomes possible to begin study in the actual reading of music. There are two standards in the reading of music: the first in which the performer looks at a given note and reacts by depressing the correct key on his instrument, and the second in which the performer looks at a given note and knows before playing it how that note will sound. For musicians, the ultimate goal is the accomplishment of the second standard. An important attribute of the accomplished musician is his ability to read music of varying complexities, including a single melodic line, the two staves of notation necessary for piano music, or even an orchestral score consisting of a full page of staves representing all the instruments of the symphony orchestra. An effective approach to the ultimate skills of music reading is through the technique of singing a melody at sight. Singing is preferred over performance at an instrument because in singing it is impossible to fall back on any mechanical help (such as a key) to help locate a correct pitch.

In singing at sight (sightsinging) two kinds of reading are necessary: (1) reading note values and (2) reading pitches. We will begin by learning to read the durations of different note values. Most students have found their study made easier if they can actually feel the metrical grouping as they perform. This can be accomplished by the use of *conductor's beats*.

Conductor's Beats

Conductor's beats are patterns of hand gestures used to indicate groupings of beats.[1] While the motions or diagrams of the beats may vary among conductors, certain basic movements are so standardized as to be accepted by musicians throughout the world.

The following right-hand diagrams for conductor's beats are recommended because the *points* of all beats occur approximately on the same horizontal plane. For the student seated in a classroom this horizontal plane might be the desk-top.

---

[1] Herman Scherchen (*Handbook of Conducting*, Oxford University Press, London, 1933) considers that there are three distinct purposes in conducting: (1) to present the metric course of the music; (2) to indicate its expressive, structural features; and (3) to actually guide the musicians—preventing faulty performance and correcting fluctuations or inequalities. In this present course of study, the student will be concerned only with the first purpose, to present the metric course of the music.

FIGURE 8.1. *Conductor's Beats.*[2]

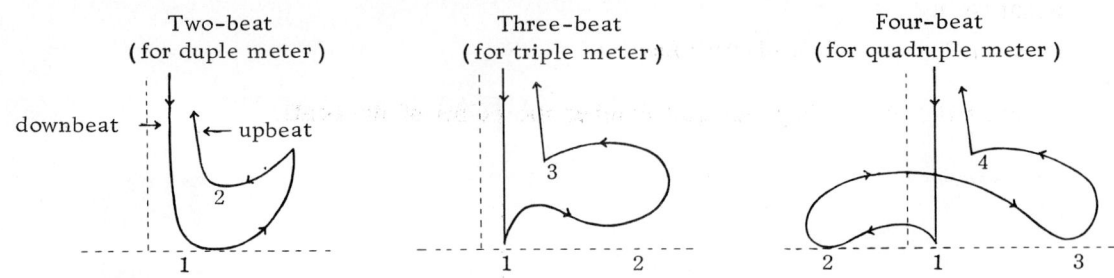

The numbers indicate the *points* of the beats. The first beat in all diagrams is called the *downbeat* and always coincides with the first beat of a measure. In any of these patterns, the last beat is described by an upward motion of the hand and is called an *upbeat*.

The two-beat can be used for duple simple meter signatures (numerator of 2) or duple compound signatures (numerator of 6). In the same way, the three-beat can be used for meter signatures with numerators of 3 or 9, and the four-beat for meter signatures with numerators of 4 or 12.

FIGURE 8.2. *Meter Signatures and Accompanying Conductor's Beats.*

	Meter Signatures						Accompanying Conductor's Beats
	Simple			Compound			
DUPLE	$\frac{2}{8}$	$\frac{2}{4}$	$\frac{2}{2}$	$\frac{6}{16}$	$\frac{6}{8}$	$\frac{6}{4}$	TWO-BEAT
TRIPLE	$\frac{3}{8}$	$\frac{3}{4}$	$\frac{3}{2}$	$\frac{9}{16}$	$\frac{9}{8}$	$\frac{9}{4}$	THREE-BEAT
QUADRUPLE	$\frac{4}{8}$	$\frac{4}{4}$	$\frac{4}{2}$	$\frac{12}{16}$	$\frac{12}{8}$	$\frac{12}{4}$	FOUR-BEAT

Use of the conductor's beats alone does not differentiate simple and compound meter. While conducting with the right hand, the difference can be demonstrated by tapping with the left hand. Two taps with the left hand for each of the beats in the right hand will describe simple meters; three taps with the left hand for each of the beats in the right hand will describe compound meters.

Using the conductor's beat and tapping with the left hand simultaneously is basically the same procedure shown in Chapter 5 in the diagrams, Figure 5.4, and practiced in Exercises 5.1–5.4. The only difference is in the right hand, where the conductor's beat is substituted for the beat-tap.

---

[2] In addition to two, three, and four, there are other beat-patterns for one, five, six, etc. The student can expect to study these other beat-diagrams in later theory or conducting courses.

_____ NAME

EXERCISE 8.1
Drawing Diagrams of Conductor's Beats

Draw right-hand diagrams and number the points of the beats.

(a) Two-beat

(b) Three-beat

(c) Four-beat

NAME _____

EXERCISE 8.2
Selecting the Conductor's Beat According to Meter Signature

What conductor's beat would be used to accompany the following meter signatures?

Example: 2   *Answer:*
        8   two-beat

(a) 4/4 _____

(b) 9/8 _____

(c) 2/2 _____

(d) 6/8 _____

(e) 12/4 _____

(f) 2/4 _____

(g) 6/16 _____

(h) 9/4 _____

(i) 3/8 _____

(j) 4/2 _____

(k) 3
    4   _____

(l) 12
    16 _____

(m) 6
    4   _____

(n) 12
    8   _____

(o) 9
    16 _____

(p) 4
    8   _____

(q) 3
    2   _____

EXERCISE 8.3

Practicing Conductor's Beats

Practice the two-, three-, and four-beats. Practice sometimes in front of a mirror. Have other students criticize your beats. Observe especially the clarity of diagrams which you execute and the preciseness of the points of the beats.

EXERCISE 8.4

Conducting and Tapping Simple Meters (without music)

While conducting two (duple), three (triple), or four (quadruple), tap the simple division of the beat (division of two) with the other hand. The student can practice alone and outside of class. Ordinarily, this exercise requires much repetitious practice before the student feels at ease.

EXERCISE 8.5T

Conducting and Tapping Simple Meters

The instructor will designate a melody from Exercise 5.3T. Observe the meter signature, make the appropriate conductor's beat, and tap the simple background in the left hand. As you continue conducting, the instructor will play the given melody. Observe that not all melodies start on the downbeat, but that some may start on other beats of the measure, or on the second division of the beat.

EXERCISE 8.6T

Conducting and Tapping Simple Meters

The instructor will announce a simple meter signature, followed by the playing of a melody in simple time. Listen for the beat grouping and the location of the downbeat. On the second hearing, conduct with the right hand using the appropriate conductor's beat. On the third playing, continue to conduct, but add the simple background of the beat (division of two) by tapping with the left hand.

EXERCISE 8.7

Conducting and Tapping Compound Meters (without music)

While conducting two, three, or four, tap the compound division of the beat (division of three) with the other hand. The student can practice alone and outside of class.

EXERCISE 8.8T

Conducting and Tapping Compound Meters

The instructor will designate a melody from Exercise 5.4T. Observe the meter signature, make the appropriate conductor's beat, and tap the compound background in the left hand. Observe that the melody may begin on any beat, or on a division of a beat (if on a division of a beat, usually the third division). As you continue conducting, the instructor will play the melody.

EXERCISE 8.9T
Conducting and Tapping Compound Meters

The instructor will announce a compound meter signature, followed by the playing of a melody in compound time. Listen for the beat grouping and the location of the downbeat. On the second hearing, conduct with the right hand using the appropriate conductor's beat. On the third playing, continue to conduct, but add the compound background of the beat (division of three) by tapping with the left hand.

EXERCISE 8.10T
Conducting and Tapping Simple or Compound Meters

Listen to a melody played by the instructor. Listen for meter (beat grouping and background) and location of downbeat. Conduct with the right hand and tap the background with the left hand. Use the music supplied for Exercise 5.5T. For additional material, use the following melodies from *Music for Sight Singing*. Observe the recommended metronome indications.

(1)   5 M.M. 92
(2) 59 M.M. 84
(3) 15 M.M. 108
(4) 27 M.M. 116
(5) 116 M.M. 80
(6) 68 M.M. 69
(7) 176 M.M. 112
(8) 182 M.M. 100

(9) 199 M.M. 60
(10) 341 M.M. 80
(11) 212 M.M. 86
(12) 95 M.M. 92
(13) 66 M.M. 92
(14) 83 M.M. 100
(15) 201 M.M. 69
(16) 113 M.M. 112

CHAPTER NINE

TIME
(continued)

Rhythm
Anacrusis
Repeat Signs
Rhythmic Reading

In our exercises in listening to melodies, you have analyzed beats and beat groupings. But you have also noticed that the pitches of the melody are of various durations, some the same as the beat, some the same as the background, and still others of lengths different from the beat or background. This feature of musical composition is called *rhythm*.

Rhythm

The occurrence of a series of sounds of varying durations is known as *rhythm*. In our previous study, the regularly recurring beats of music were shown to designate meter. Now we shall see that varying durations comprise the rhythm of the music.

FIGURE 9.1. *Rhythm and Meter.*

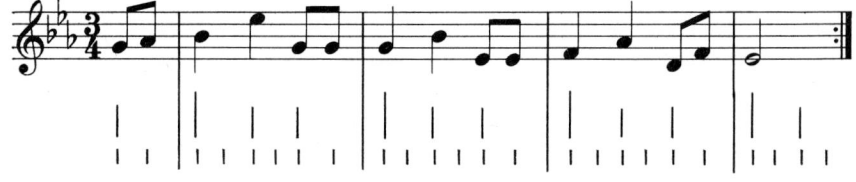

Rhythm, the occurrence of various note values, is revealed in the melody.

Meter is the regularly recurring pulsations of beats and backgrounds.

Observe that the music in Figure 9.1 contains two factors not previously defined: (1) the melody does not start on the first beat of a measure; it begins with an *anacrusis;* and (2) the melody ends with a *repeat sign*.

Anacrusis

The *anacrusis* is that part of the music occurring before the downbeat of the first complete measure. It may be described as an incomplete measure before the first full measure, and it may consist of one, two, or several notes. When the anacrusis occurs on the last beat or fraction of the last beat before the first complete measure, it is often called the "upbeat" or "pick-up."

The anacrusis is usually written as an incomplete measure, in which case, its value and the note values found in the final measure are equal to one full measure. In Figure 9.1 the value of the anacrusis, ♩ ♩, added to the value of the final measure, 𝅗𝅥, is equal to a full measure of $\frac{3}{4}$ meter.

Repeat Signs

(1) Double Bar and Dots. A repeat sign consists of a double bar preceded by two dots around the third line, and indicates a repetition of the music preceding the sign. Upon reaching the repeat sign the second time, continue on to the next measure.

FIGURE 9.2. *Repeat Sign at the End of a Measure.*

When the section to be repeated ends before the end of the measure, the repeat sign (double bar with dots) will be found between the two single bar-lines of the measure.

FIGURE 9.3. *Repeat Sign (Double Bar and Dots) Within a Measure.*

If the section to be repeated begins after the beginning of the composition, the section is enclosed by double bars, the first with dots to the right of the double bar and the second with the dots to the left of the double bar.

FIGURE 9.4. *Indication of Repetition of a Section Within a Composition.*

102

(2) First and Second Endings

FIGURE 9.5. *First and Second Endings.*

The first ending (⌜1.⎯⌉) indicates a return to the beginning, or to a previous repeat sign (‖:) . During the repetition, the music of the first ending is skipped and the piece continues with the second ending (⌜2.⎯⌉) .

(3) D.C., D.S., and Fine

(a) Da capo (It. *da capo,* literally, "from the head"), abbreviated D.C., indicates a repeat from the beginning of the composition. See Figure 9.6.

(b) Dal segno (It. *dal segno,* "from the sign"), abbreviated D.S., indicates a repeat from the sign 𝄋. See Figure 9.7.

(c) Fine (It. *fine,* "end," pronounced *fee'-nay*) indicates the place where the composition ends after using D.C. or D.S. These combinations are often used: *D.C. al fine* (from the beginning, then to the end) and *D.S. al fine* (from the sign, then to the end). A double bar is used with the *fine*. See Figures 9.6 and 9.7.

FIGURE 9.6. *The Da Capo.*

FIGURE 9.7. *The Dal Segno.*

Several of the devices for musical repeats are shown in the three folksongs of Figure 9.8.

FIGURE 9.8. *Examples of Repeat Signs.*

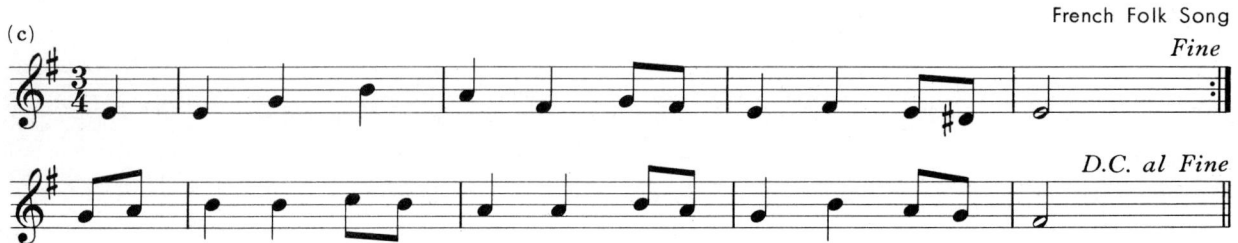

Having now defined meter and rhythm, and having recognized certain signs found in music, we will combine these in a practical application known as *Rhythmic Reading.*

Rhythmic Reading

Rhythmic Reading, or rhythmic recitation, is a process in music by which note durations only, not pitches, are expressed in vocal sounds. Rhythmic reading is based on these principles:

(1) Any note occurring on a beat is recited by the number of that beat.

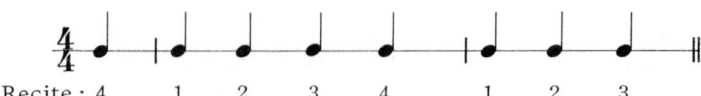

(2) Any note, not recited by number, occurring on a fraction of a beat is recited by the syllable *ta* (tah).

(3) The syllable which originates with a note is held for the duration until the next appropriate syllable is articulated.[1]

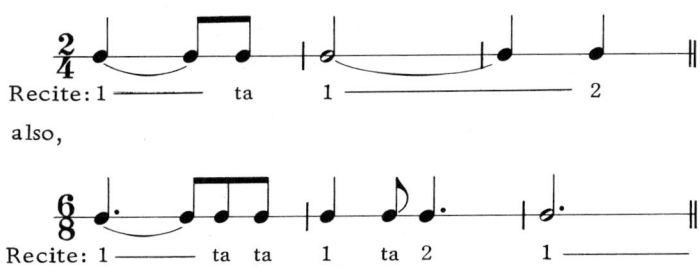

(4) At the occurrence of a rest, the reader remains silent.

---

[1] The *tie* (bind) is a curved line which connects two notes of the same pitch. The second note is not articulated and the result is a sustained unbroken sound equal to the duration of both notes.

_____ NAME

EXERCISE 9.1
Anacrusis

In the last measure of each example, place one note which will make a complete measure when added to the anacrusis.

EXERCISE 9.2
Repeat Signs

Write repeat sign(s) as directed for each example.

(a) Place repeat sign(s) so that the first four measures will be repeated.

(b) Place repeat sign(s) so that measures 4–5 will be repeated.

(c) Place repeat sign in measure four so that four complete measures will be repeated.

(d) Place first and second endings so that measures 1–3 will be repeated.

EXERCISE 9.3
Writing Rhythmic Syllables

Below each note write the rhythmic syllable.

Example:

NAME

EXERCISE 9.4

Rhythmic Reading (with the syllables written out)

While conducting and tapping the meter, read aloud the rhythmic syllables for each of the examples in Exercise 9.3.

EXERCISE 9.5

Rhythmic Reading, Simple Meter

While conducting and tapping the meter, read with rhythmic syllables the rhythm of the melodies found in Exercise 5.3. For additional practice, read the rhythm of melodies from *Music for Sight Singing,* Chapters 1, 3, and 6.

EXERCISE 9.6

Rhythmic Reading, Compound Meter

While conducting and tapping the meter, read the rhythm of the melodies found in Exercise 5.4. For additional practice, read melodies from *Music for Sight Singing,* Chapters 2, 4, and 7.

EXERCISE 9.7

Rhythmic Reading, Simple and Compound Meters

While conducting and tapping the meter, read the rhythm of the melodies found in Exercise 5.5. For additional practice, read melodies from *Music for Sight Singing,* Chapter 9.

CHAPTER TEN

TIME
(continued)

Beams in Notation
Rests in Notation
Rhythmic Dictation
Rhythmic Transcription

The next skill to be developed after rhythmic reading is the ability to identify the rhythm of a melodic line when you hear it, and to write it as notation on paper. This process of writing the rhythmic pattern you hear is called *rhythmic dictation.* Just as in the world of business a stenographer "takes dictation," in music the student also "takes dictation." Rhythmic dictation is in a sense the reverse process of rhythmic reading. While in rhythmic reading, notation is transferred into sound, in rhythmic dictation, sound is transferred into notation. In order to write clearly the rhythm you hear, you must understand certain principles of the use of *beams* and *rests in notation.*

Beams in Notation

Beams have been previously described as heavy lines connecting stems of notes. In making notation easier to read, beams serve to (1) eliminate long series of flagged notes and (2) to clarify the location of the beats in a measure. Figure 10.1 shows a measure of 9/8 meter containing nine eighth notes written in three different ways. In Figure 10.1a the notation is correct, but in Figure 10.1b the notation is easier to read because the beams make clear the location of each of the three beats in triple compound meter. Incorrect beaming, as in Figure 10.1c, actually makes the same rhythmic pattern more difficult to read, because the beginnings of beamed groups do not coincide with the second and third beats of triple compound meter.

FIGURE 10.1. *Use of Beams.*

A beam, once begun, ordinarily does not extend into the next beat unit. If additional notes are to be beamed, a new beam starts at the new beat, as shown in Figure 10.2. The following examples show various correct and incorrect applications of this principle. The bracket (⌐⎯⌐) indicates the duration of a beat.

FIGURE 10.2. *Correct and Incorrect Uses of Beams.*

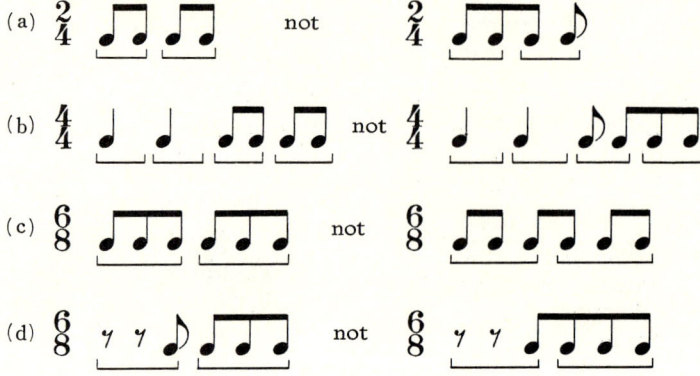

Rests in Notation

(1) *Dotted Rests.* Rests, like notes, may be dotted. The dot increases the value of the rest by one-half, e.g., 𝄽· = 𝄽 𝄾 𝄾· = 𝄾 𝄾 ▬· = ▬ 𝄽 ; etc.

(2) *The Whole Rest.* Whenever an entire measure is to be silent, a whole rest is written, whatever the meter signature in use at the time.

FIGURE 10.3. *Use of the Whole Rest.*

(a) 3/4 𝅗𝅥. | ▬ | 𝅗𝅥. ‖

(b) 6/8 𝅗𝅥. 𝅗𝅥. | ▬ | 𝅗𝅥. ‖

(3) *Separate or Combined Rests.* (A) When a period of silence lasts more than one beat, individual (separate) rests may be used for each beat, or two or more rests may be combined and shown as a single rest; for example,

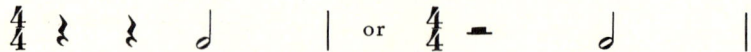

(B) When, however, a combining of rests would make less clear the location of the beats of a measure, separate rests are used. In Figure 10.4 each example in the right-hand column contains a rest which obscures the location of one of the beats of the measure.

FIGURE 10.4. *Correct and Incorrect Uses of Rests.*

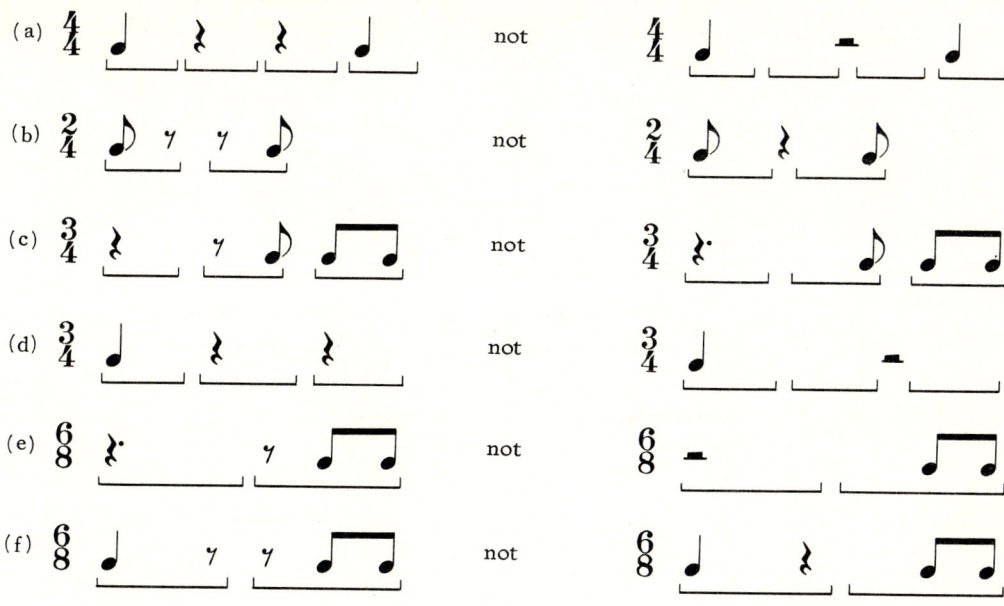

(C) In compound meter, separate rests are ordinarily used for the second and third divisions of the beat; for example,

Before continuing this chapter, go to Exercises 10.1–3 which will give you practice in the correct writing of beams and rests. You will then be ready to begin *rhythmic dictation*.

Rhythmic Dictation

We are now ready to listen to a melody and to write the rhythm of this melody, using notation, on paper. To develop most efficiently the skill of taking rhythmic dictation, follow these systematic steps in *listening to a melody* and *writing the rhythm*.

Listening to a Melody. When the instructor is ready to play a melody for rhythmic dictation, observe this procedure:

Step 1. The meter signature will be announced. Using the appropriate conductor's beat and tapping the background, follow the instructor's lead in establishing the meter. Students continue to conduct and tap throughout Steps 2, 3, and 4.

Step 2. As the instructor plays, listen to the melody and commit it to memory.

Step 3. Sing back the melody, using the neutral syllable *la*.

Step 4. Sing the melody again, this time using rhythmic syllables, *or*, recite without pitch using rhythmic syllables. For Figure 10.6 these syllables would be "one two three-ta four-ta / one two three."

Writing the Rhythm

For the first exercises in rhythmic dictation, diagrams are supplied to help you in writing the notation. Each diagram consists of three lines:

The top line shows the beat durations of each measure (the same as the right-hand conductor's beat)

The bottom line shows the beat divisions of each measure (the same as the left-hand background)

On *the middle line* you are to write the rhythm.

FIGURE 10.5. *Rhythmic Dictation: Meter Diagram.*

Quadruple simple meter with the signature 4/4:

Figure 10.6a shows a rhythmic dictation problem as played by the instructor. The solution (b) is the rhythmic pattern placed on the middle line of the diagram.

FIGURE 10.6. *Example of Rhythmic Dictation.*

(a) Problem played by the instructor:

(b) Solution written on the middle line:

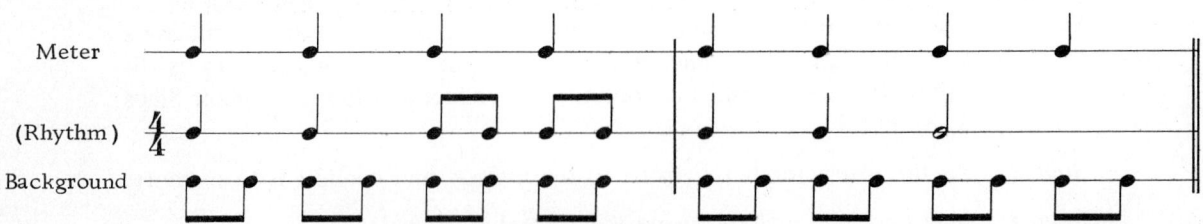

Material for rhythmic dictation will be found at the end of this chapter beginning with Exercise 10.4.

Rhythmic Transcription

Rhythmic transcription is the rewriting of a piece using a meter signature with the same numerator but a different denominator. This will produce a notation which looks different from the original, but in performance will sound identical to the original. When, for example, you hear a rhythmic pattern in quadruple simple time, there is no way of knowing what the notation will be until you are told, or decide for yourself, the bottom number of the meter signature. A pattern in quadruple simple meter can be written with a half note, a quarter note, or an eighth note as the beat unit, and, although the notation for each looks different, each one will actually sound exactly like the others, assuming all have the same tempo indication. In Figure 10.6, where 4/4 was given as the meter signature, you used the quarter note as the beat unit. If 4/2 had been announced, your solution would have appeared:

or, if 4/8 had been announced your solution would have appeared:

These solutions are identical in sound (when the tempo for the beat unit is the same); only the notation is different.

FIGURE 10.7. *Rhythmic Transcription.*

Rhythmic transcription is included in exercises at the end of this chapter where you are instructed to write the rhythm of the given melody in three ways, using three meter signatures each with identical numerators but different denominators.

EXERCISE 10.1
Improving Notation by Use of Beams

Rewrite each rhythmic pattern by using beams where feasible.

EXERCISE 10.2
Correcting Examples Showing Incorrect Use of Beams

Rewrite each exercise with correct beaming.

(d) 9/8 sheet music example

(e) 4/8 sheet music example

NAME

EXERCISE 10.3
Correcting Examples Showing Incorrect Use of Rests

Rewrite each exercise with correct rests.

EXERCISE 10.4T

Rhythmic Dictation, Simple Meter

Follow basic directions given on pages 115–116. Observe headings below which list contents of exercises and/or changes in method of writing dictation. The instructor will play from correspondingly numbered melodies on pages 133–134. Upon completion of an exercise, the student may turn to these pages to check his answer.

Duple simple time, ♩ = 1 beat. Begin on the downbeat. Use diagram.

Write answer when only center line of diagram is given.

(3) 2/4

(4) 2/4

(5) 2/4

Duple simple time. Begin on upbeat. Use diagram.

123

Write answer when only center line of diagram is given.

Duple simple time. Denominators other than 4 will be used. Use diagram.

Write answer when only center line of diagram is given.

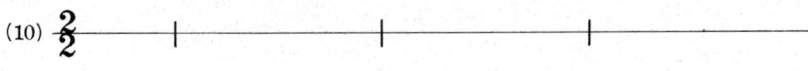

Triple simple time. Use diagram.

Write answer when only center line of diagram is given. Note increase in length of melody.

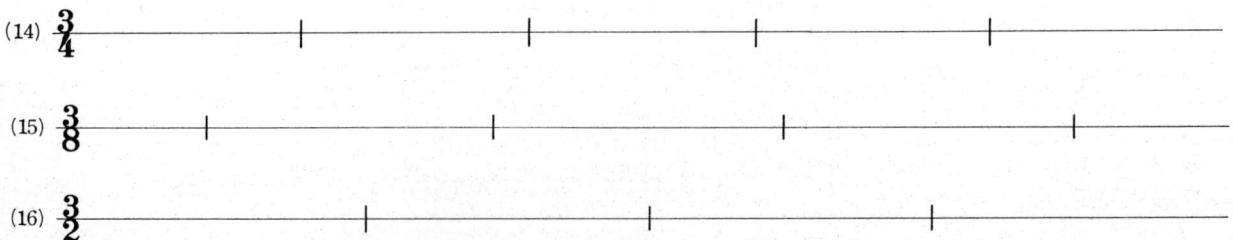

_____ NAME

Quadruple simple time. Use diagram.

(17)

Rests are now added. Use diagram.

(18)

Write answer when only center line of diagram is given.

(19)

(20)

(21)

(22)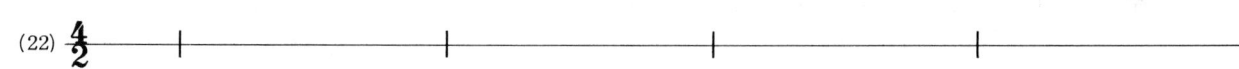

Various simple meter signatures. Write exercises without center line, supplying your own bar-lines.

(23) 2
4

(24) 3
2

Write the dictation answer for the first of the three meter signatures given. Then write the same rhythmic pattern using each of the other two meter signatures.

(25) 4/4

4/2

4/8

(26) 4/8

4/4

4/2

(27) 3/8

3/4

3/2

(Instructor: For additional material in dictation of simple meters, use melodies or excerpts of melodies from *Music for Sight Singing,* Chapters 1, 3, and 6.)

NAME _____

EXERCISE 10.5T

Rhythmic Dictation, Compound Meter

Follow basic directions given on pages 115–116. Observe headings below which list contents of exercises and/or changes in method of writing dictation. The instructor will play from correspondingly numbered melodies on pages 134–135. Upon completion of an exercise, the student may turn to these pages to check his answer.

Duple compound meter, ♩. = 1 beat. Begin on downbeat. Use diagram.

Write answer when only center line of diagram is given.

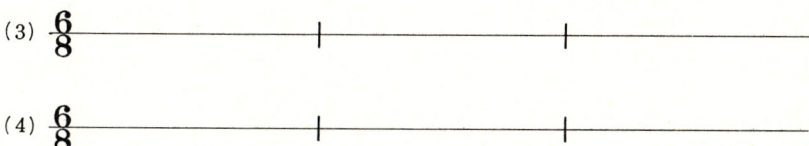

Duple compound meter. Begin on upbeat. Use diagram.

127

Write answer when only center line of diagram is given.

(7)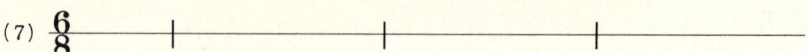

Duple compound meter. Denominators other than 8 will be used. Use diagram.

(8)

Write answer when only center line of diagram is given.

(9)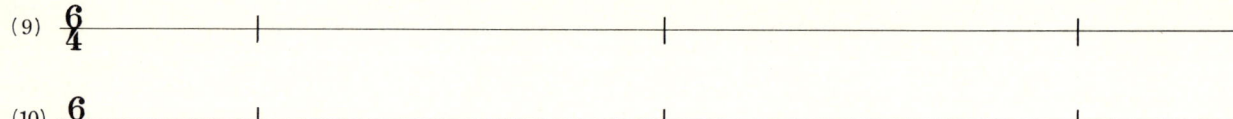

(10)

Triple compound meter. Use diagram.

(11)

(12)

Write answer when only center line is given. Note increase in length of melody.

(13)

(14)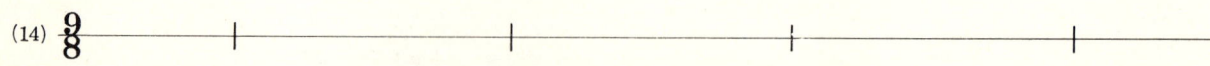

(15)

Quadruple compound meter. Use diagram.

Write answer when only center line of diagram is given.

_____ NAME

Various meter signatures. Rests are added. Use center line only.

(18) $\frac{6}{8}$

(19) $\frac{9}{8}$

Write exercises without center line, supplying your own bar-lines.

(20) $\frac{6}{8}$

(21) $\frac{6}{4}$

Write the dictation answer for the first of the three meter signatures given. Then write the same rhythmic pattern using each of the other two meter signatures.

(22) $\frac{6}{16}$

$\frac{6}{8}$

$\frac{6}{4}$

(23) $\frac{9}{8}$

$\frac{9}{16}$

$\frac{9}{4}$

(24) $\frac{12}{8}$

$\frac{12}{4}$

$\frac{12}{16}$

131

(25) 6
     8

    6
    16

    6
    4

(Instructor: For additional material in dictation of compound meters, use melodies or excerpts of melodies from *Music for Sight Singing,* Chapters 2, 4, and 7.)

Dictation material for Exercise 10.4T.

25

26

27

Dictation material for Exercise 10.5T.

1

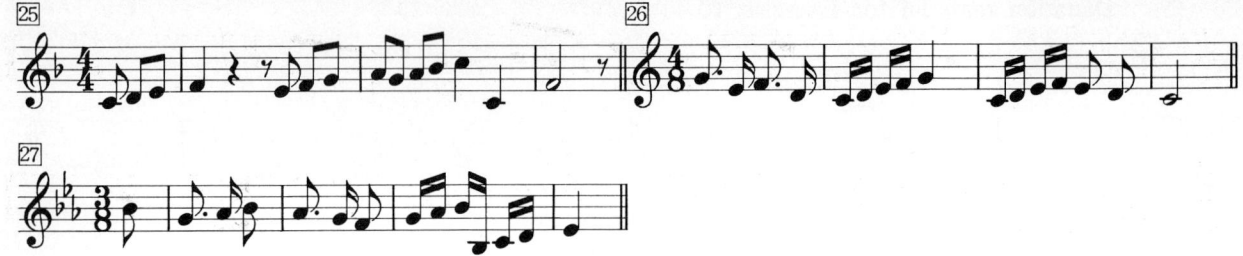

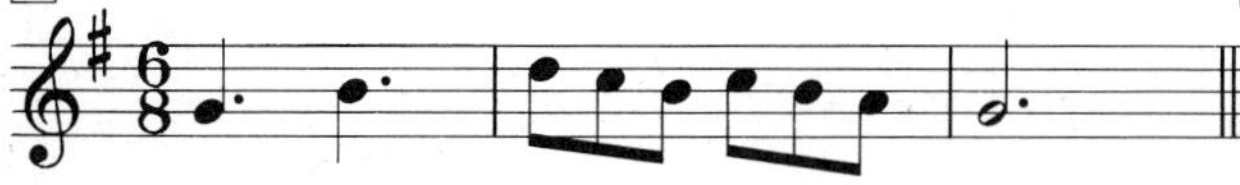

2

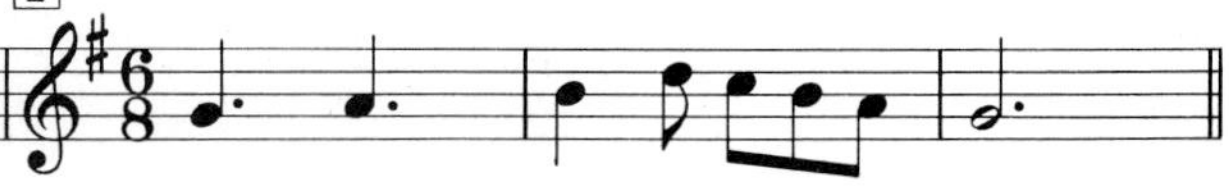

3

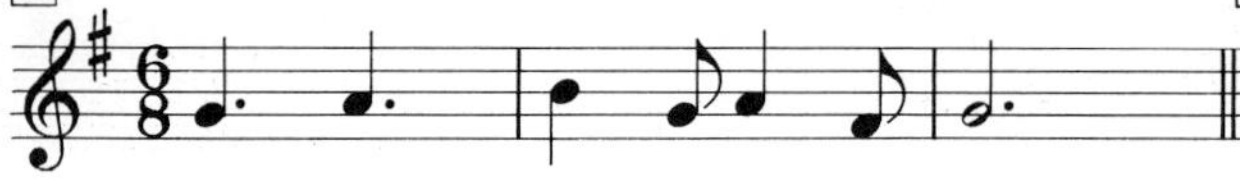

4

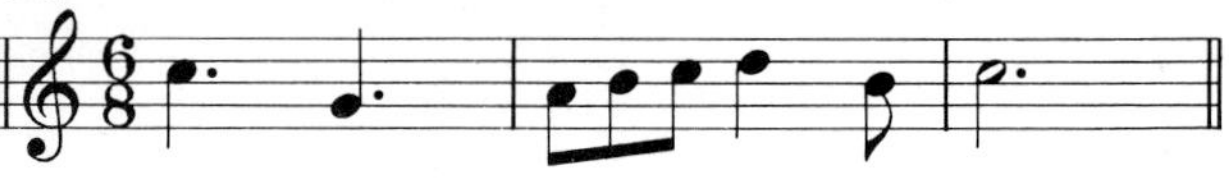

5

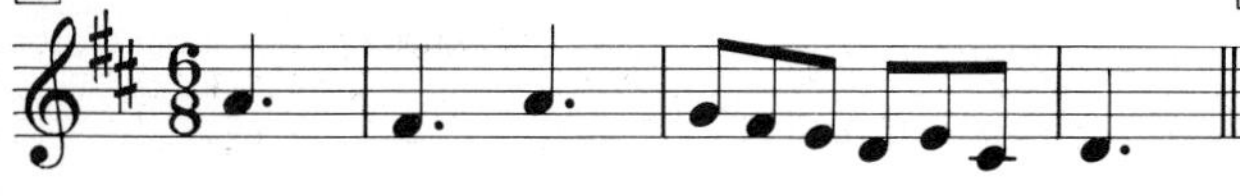

6

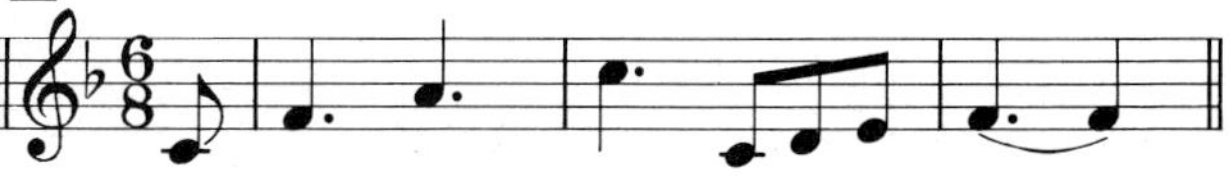

7

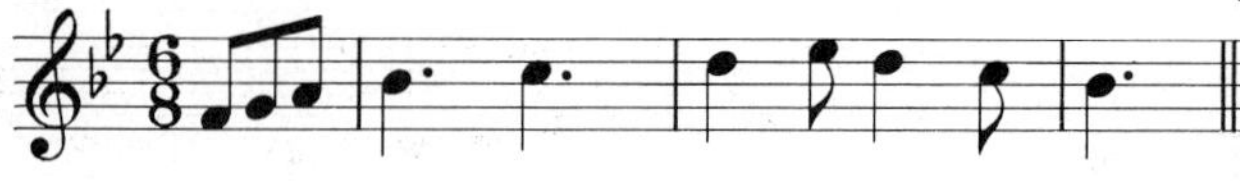

8

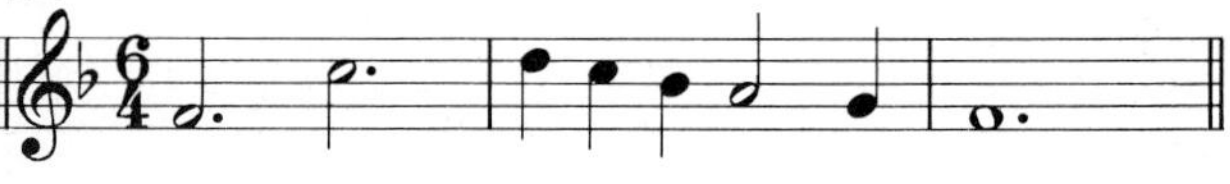

9

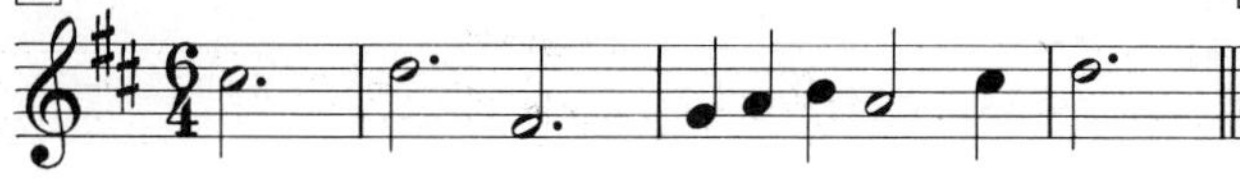

10

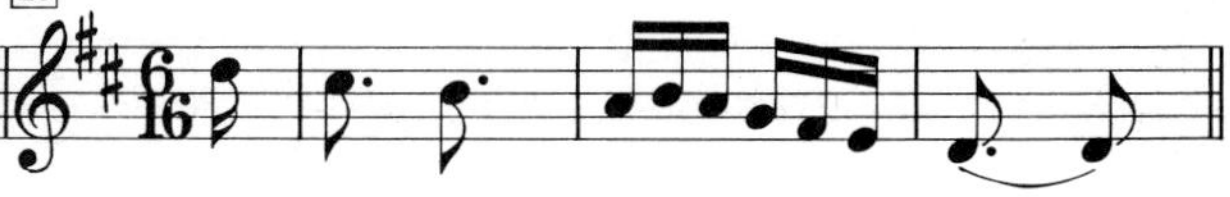

11

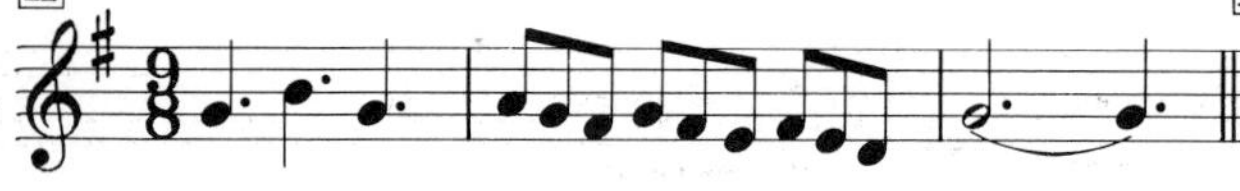

12

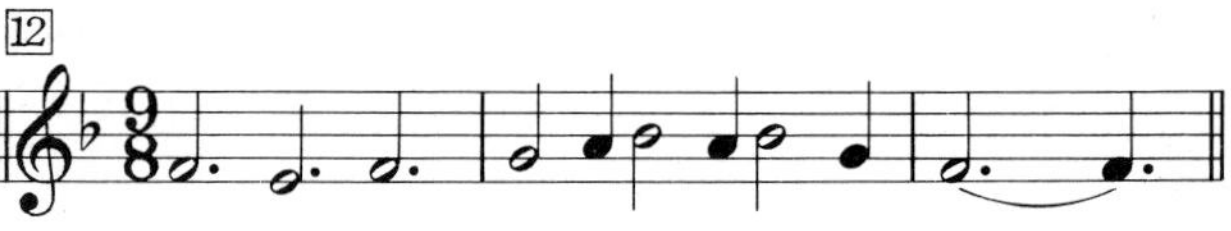

13

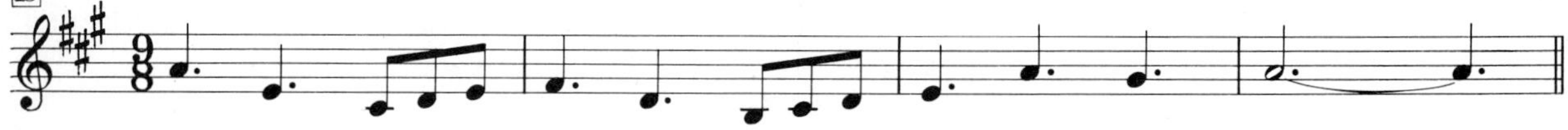

14

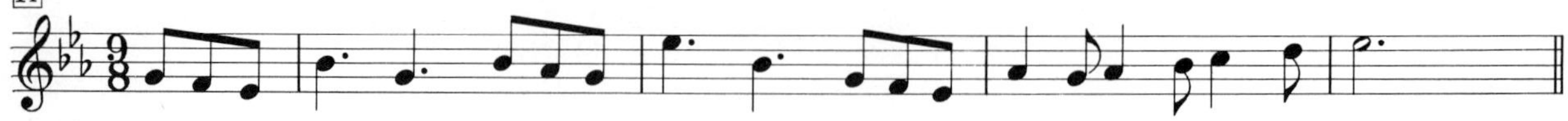

15

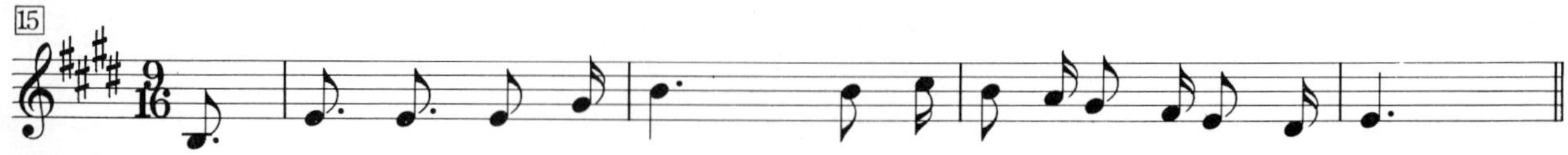

16

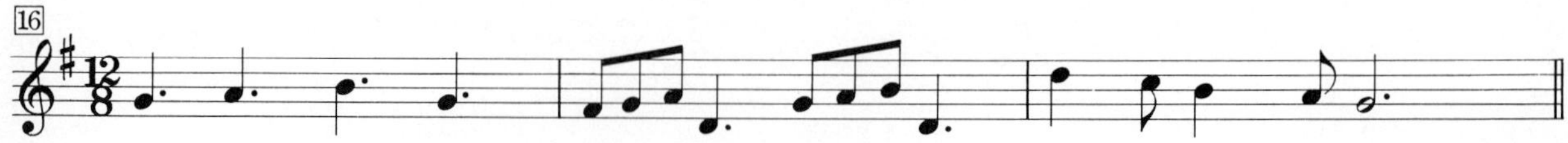

CHAPTER ELEVEN

MAJOR SCALES

Like rhythm, the resources of pitch in music can be organized into well-defined patterns. A pattern commonly used to express organization of pitch is the scale (Latin, *scala,* ladder). A scale is an orderly graduated arrangement of ascending or descending pitches. There are many kinds of scales used in music depending on historical period or geographical culture. Most scales in Western music, including those which we will study here, ascend and descend through a series consisting of half-steps and whole-steps [1] with each pitch named by a successive letter of the musical alphabet.

For purposes of study, a scale is limited to the series of eight notes encompassing the interval of an octave, so that the first and last notes of each scale have identical letter names.[2] Scales differ from each other because the relative placement of the half-steps and whole-steps within the octave may be different. This can be demonstrated at the piano by choosing a single white key at random and playing a series of eight ascending white keys. If we choose any *a,* the resulting scale would be

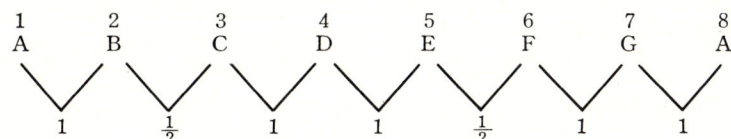

with half-steps between 2 and 3 and between 5 and 6, and the remaining steps whole-steps.[3] If we choose any *c* a different scale would result:

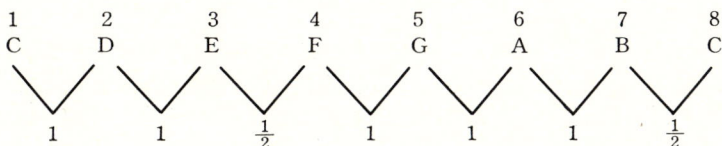

in which the half-steps occur between 3 and 4 and between 7 and 8. By playing white-key scales from each of the seven letter names, seven different scale constructions would result. For present purposes, two scale formations, named *major* and *minor* will be considered. We will begin with the *major scale.*

---

[1] Half-steps and whole-steps were first discussed in Chapter 2, pages 21-22.
[2] A scale once established in one octave will look, sound, and be spelled the same at any other octave.
[3] The ascending scale pitches are numbered 1 through 8, and intervals are represented by 1 for a whole-step and ½ for a half-step.

The Major Scale

The major scale is a series of eight pitches with the intervals between successive pitches being whole-step, whole-step, half-step, whole-step, whole-step, whole-step, and half-step.

FIGURE 11.1. *Structure of the Major Scale.*

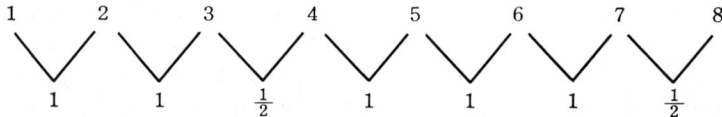

It can be seen that the major scale consists of whole-steps excepting between the third and fourth and the seventh and eighth pitches, where the intervals are half-steps.

A scale may be shown on the staff by placing the eight pitches, each known as a scale degree, on eight successive lines and spaces. Each whole-step and each half-step is represented on the staff by two notes on adjacent lines and spaces. The scale is identified by the relative location of whole-steps and half-steps, and by the first note of the scale. In Figure 11.2 the scale is major because the half-steps occur between 3 and 4 and between 7 and 8 (compare with Fig. 11.1), and it is a *c* major scale because the first scale degree is *c*.

FIGURE 11.2. *The C Major Scale.*

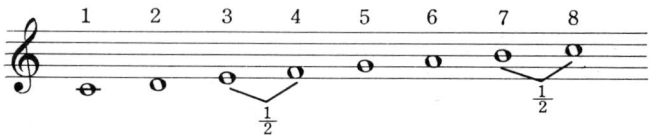

Notice that the major scale starting on *c* involves only white keys because the half-steps 3–4 and 7–8 coincide with the white keys e–f and b–c. The major scale on *c* is the only major scale consisting entirely of white keys. But the sound of the major scale is not restricted to that beginning on *c*. The characteristic sound of the major scale can be reproduced beginning on any pitch name or on any key of the piano. When starting on a pitch other than *c,* however, we must employ one or more accidentals to maintain the characteristic half-step and whole-step arrangement of the major scale shown first in Figure 11.1. Accidentals are added so that the half-steps will appear in their proper location between 3 and 4 and between 7 and 8, and so that the remaining steps will be whole-steps. To illustrate, a white key scale on *g* produces a scale with half-steps between 3 and 4 and between 6 and 7:

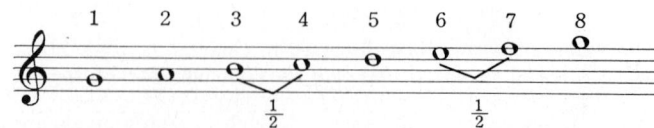

Raising *f* to *f♯* places the half-steps between 3 and 4 and between 7 and 8, and the scale is major.

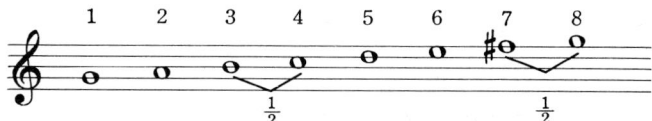

Care should be taken that incorrect spellings of pitches by enharmonics are not used. In the *g* major scale shown below, writing *g♭* instead of *f♯* for the seventh scale degree is incorrect for two reasons: (1) the complete musical alphabet is not employed (the letter *f* is missing), and (2) the whole-step between 6 and 7 does not occur on adjacent staff degrees.

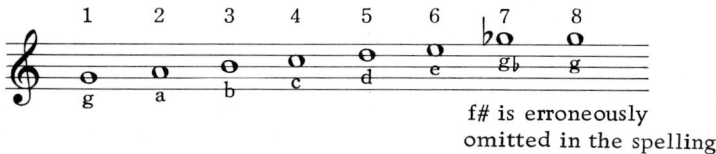

A white-key scale on *f* produces a scale with half-steps between 4 and 5 and between 7 and 8:

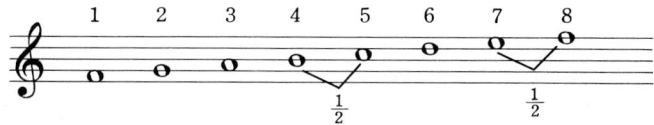

Lowering the *b* to *b♭* places the half-steps between 3 and 4 and between 7 and 8, and the scale is major.

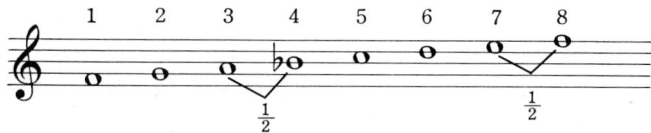

Major scales may begin on black keys, or on letter names containing an accidental. The scale is produced as before, with half-steps between 3 and 4 and between 7 and 8, for example,

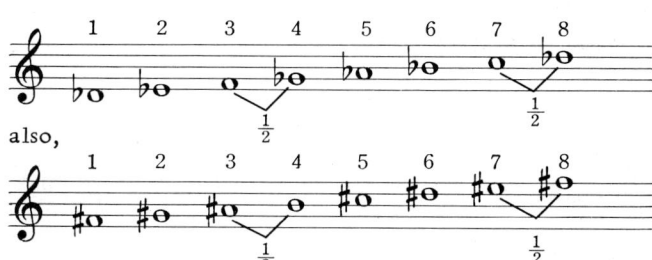

also,

Although a major scale can theoretically start on any letter name containing an accidental, for practical purposes, scales that would require more than seven sharps or seven flats are not used. We will not consider scales requiring double sharps or double flats. For example, a major scale on *g♯* would require eight sharps: g , a , b , c , d , e , f , g , where f is sharped twice and indicated as f𝄪 .

Since there are but seven letter names, the maximum number of scales containing sharps will be seven, and the maximum number of scales containing flats will also be seven. These, with *c* major, comprise the fifteen major scales.

FIGURE 11.3. *Table of Major Scales and Numbers of Accidentals.*

Scale	C	G	D	A	E	B	F♯	C♯
Accidentals	none	1♯	2♯	3♯	4♯	5♯	6♯	7♯
Scale		F	B♭	E♭	A♭	D♭	G♭	C♭
Accidentals		1♭	2♭	3♭	4♭	5♭	6♭	7♭

You will observe in Figure 11.3 that there is a definite relationship between the number of accidentals used in a scale and the name of the starting pitch of the scale. By counting *up* five notes from the starting note (and including the starting note), a new scale at this point will have one sharp more than the preceding scale. This additional sharp will always occur on the seventh scale degree.

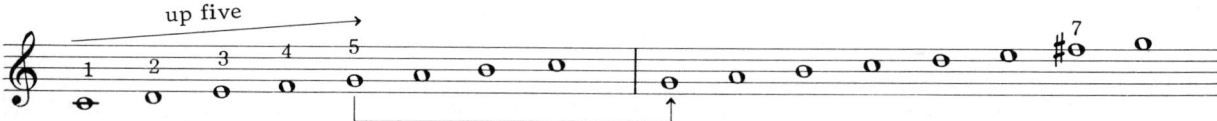

By counting *down* five notes, the new scale at this point will have one flat more than the preceding scale. This additional flat will always occur on the fourth scale degree.

Before proceeding to the exercises at the end of this chapter, review Chapter 2 with special attention to pages 21–22.

CHAPTER TWELVE

MAJOR SCALES
(continued)

Names of Scale Degrees

The scale has been shown to be composed of eight successive pitches, each known as a scale degree. The terms *scale tone* and *scale step* are often used synonymously with *scale degree*. For example, in the scale of c major, the fifth degree, g, may be called the fifth scale tone or fifth scale step. In addition to these general designations, each tone, step or degree of the scale can be identified by a specific name of its own. Here, with a discussion of the significance of each, are the *names of the scale degrees*.

Names of the Scale Degrees

The name of the first scale degree is *tonic* (Greek, *tonikos* [1]). It is the main tone, the tone which gives the scale its identity. In the c major scale, c is the tonic tone.

Since the tonic is the most important tone, all other scale degrees are signified by their relationships to it.

In rank of importance after the tonic is the fifth scale tone which is called the *dominant*. It dominates or is dominant to all the other scale tones excepting tonic. The dominant is the fifth degree above tonic. In the c major scale, g is the dominant tone.

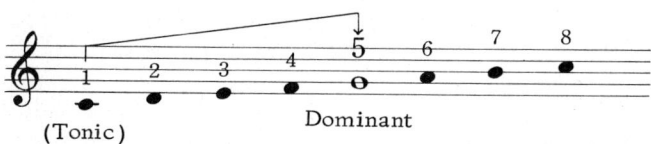

The scale tone five steps below the tonic and ranking next in importance to the dominant is called *subdominant*. The prefix *sub* means under or below the tonic.

---

[1] *tonikos*, stretching, referring to the fact that a string must be stretched to produce a tone. Greek, *tonos*, Latin, *tonus*, tone.

Notice that while the dominant is five steps above the tonic, the subdominant is five steps below the tonic. In the c major scale, *f* is the subdominant tone, the fourth scale degree.

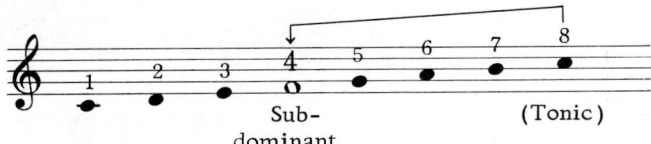

The third scale tone, midway or the middle or median tone between the tonic and dominant, is called *mediant*. In the c major scale, *e* is the mediant tone.

The sixth scale tone, the middle or median tone between the tonic and subdominant, is called *submediant*. Notice that while the mediant is three steps above the tonic, the submediant is three steps below the tonic. In the c major scale, *a* is the submediant tone.

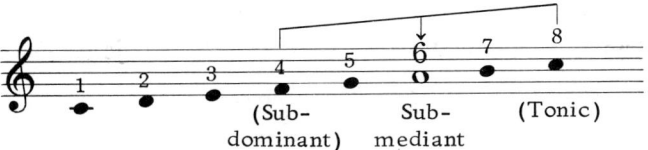

The seventh tone in the major scale, because of its strong tendency to ascend or lead upward to the tonic, is called *leading tone*. It is also referred to, though less commonly, as *subtonic* since it is the tone immediately below tonic. In the c major scale, *b* is the leading tone.

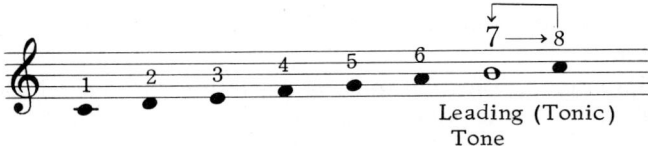

The second scale tone, the scale degree immediately above tonic, is called *supertonic*. Notice that while the leading tone, or subtonic, is the tone next below tonic, the supertonic is the tone next above tonic. In the c major scale, *d* is the supertonic tone.

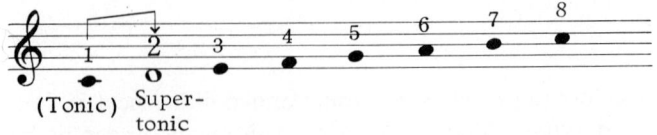

In ascending order, the names of the scale tones are shown in Figure 12.1.

FIGURE 12.1. *Names of the Scale Tones.*

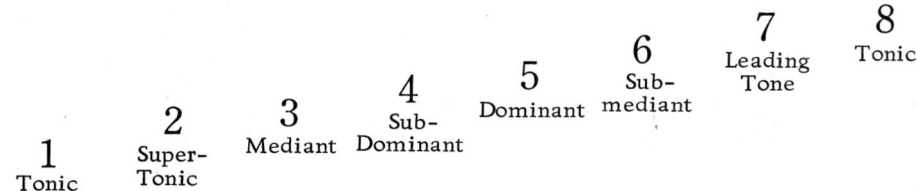

In Figure 12.2, names of the scale tones in ascending consecutive order are shown for c major.

FIGURE 12.2. *Names of the Scale Tones, C Major.*

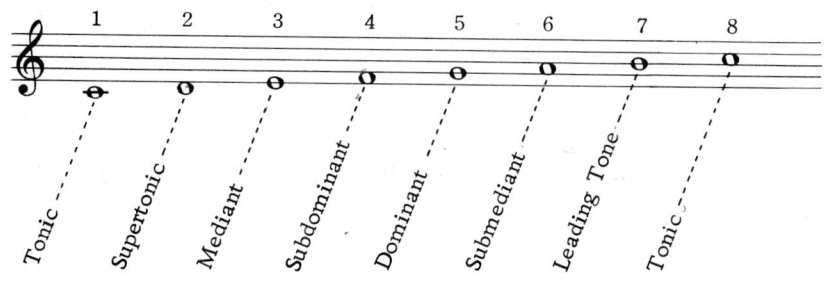

Scale tone names are applied in similar manner for all major scales.

1 Tonic

2 Super tonic

3 mediant

4 Subdominant

5 Dominant

6 Submediant

7 Leading tone

8 tonic

CHAPTER THIRTEEN

MAJOR SCALES
(continued)

Playing Scales at the Keyboard

With the construction and terminology of major scales well-established, we will now set out to perform major scales on the piano and by singing. In performing a scale it is of utmost importance to keep in mind the series of whole-steps and half-steps that produce the major scale. Though this may not seem of particular importance when playing the scale on the piano where the keys play fixed pitches, it becomes essential in singing or when playing such instruments as violin or trombone where the performer is responsible for fixing the pitches, or in recognizing by ear whether a series of pitches produces a major scale or some other variety of scale. Development of the ability to produce or to differentiate whole-steps and half-steps is an important result of *playing scales at the keyboard*.

Playing Scales at the Keyboard [1]

(a) The C Major Scale. By playing the white key *c* and the next seven white keys above it, a *c* major scale will be produced. Playing only white keys from this given pitch *c* automatically places the half-steps in their correct scale locations, between 3 and 4 and between 7 and 8, as shown in Figure 13.1.

FIGURE 13.1. *Playing the C Major Scale.*

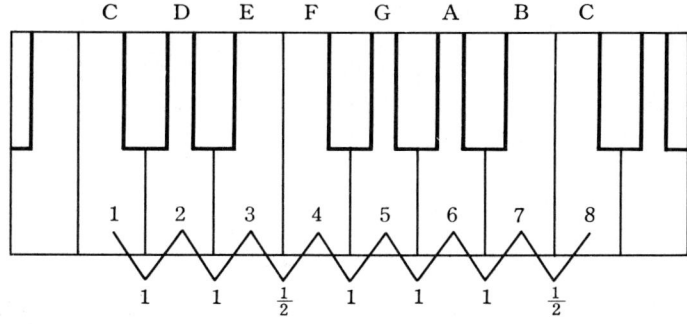

[1] Keyboard performance of scales may be studied from one of two points of view: (1) simply for knowledge of scale construction and sound, in which case the fingering of the scale is not a primary consideration; or (2) for achieving skill in performance, in which case fingering is a vital consideration. Correct scale fingerings are shown in Appendix 1, pages 299-300.

(b) *Major Scales on G, D, A, E, B, F, B♭, E♭, A♭, D♭.* These scales (with *c* major) include all those written in Exercise 11.1 except *c♯, c♭, f♯,* and *g♭,* which will be considered in section (c). Playing major scales other than *c* involves use of black keys. Practice in playing these scales should be done in each of these three ways:

1. Play the scales listed in this section, reading from the scales you wrote in Exercise 11.1. Spell the scale orally as you play it.
2. Without the music, choose one of the starting pitches listed in this section. Play each note in succession by determining if the next note will be a whole-step or a half-step. For example, choose *d*. Figure 13.2 shows the whole-steps and half-steps, and the keys necessary to play these intervals. Spell each scale orally as you play it.

FIGURE 13.2. *Playing the D Major Scale.*

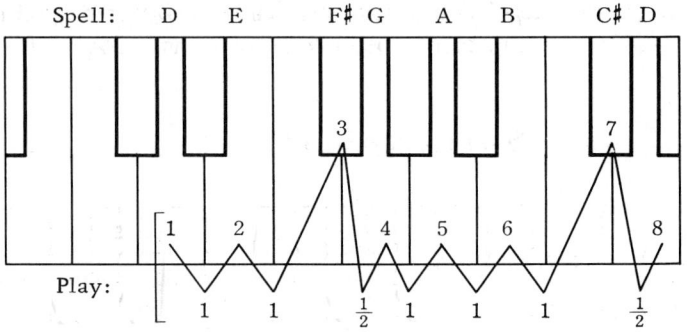

3. Choose a note as tonic. Spell the scale orally and play each key as you spell it. For example, spell the *e♭* major scale, playing each note as you spell it.

FIGURE 13.3. *Playing the E♭ Major Scale.*

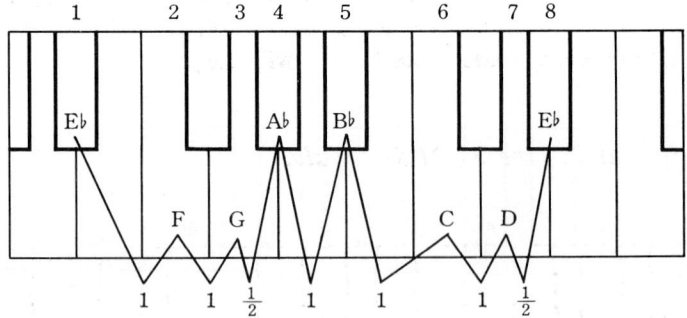

(c) *Major Scales on F♯, G♭, C♯, and C♭.* These scales require enharmonic spellings of white keys. In previous study you learned that black keys can be spelled enharmonically.[2] All white keys may also carry enharmonic spellings, but at this time we shall limit ourselves to those on the white key half-steps, *e–f,* and *b–c.*

[2] First mentioned on page 24.

Up to now the white key a half-step above *e* has been called *f*, but enharmonically it can be called *e♯*; likewise the half-step above *b* can be called *c* or *b♯*, as in Figure 13.4.

FIGURE 13.4. *E♯ and B♯ on the Keyboard.*

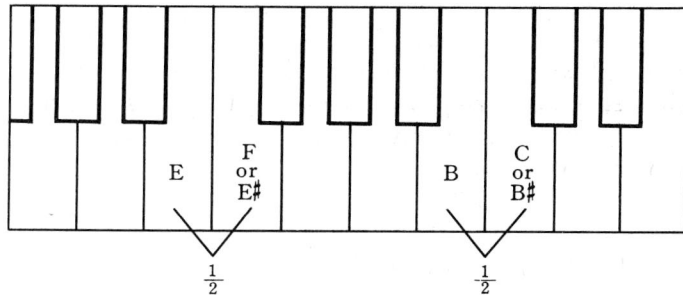

The white key a half-step below *f* has been called *e*, but it may also be called *f♭*; likewise the half-step below *c*, may be called *b* or *c♭* as in Figure 13.5.

FIGURE 13.5. *F♭ and C♭ on the Keyboard.*

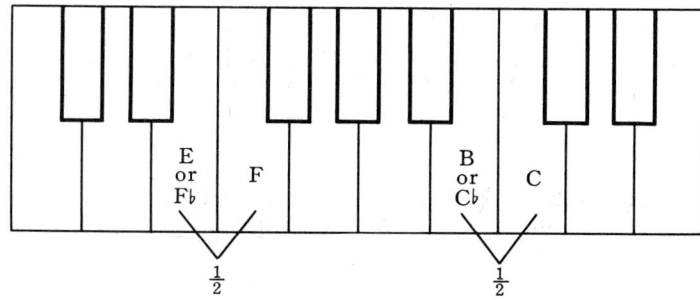

The scales of *f♯*, *g♭*, *c♯*, and *c♭* will make use of these enharmonic spellings; for example, the *f♯* major scale, where the enharmonic white key *e♯* is used (see Fig. 13.6). The *g♭* scale will use *c♭*, the *c♯* scale will use *e♯* and *b♯*, and the *c♭* scale, starting on the enharmonic white key *c♭*, will use *f♭*.

FIGURE 13.6. *Playing the F♯ Major Scale.*

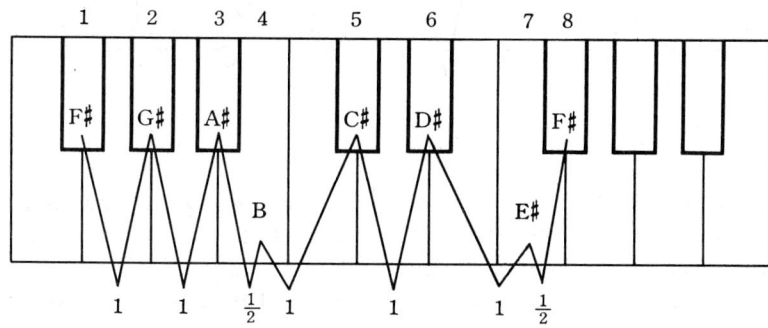

CHAPTER FOURTEEN

MAJOR SCALES
(continued)

Singing Major Scales

Singing Major Scales

Singing is ordinarily the vocal performance of a musical setting of a literary text, usually poetry, called a song. However, in a course of study in music theory and in the preparation and training of a musician, the student will often be required to sing, not songs with words having artistic expression, but exercises with vocal sounds having theoretical significance. Singing major scales is such an exercise. The vocal sounds can be expressed three ways:

(1) *By numbers*. Any major scale, ascending and descending, can be sung by numbers. Figure 14.1 shows application for the *c* major scale.

FIGURE 14.1. *Singing the Scale by Numbers, C Major.*

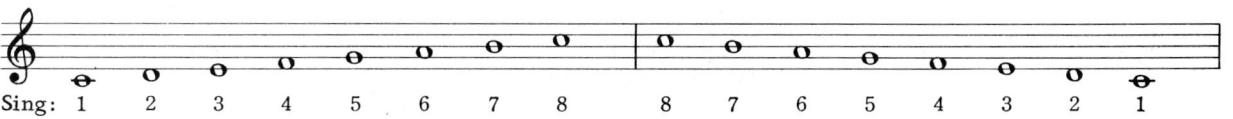

(2) *By letter names*. Any scale can be sung using for vocal sounds the letter names of the scale degrees. Figure 14.2 shows application for the *d* major scale. When a letter name includes an accidental, sing on two repeated pitches, e.g., "f–sharp."

FIGURE 14.2. *Singing the Scale by Letter Names, D Major.*

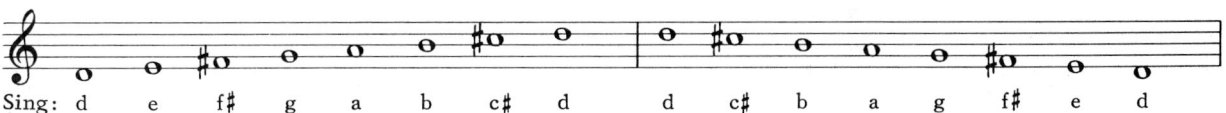

(3) *By syllables*. Any scale can be sung using for vocal sounds the traditional syllables for the scale degrees. Singing with syllables is known as *solmization,* two important systems of which are known as *tonic sol-fa* and *solfeggio*.[1] Figure 14.3 shows a solmization of the c major scale.

FIGURE 14.3. *Singing the Major Scale by Syllables, C Major.*

The syllables are pronounced:

do — *doe*
re — *ray*
mi — *me*
fa — *fah*
sol — *soh*
la — *lah*
ti — *tee*

EXERCISE 14.1
Singing Major Scales

Choose any single pitch which can be used as the tonic tone of a major scale. Sing the scale in three ways: (1) by numbers, (2) by letter names and (3) by syllables, as shown in Figures 14.1–3. Sing each of the fifteen major scales in this manner. You may sing these from the scales you wrote in Exercise 11.1. If necessary, play the scale as you sing until you feel able to sing without the piano. Use the piano at any time to check your accuracy.

EXERCISE 14.2T
Singing Whole-Steps and Half-Steps

From any given pitch sing a whole-step up or down, or a half-step up or down. Each of these intervals can be sung easily if you think of it as part of the scale:

whole-step up	1 up to 2	or	*do* up to *re*
whole-step down	2 down to 1	or	*re* down to *do*
half-step up	7 up to 8(1)	or	*ti* up to *do*
half-step down	8(1) down to 7	or	*do* down to *ti*

[1] In the tonic sol-fa system the syllables are moveable, that is, "do" is always the tonic note of the scale. In solfeggio, the syllables are fixed: C, for example, is always "do" regardless of its location in the scale. This text will make use only of tonic sol-fa.

Accounts of the invention of a system of solmization by Guido d'Arezzo (A.D. 980–1050) and its development into modern syllable systems may be found in music history books, encyclopedias, or dictionaries.

For practice, play any note at the keyboard, sing that note and the chosen interval. Check your accuracy by playing the interval at the keyboard.

Example: Sing a whole-step up from *c*.

   (1) Play and sing *c* by number (one) or syllable (do).
   (2) Sing a whole-step up by numbers (one-two) or by syllables (do-re).
   (3) Play the whole-step on the piano (*c–d*).
   (4) Did your whole-step (one-two or do-re) match the whole-step on the piano (*c–d*)?

Example: Sing a whole-step down from *f*.

   (1) Play and sing *f* by number (two) or syllable (re).
   (2) Sing a whole-step down by numbers (two-one) or syllables (re-do).
   (3) Play the whole step on the piano (*f–e♭*, if *f* is supertonic then *e♭* is tonic).
   (4) Did the whole-step (two-one or re-do) match the whole-step on the piano (*f–e♭*)?

Example: Sing a half-step up from *f♯*.

   (1) Play and sing *f♯* by number (seven) or syllable (ti).
   (2) Sing a half-step up by numbers (seven-eight) or syllables (ti-do).
   (3) Play the half-step on the piano (*f♯-g*, if *f♯* is leading tone, then *g* is tonic).
   (4) Did the half-step (seven-eight or ti-do) match the half-step on the piano (*f♯-g*)?

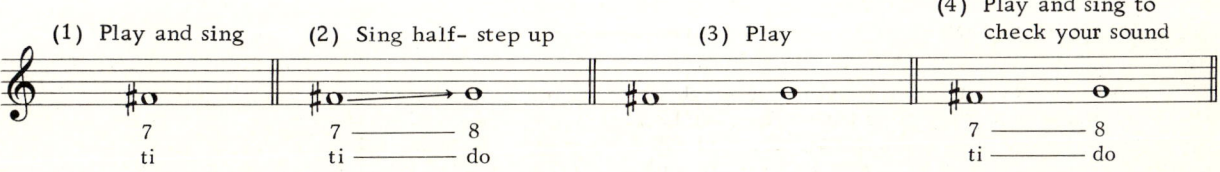

Example: Sing a half-step down from b♭.

(1) Play and sing b♭ by number (eight or one) or syllable (do).
(2) Sing a half-step down by numbers (eight- or one-seven) or syllables (do-ti).
(3) Play the half-step on the piano (b♭-a).
(4) Did the half-step (eight-seven or do-ti) match the half-step on the piano (b♭-a)?

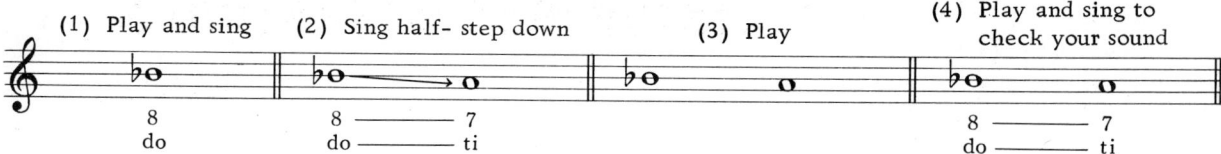

EXERCISE 14.3T
Singing the Major Scale from a Beginning Note Other Than One or Do

You will hear a pitch with its identification as a number other than "1" or a syllable other than "do." By using your knowledge of scale construction and your ability to sing whole-steps and half-steps, sing up or down the scale as directed, ending on the tonic.

Example: The instructor calls the given pitch "6" with directions to sing down the scale.

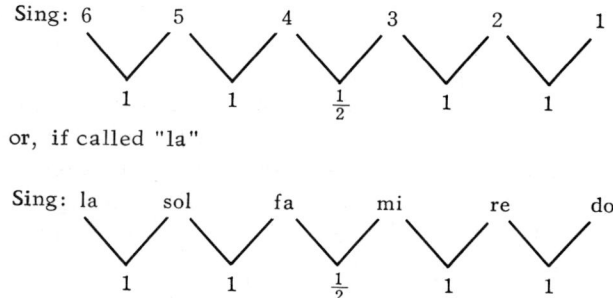

When practicing this exercise at the piano, check your response by playing the necessary portion of the scale. For example, with c given as "6" or "la,"

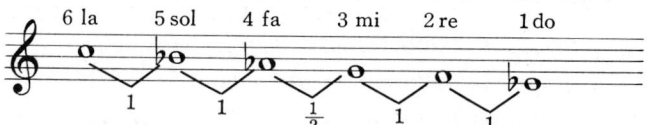

For practice, use these pitches, or choose your own combinations.

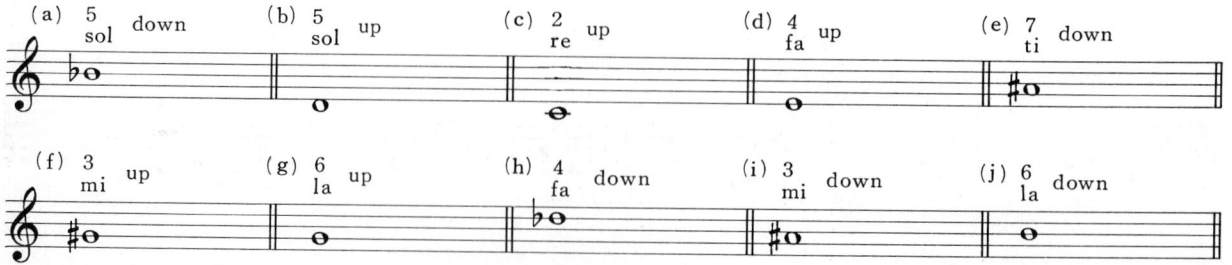

CHAPTER FIFTEEN

MAJOR KEY SIGNATURES

**Key
Key Signature
Circle of Fifths
Order of Sharps and Flats on the Staff**

The major scale, with its characteristic locations of half-steps and whole-steps, constitutes a musical pattern having its own unique aural quality. We have found that the major scale pattern can be written with fifteen different locations (letter names) as tonic, each location other than that of *c* requiring a varying number of sharps or flats to maintain the correct half-step and whole-step relationships. Since each of these fifteen scales has the same characteristic sound, there are not really fifteen different scales; there is simply *one* major scale structure which can be written or played at fifteen different locations.

Much music commonly performed today (including most music of the 17th–19th centuries) is based on either one of two scale patterns: the major scale as already studied, and the minor scale, to be studied in Chapter 16. Music is said to be in *major* when the pitches used can be arranged in alphabetical order with a resulting major scale pattern. In "Joy to the World" (George F. Handel, 1685–1759), the first line of the melody already assumes the pattern of the *d* major scale.

FIGURE 15.1. *"Joy to the World," D Major Scale.*

In the folksong in Figure 15.2, we find the same tones in a different order but still resulting in the same *d* major scale.

FIGURE 15.2. *Folksong, D Major Scale.*

Both of these tunes are said to be *in major* because they are based on the construction of the major scale.

It is possible to begin "Joy to the World" on a different note, with a resulting change in scale spelling.

FIGURE 15.3. *"Joy to the World," B♭ Major Scale.*

We also can write the folksong in Figure 15.2 based on any other major scale. In Figure 15.4 the scale is built on a tonic of f♯.

FIGURE 15.4. *Folksong, F♯ Major Scale.*

It is easy to see that each of these tunes could be written using any of the fifteen major scale locations. We could identify a piece of music by saying it uses a certain scale (Fig. 15.1 uses a *d* major scale), but instead, we say the music is in a certain *key*.

Key

The term *key* refers to the letter name of the tonic (first degree) of that scale upon which the composition is based. The letter name of the tonic is also called *keynote*. Figures 15.1 and 15.2 are therefore in the *key* of D major because (1) each uses a major scale and (2) the tonic, or keynote, of each scale is D. In similar manner we would identify "Joy to the World" in Figure 15.3 as in the key of B♭ major, and the folksong in Figure 15.4 as in the key of F♯ major.

Music could be written with the correct accidentals placed before each note where needed, as in the preceding figures, but this is obviously cumbersome and makes the music appear unduly complicated. To facilitate the notation of accidentals, we use a device called *key signature*.

Key Signatures

The *key signature* is a group of accidentals found on the staff at the beginning of a composition. This group consists of the accidentals used in the scale of the composition, and, when the music uses a major or minor scale, the signature can be used to identify the key of the composition. If we rewrite Figure 15.4 by placing the sharps in a certain order at the beginning of the staff, we find we have a key signature of six sharps, which, as we will learn, will designate the key of F♯ major. The key signature is placed before the time signature.

FIGURE 15.5. *Folksong, Key Signature for F♯ Major.*

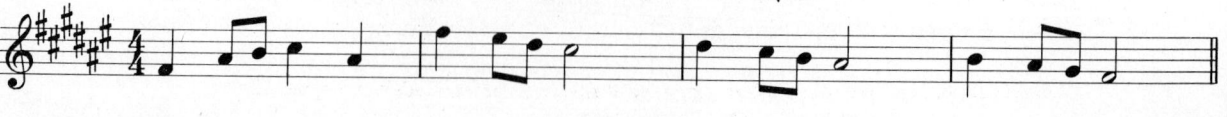

By extracting the accidentals from each major scale in this way, we can find the number and names of sharps or flats for each major key, and the key signature for each. Including C (no sharps and no flats), there are fifteen major keys, just as there are fifteen locations of the major scale.

FIGURE 15.6. *Number and Names of Accidentals for Major Key Signatures.*

Name of key (Name of tonic or keynote)	Number of #'s or ♭'s in key signature	Names of #'s or ♭'s
C	none	
G	1#	f#
D	2#	f#, c#
A	3#	f#, c#, g#
E	4#	f#, c#, g#, d#
B	5#	f#, c#, g#, d#, a#
F#	6#	f#, c#, g#, d#, a#, e#
C#	7#	f#, c#, g#, d#, a#, e#, b#
(C)	(none)	
F	1♭	b♭
B♭	2♭	b♭, e♭
E♭	3♭	b♭, e♭, a♭
A♭	4♭	b♭, e♭, a♭, d♭
D♭	5♭	b♭, e♭, a♭, d♭, g♭
G♭	6♭	b♭, e♭, a♭, d♭, g♭, c♭
C♭	7♭	b♭, e♭, a♭, d♭, g♭, c♭, f♭,

A common way of illustrating the order of key signatures, with the numbers of accidentals in each, is through the *circle of fifths*.

Circle of Fifths

To understand the *circle of fifths,* the student must first be able to measure the interval of a perfect fifth.[1] A perfect fifth spans five staff degrees and is comprised of three whole-steps and one half-step, or seven half-steps. However, rather than counting steps, a perfect fifth can be calculated more quickly by using information already learned in connection with the scale (Chapter Eleven, p. 140). Consider

[1] Interval names, including other kinds of fifths, will be studied in Chapter 22.

the note from which the measurement is to be made as tonic. From a tonic note up to its dominant note is an ascending perfect fifth.

FIGURE 15.7. *Ascending Perfect Fifths.*

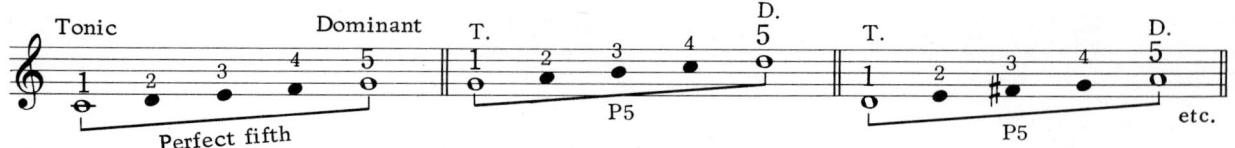

From a tonic note down to its subdominant note is a descending perfect fifth.

FIGURE 15.8. *Descending Perfect Fifths.*

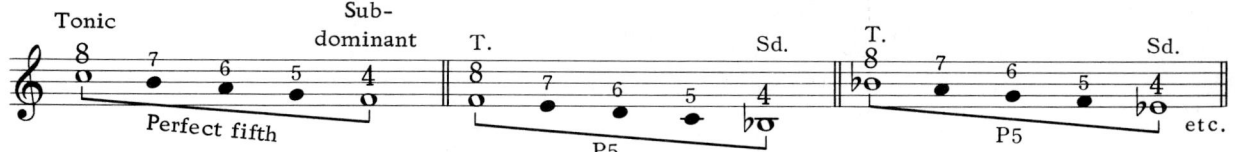

It is through the interval of the perfect fifth that keys are related to each other, as shown in Figures 15.6 and 15.9. Starting with C, we count *up* a perfect fifth to find the keynote (G) for the scale with *one* sharp; we count up a perfect fifth from G to find the keynote (D) for the scale with *two* sharps, and so on until we reach C♯ with *seven* sharps. The flat keys are related in a similar manner. Starting with C, we count *down* a perfect fifth to find the keynote (F) for the scale with *one* flat; we count down a perfect fifth from F to find the keynote (B♭) for the scale of *two* flats, and so on until we reach C♭ with *seven* flats. This process is diagrammed as shown in Figure 15.9, where it can be seen that each progression up by fifth adds one new sharp, and each progression down by fifth adds one new flat.

FIGURE 15.9. *Progressions by Fifths from C.*

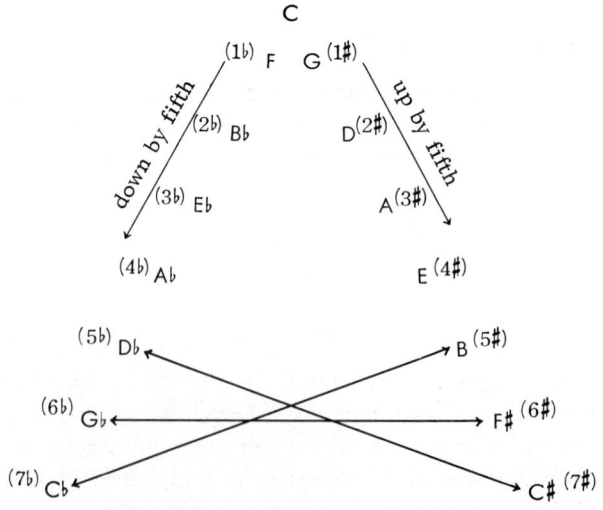

Further observation of Figure 15.9 shows that the key names used for 5, 6, and 7 sharps have enharmonic equivalents in the names for keys of 5, 6, and 7 flats: B (5 sharps) and C♭ (7 flats); F♯ (6 sharps) and G♭ (6 flats); C♯ (7 sharps) and D♭ (5 flats). By reconstructing Figure 15.9 so that these enharmonic keys coincide, the *circle of fifths* for major keys is produced.

FIGURE 15.10.   *Circle of Fifths for Major Keys.*

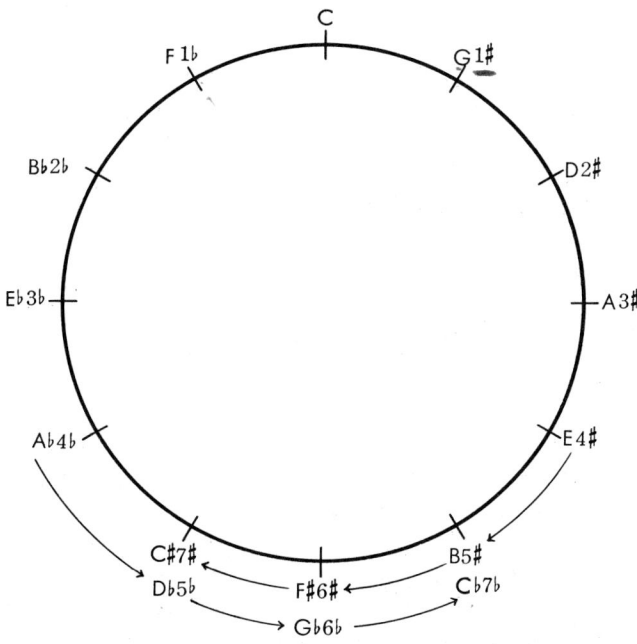

This circle includes all the major key names with the sharp keys reading clockwise from C, and the flat keys reading counterclockwise from C. The circle is joined by the three enharmonic keys. The number of sharps or flats for each key can be determined by counting the number of fifths away from C. For example, A has 3 sharps because it is the third key clockwise from C; D♭ has 5 flats because it is five keys counterclockwise from C.

The circle also indicates the *order of sharps and flats on the staff.*

Order of Sharps and Flats on the Staff

The accidentals of the key signatures are placed on the staff in the same order of appearance as in the circle of fifths. For sharp keys the first sharp appears on f^2 (treble clef) and on small f (bass clef).

This sharp applies to any f in the musical composition whether on the same lines or on any other locations, and this same principle is observed for any other sharps (or flats) of the key signature. All sharps are placed as shown in Figure 15.11. Notice that the sharps progress in an orderly arrangement from left to right. For quick identification of a major key in a signature of sharps, the keynote occupies that staff degree immediately above the last sharp.

175

FIGURE 15.11. *C Major and Sharp Key Signatures.*

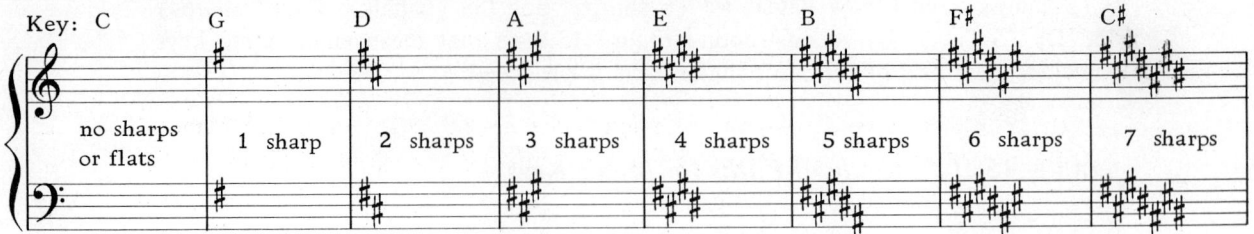

For flat keys, the first flat appears on b¹ (treble clef) and on great B (bass clef).

All flats are placed as shown in Figure 15.12. For quick identification of a major key in a signature of two or more flats, the keynote is identical with the penultimate (next-to-last) flat.

FIGURE 15.12. *C Major and Flat Key Signatures.*

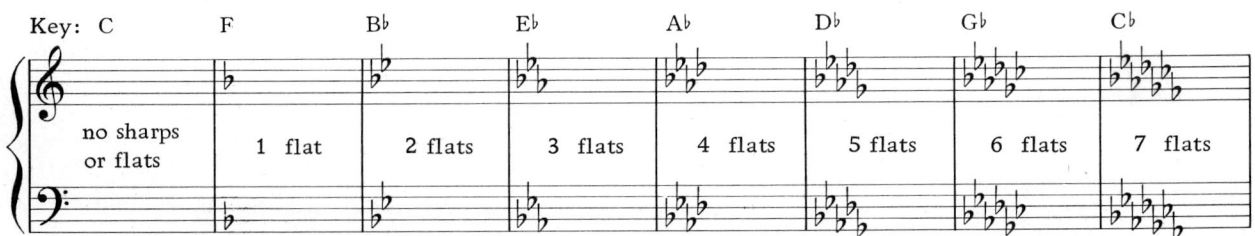

The key signatures may now be used to identify the key. When it is known that the music is in a major key, the number of sharps or flats in the signature will indicate the name of that major key as shown in Figures 15.11–12. For example, when the key is major, four sharps always indicates the key of E.

EXERCISE 15.1
Identifying Key Signatures from the Circle of Fifths

On the circle of fifths below, the key names are given. Beside each key name write the correct number of sharps or flats. The answer for G major is given.

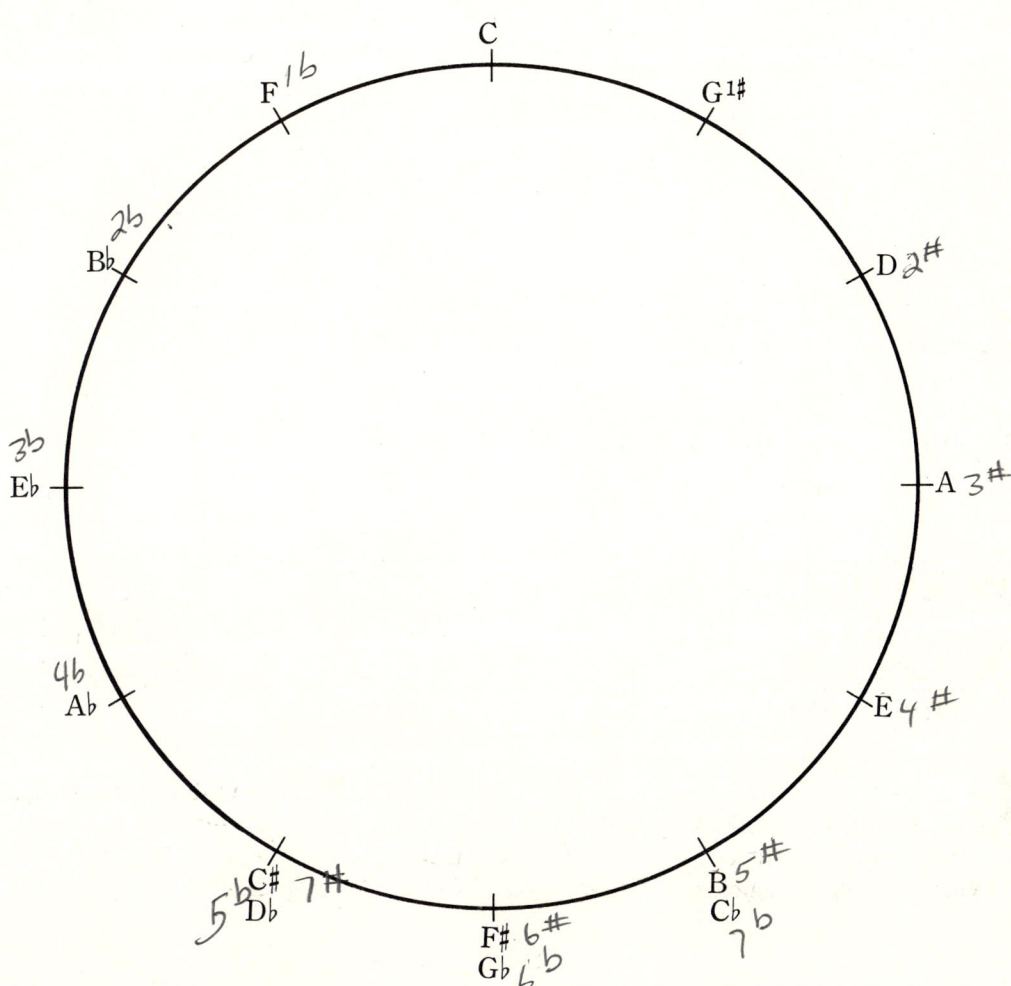

EXERCISE 15.2
Identifying the Name of the Key from the Circle of Fifths

On the circle below, the key signatures are given. Beside each, give the name of the major key. The answer for one flat is given.

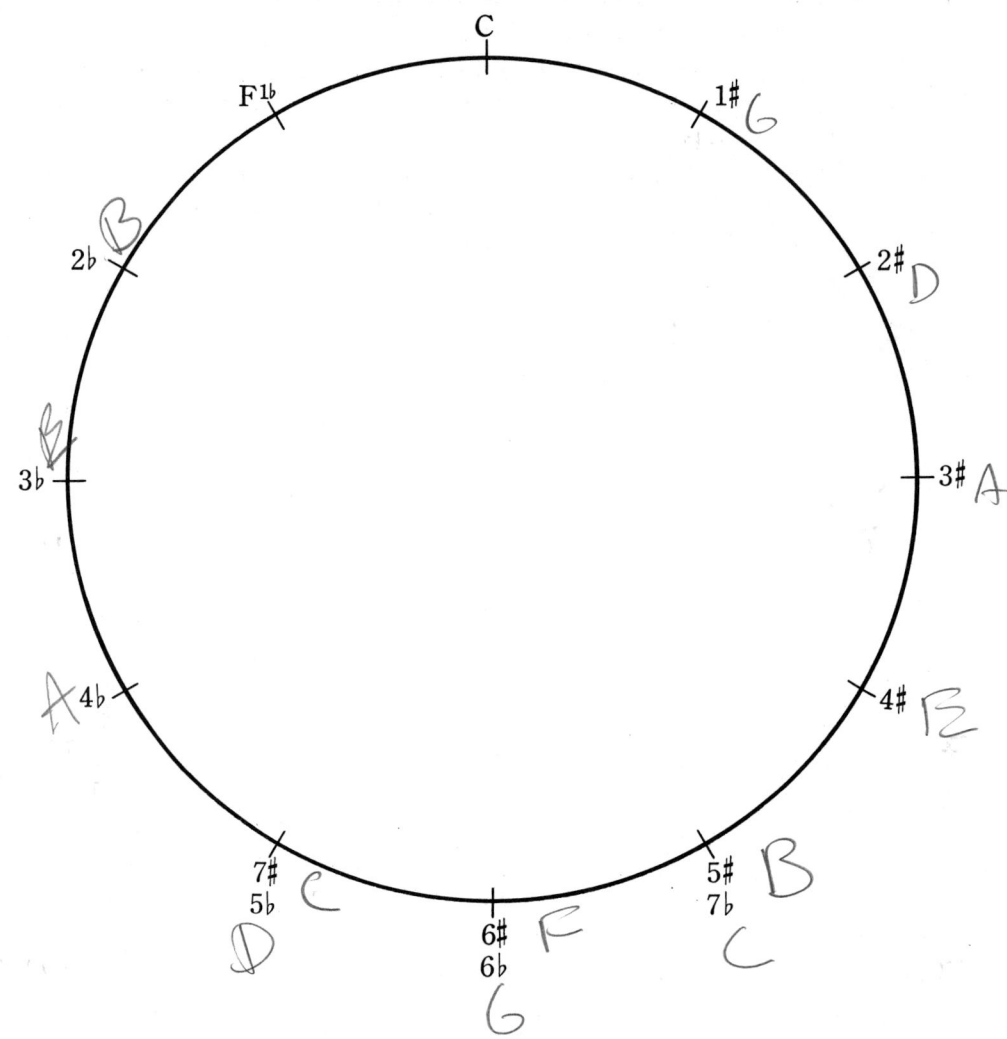

EXERCISE 15.3
Procedure for Constructing the Circle of Fifths for Major Keys

1. On the circle below, mark twelve points like the face of a clock. This provides places for all fifteen keys including three enharmonic keys.
2. At 12 o'clock place C (no sharps or flats).
3. Proceeding clockwise, at 1 o'clock place the letter name of the key a fifth above C, which is G (1 sharp); continue clockwise in fifths and add sharps through the key of C♯ (7 sharps).
4. Proceeding counterclockwise, at 11 o'clock place the letter name of the key a fifth below C, which is F (1 flat); continue counterclockwise in fifths and add flats through the key of C♭ (7 flats).

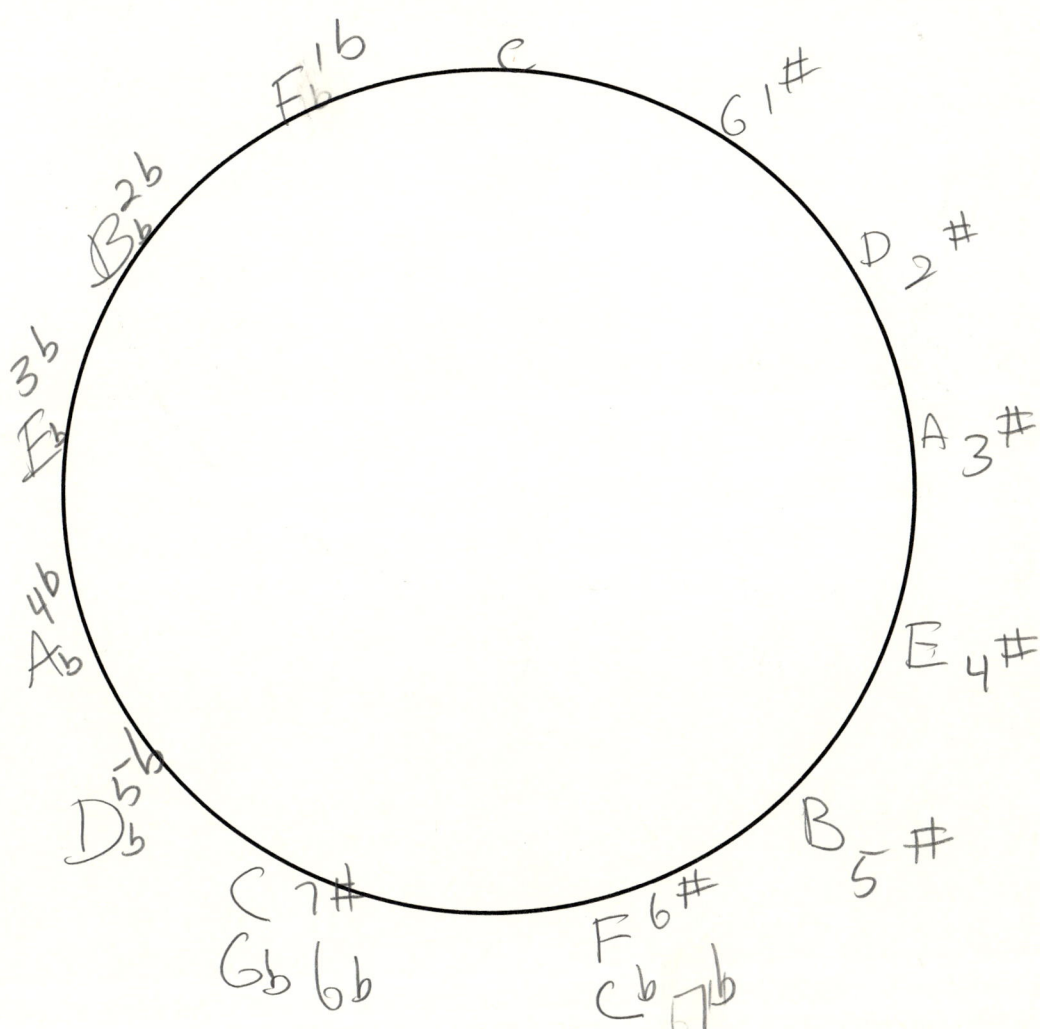

_____ NAME

EXERCISE 15.4

Constructing the Circle of Fifths for Major Keys

Construct from memory the circle of fifths for major keys. You should be able to demonstrate the circle on paper or at the board in *one minute*. To check your work, see Figure 15.10.

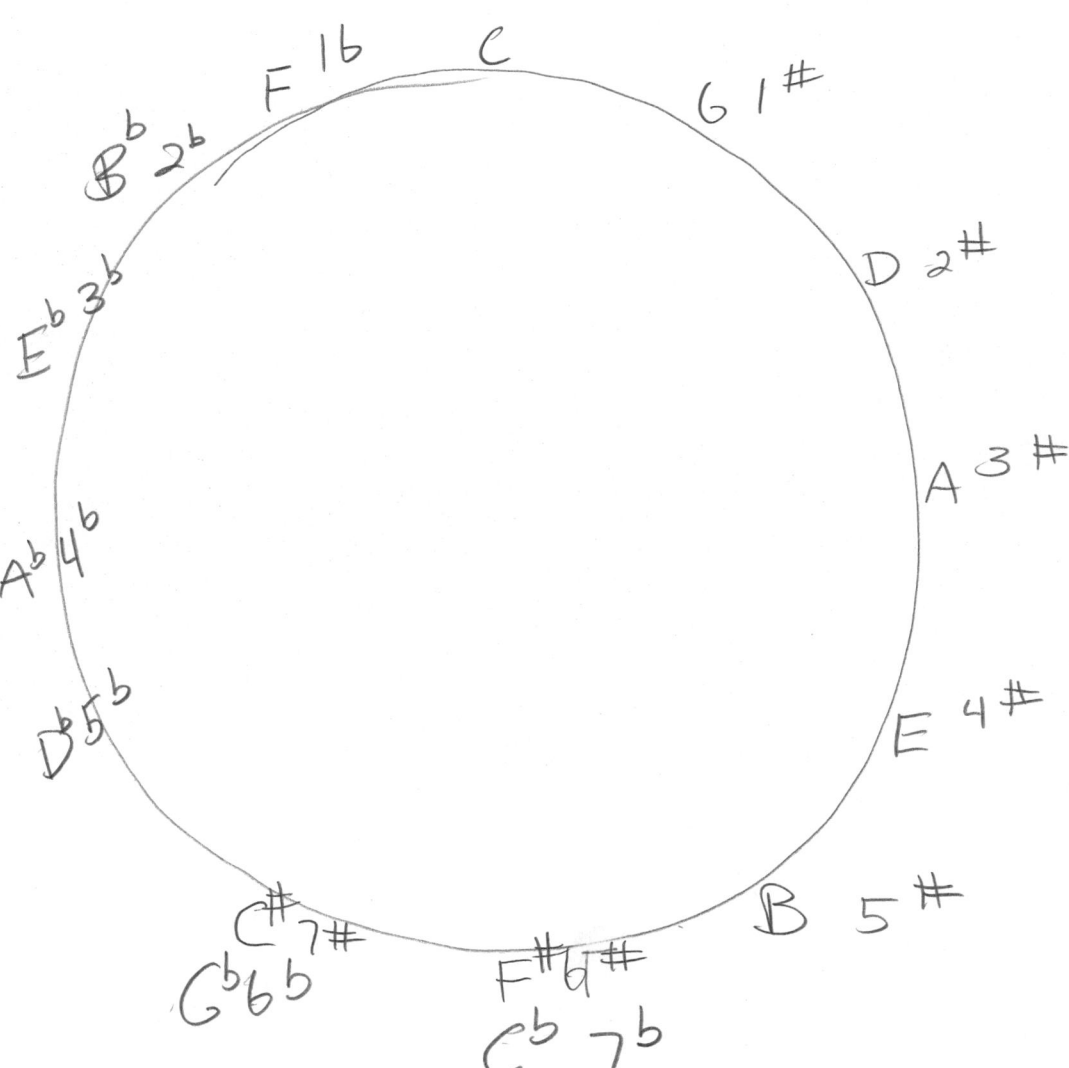

181

CHAPTER SIXTEEN

MINOR SCALES

Accidentals, continued
Minor Scales: Natural (Pure), Harmonic and Melodic Forms
Historical Derivation of Major and Minor Scales

It was observed in Chapter Fifteen that much of the music commonly performed today is based on two different scales, major and minor. We have learned that the sound of a scale is determined by the location of half-steps and whole-steps in the scale. Therefore, we can expect that the minor scale, which sounds different from the major scale, will have a different arrangement of half-steps and whole-steps. Not only is this true, but there are three different forms of the minor scale. When you have learned the construction of each form and have completed exercises in writing minor scales, we will investigate some of the history of scales to show why these three forms exist.

Writing certain minor scales requires use of accidentals other than the sharp or flat. Therefore we will first study the remaining accidentals: the *double sharp, double flat,*[1] and *natural sign* (listed on page 22).

Double Sharp, Double Flat, and Natural Sign

The *double sharp*, ×, raises the pitch of a note two half-steps or one whole-step.

FIGURE 16.1. *The Double Sharp.*

It can be seen that a note carrying a double sharp will always be enharmonic with another pitch name. In Figure 16.1, *f* × is enharmonic with the pitch *g*; *c* × is enharmonic with *d*.

The *double flat*, ♭♭, lowers the pitch of a note two half-steps or one whole-step.

---

[1] Though not found in major or minor scale spelling, the double flat is included here to complete the study of accidentals.

187

FIGURE 16.2. *The Double Flat.*

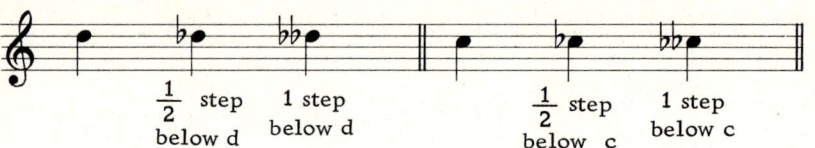

$D\flat\flat$ is enharmonic with c; $c\flat\flat$ is enharmonic with $b\flat$.

The *natural sign,* ♮ , cancels a previously used accidental, or the accidental in the key signature.

FIGURE 16.3. *The Natural Sign.*

Considerations in Using Accidentals

(a) Any accidental placed before a note affects the pitch on that line or space only.

(b) The effect of an accidental lasts only until the next bar line.

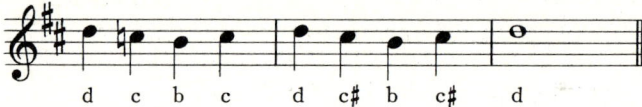

(c) An accidental may be used optionally as a reminder. The preceding illustration is repeated with the reminder in measure two. The ♯ before c does not imply double sharp.

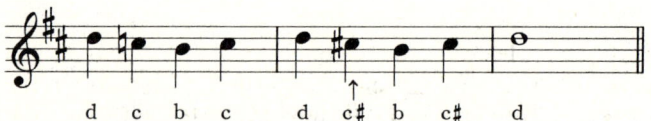

(d) When it is necessary that a note carry a double sharp or a double flat, the symbol 𝄪 or ♭♭ is always used, even if there is already a sharp or flat in the signature.

(e) When it is necessary to place a sharp or double sharp before a note already carrying a flat, or to place a flat or double flat before a note already carrying a sharp, the natural sign precedes the new accidental.

Now that we are informed in the use of accidentals, we are ready to proceed to the study of the minor scale and its three forms, *natural (pure), harmonic,* and *melodic.*

The Natural (Pure) Form of the Minor Scale

The *natural (pure)* form of the minor scale consists of a series of eight tones with the intervals between tones being whole-step, half-step, whole-step, whole-step, half-step, whole-step, whole-step.

FIGURE 16.4. *Structure of the Natural (Pure) Minor Scale.*

It can be seen that the natural minor scale consists of whole-steps excepting between the second and third degrees and the fifth and sixth degrees where the intervals are half-steps. Notice that the natural minor scale starting on *a* involves only white keys because the half-steps 2–3 and 5–6 coincide with the white keys b–c and e–f.

FIGURE 16.5. *The A Minor Scale, Natural Form.*

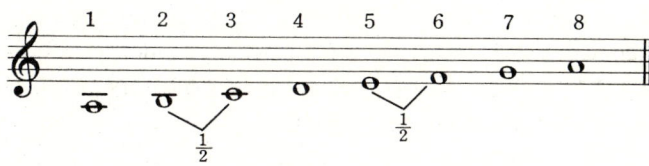

All natural minor scales starting on pitches other than *a* require one or more accidentals in order to maintain the characteristic half-step and whole-step arrangement of the scale structure shown in Figure 16.4. For example, the natural minor scale of *e* requires one sharp.

FIGURE 16.6. *The E Minor Scale, Natural Form.*

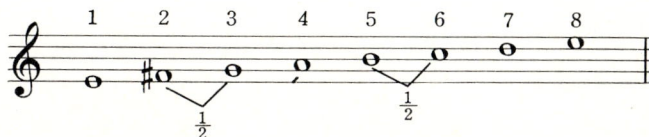

As with major scales, there are seven natural minor scales containing sharps and seven containing flats, which, together with *a* minor (no sharps or flats) comprise the fifteen natural minor scales.

FIGURE 16.7. *Table of Minor Scales and Numbers of Accidentals for the Natural Form.*

Scale	A	E	B	F♯	C♯	G♯	D♯	A♯
Accidentals	none	1♯	2♯	3♯	4♯	5♯	6♯	7♯
Scale		D	G	C	F	B♭	E♭	A♭
Accidentals		1♭	2♭	3♭	4♭	5♭	6♭	7♭

Figure 16.7 also shows relationship by fifths between minor scales such as we saw earlier in major scales (pp. 140, 173 ff.). The circle of fifths for minor will be studied in Chapter 20.

Harmonic Form of the Minor Scale

The *harmonic form* of the minor scale is derived from the natural form. It is the natural form but with a raised seventh degree.

FIGURE 16.8. *The A Minor Scale, Harmonic Form.*

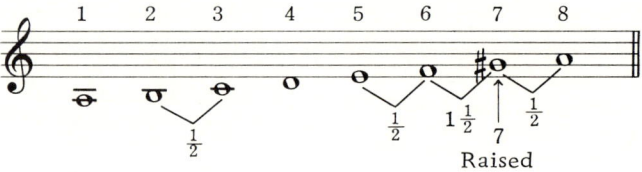

Notice that by raising the seventh, the interval between 6 and 7 becomes a step-and-a-half (three half-steps), and the interval between 7 and 8 becomes a half-step. Any natural minor scale can be changed to the harmonic form by raising the seventh scale degree. For example, the E natural minor scale shown in Figure 16.6 becomes the harmonic form when the seventh, *d,* is raised by the sharp.

FIGURE 16.9. *The E Minor Scale, Harmonic Form.*

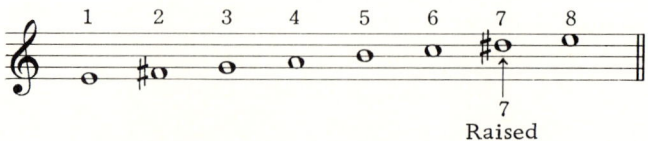

Melodic Form of the Minor Scale

The *melodic form* of the minor scale is derived from the natural form. Unlike all other major and minor scales, its ascending and descending forms are different. The ascending form of the melodic minor scale is the natural form but with *raised sixth and raised seventh degrees*. The descending form is the same as the natural form; the *seventh and sixth degrees are lowered* from their ascending form.

FIGURE 16.10.   *The A Minor Scale, Melodic Form.*

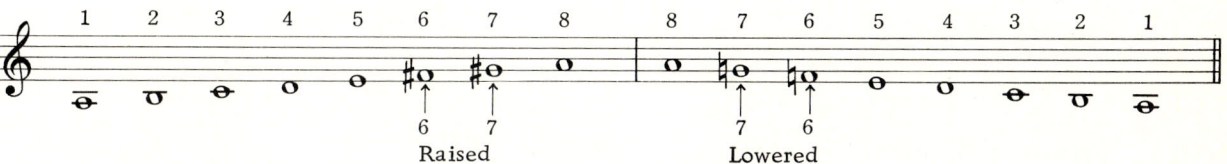

Any natural minor scale can be changed to the melodic form by (1) raising the sixth and seventh degrees in the ascending scale structure and (2) by lowering the sixth and seventh scale degrees to their natural form in the descending scale structure. For example, the E natural minor scale shown in Figure 16.6 becomes the ascending melodic form shown in Figure 16.11 when the sixth scale degree *c* and the seventh scale degree *d* are raised by sharps; in descending, the seventh and sixth are lowered by natural signs and the descending scale is identical to the natural form.

FIGURE 16.11.   *The E Minor Scale, Melodic Form.*

Figure 16.12 shows a comparison of the three different forms of the minor scale.

191

FIGURE 16.12. *A Minor: Natural, Harmonic and Melodic Forms.*

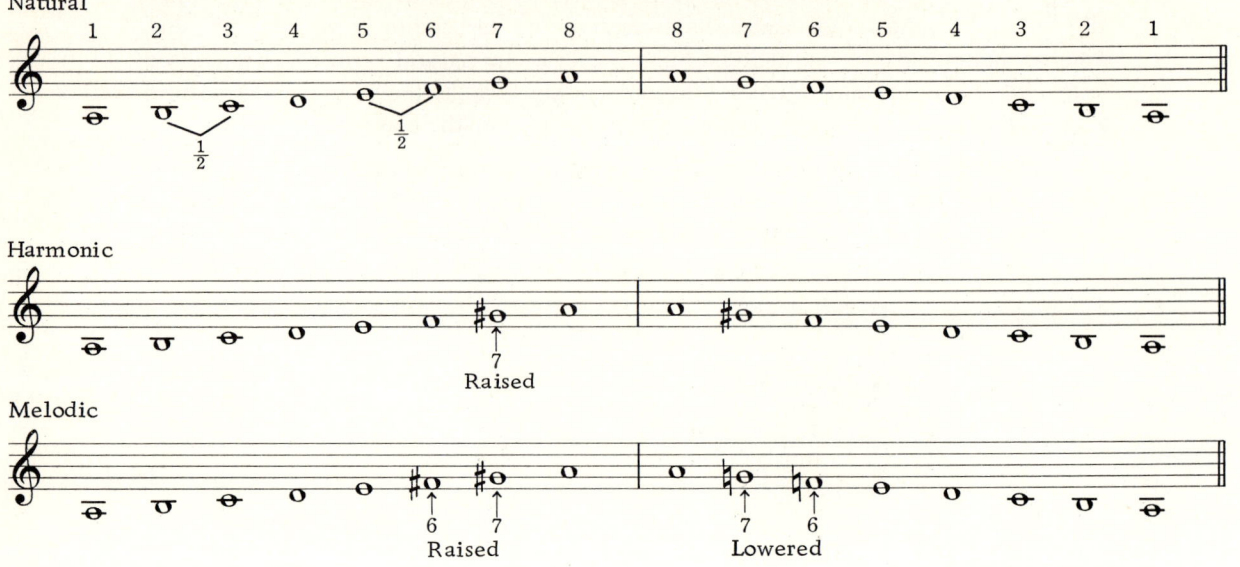

Several minor scales require use of the double sharp, as in the G♯ minor scale, harmonic form:

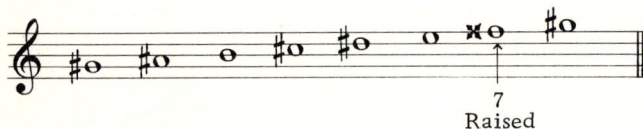

The natural sign is sometimes required to raise a pitch, as in the B♭ minor scale:

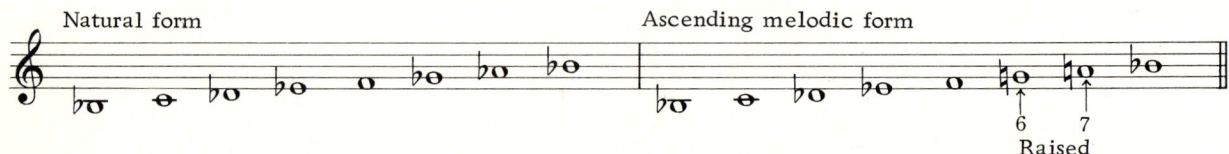

You are now ready to write minor scales as provided in the exercises at the end of this chapter. When you have gained understanding of the construction and proficiency in writing these scales, you will find the following historical account of the reasons for the three different forms of the scale to be of particular interest.

HISTORICAL DERIVATION OF MAJOR AND MINOR SCALES [2]

It may appear to you that the system of three minor scales is unnecessarily complex. Certainly the construction of minor scales is far more complex than that of major scales. The reason for this is not arbitrary; it derives from a long evolutionary process dating back to the Medieval period in music history.

[2] This section is not necessary to the development of skills presented in this chapter; it is included to help clarify particular musical practices often found puzzling to students.

Early Scales

The structures of both our present day major and natural minor scales are identical to two scales in earlier music history. Eight-note scale systems in Western music evolved as early as the 8th century A.D., and by 1600 music was commonly written in a system of six different scales, called *modes*. These six modes can be found quickly on the piano keyboard by playing up an octave from each note given below (Fig. 16.13), using only white keys. You will observe that each mode consists of five whole-steps and two half-steps, and that the half-steps are always *e–f* and *b–c*, but each mode differs from the others because of the varying locations of the half-steps. These differences, together with the name of each mode, are shown in Figure 16.13.

FIGURE 16.13. *Modes.*

First note	White-key scale	Mode
A	a b—c d e—f g a (2–3 ½, 5–6 ½)	Aeolian
(B)[3]		(Locrian)
C	c d e—f g a b—c (3–4 ½, 7–8 ½)	Ionian
D	d e—f g a b—c d (2–3 ½, 6–7 ½)	Dorian
E	e—f g a b—c d e (1–2 ½, 5–6 ½)	Phrygian
F	f g a b—c d e—f (4–5 ½, 7–8 ½)	Lydian
G	g a b—c d e—f g (3–4 ½, 6–7 ½)	Mixolydian

Ionian and Aeolian: Major and Minor

Through evolutionary processes, the number of scale systems was reduced to two by the mid-seventeenth century. The Ionian mode became the pattern for the major scale. The Aeolian mode was also retained, and became the pattern for the basic minor scale: the pure, or natural form of the minor scale.

The Role of "Musica Ficta" in Scale Development

Of the seven possible modal scales, only two, the Ionian and the Lydian, contain a leading tone. This lack of a leading tone in ascending forms of the other

---

[3] Theoretically, a mode called Locrian can be constructed on B, but it was not used in musical practice.

modes was recognized very early in the history of the use of modes. Performers often preferred the sound of leading tone to tonic rather than a whole-step, and, in performance of music written with an ascending whole-step between 7 and 8, would sometimes raise the seventh scale step to create a leading tone. This practice, part of a system known as *musica ficta* (false music), was condoned by performers and composers alike.[4]

By adding a leading tone, the Mixolydian mode displays the same scale structure as Major:

G A B C D E F♯ G;

the Aeolian the same as Minor, harmonic form:

A B C D E F G♯ A;

and the Dorian the same as Minor, melodic form:

D E F G A B C♯ D.

Figure 16.4 shows a melodic line in the Aeolian mode, with the seventh scale degree *g* raised to *g♯*. The sharp *above* the note indicates that it was *not* written by the composer but rather reflects the probable performance based on known principles of *musica ficta*.

FIGURE 16.14. *Use of Musica Ficta.*

In another practice common to *musica ficta*, *b* was lowered to *b♭* in certain circumstances. When applied to the Lydian mode, the resulting scale structure is the same as major:

F G A B♭ C D E F.

When applying both varieties of *musica ficta* (♭6 and ♯7 [5]) to the Dorian, the resulting scale structure is the same as minor, harmonic form:

D E F G A B♭ C♯ D.

Thus the three forms of the minor scale are simply a result of performance practices applied to modal structures. Even today, the minor key signature is that

---

[4] This principle was not applied to the Phrygian mode. For more detailed information, consult articles under the heading *musica ficta* in music dictionaries, or in music history books, chapters on Medieval and Renaissance music.

[5] The symbol ♯7 indicates *raised seventh*.

for Aeolian mode, while changes in the sixth and seventh scale degrees are placed in the music itself.

Characteristics of the Harmonic Minor Scale

In the harmonic form of the minor scale, the raised seventh (leading tone) has a strong tendency to ascend, and the sixth scale step has a strong tendency to descend. When, in a piece of music in minor, the seventh scale step ascends and the sixth descends, these characteristics identify the form of the scale used for the composition as Harmonic Minor.

FIGURE 16.15. *Characteristics of the Harmonic Minor Scale.*

Characteristics of the Melodic Form of the Minor Scale

When the sixth scale degree of the harmonic minor scale ascends, the next scale tone, the leading tone, is more than a whole-step up. This interval of three half-steps (a step-and-a-half [6]) has been found objectionable in melodic writing by most composers and performers. To eliminate this offending interval, the sixth scale degree is raised, eliminating the awkward step-and-a-half between 6 and 7 of the harmonic form of the scale. The interval between 6 and 7 becomes a whole-step and, at the same time, the desired leading tone is present. This accounts for the ascending form of the melodic minor scale with its raised sixth and seventh degrees.

FIGURE 16.16. *Difference Between Harmonic and Melodic Forms of the Minor Scale.*

The sensation of leading tone is peculiar to ascending melody; on the other hand, when a melody descends from the tonic note, there is no need for the leading tone. Accordingly, the descending form of the melodic minor scale is found with both the sixth and seventh scale steps lowered, and is identical to the natural form of the scale. When, in a piece of music, both raised and lowered sixth and seventh scale steps occur, these characteristics identify the form of the scale used for the composition as Melodic Minor.

[6] Called *augmented second;* included in the study of intervals, Chapter 23.

FIGURE 16.17. *Characteristics of the Melodic Minor Scale.*

Summary

(1) The natural minor scale is a hold-over from an earlier scale system and is identical to the Aeolian mode (just as the major scale is identical to the Ionian mode); (2) the harmonic form evolved from the musical practice of raising the seventh scale degree to allow for a leading tone; and (3) the ascending melodic form resulted from raising the sixth (along with the seventh) in order to eliminate the awkward interval of a step-and-a-half in the harmonic form; descending, the sixth and seventh tones were lowered to conform with natural minor.

_____ NAME

EXERCISE 16.1

Writing Minor Scales on the Staff

Write all 15 minor scales, each in the three forms, as shown in the model, Figure 16.18 below. Indicate location of half-steps in the natural minor; indicate additional accidentals needed in the harmonic and melodic forms. Observe that the scales are presented in the order of fifths as shown in Figure 16.7.

(Instructor: The student should not use key signatures in this assignment. Minor key signatures will be studied in Chapter 20.)

FIGURE 16.18. *Model for Writing Minor Scales.*

(1) A natural minor

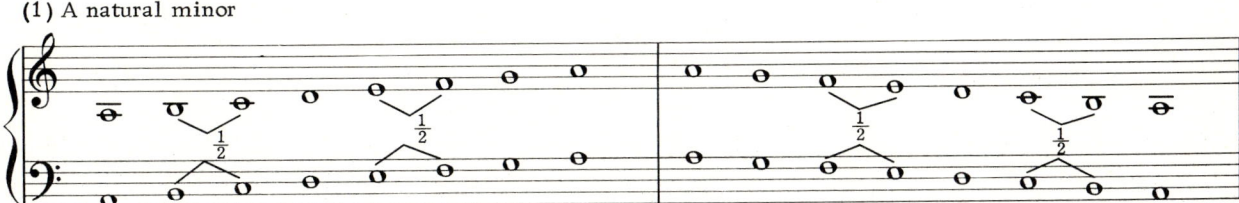

A harmonic minor

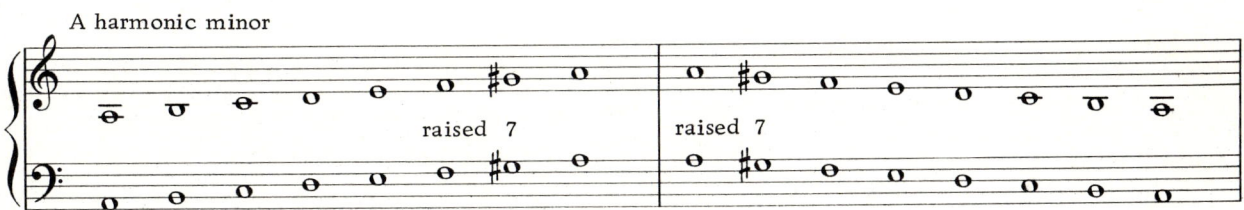

A melodic minor

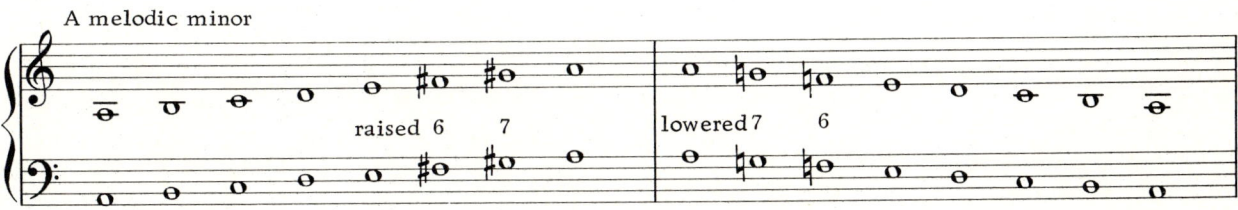

197

(2) E natural minor

E harmonic minor

E melodic minor

(3) B natural minor

B harmonic minor

B melodic minor

_____ NAME

(4) F# natural minor

F# harmonic minor

F# melodic minor

(5) C# natural minor

C# harmonic minor

C# melodic minor

(6) G# natural minor

G# harmonic minor

G# melodic minor

(7) D# natural minor

D# harmonic minor

D# melodic minor

(8) A# natural minor

A# harmonic minor

A# melodic minor

(9) D natural minor

D harmonic minor

D melodic minor

(10) G natural minor

G harmonic minor

G melodic minor

(11) C natural minor

C harmonic minor

C melodic minor

NAME _____

(12) F natural minor

F harmonic minor

F melodic minor

(13) B♭ natural minor

B♭ harmonic minor

B♭ melodic minor

(14) E♭ natural minor

E♭ harmonic minor

E♭ melodic minor

(15) A♭ natural minor

A♭ harmonic minor

A♭ melodic minor

EXERCISE 16.2
Writing Minor Scales on the Staff

Follow directions for Exercise 16.1, except that selected scales are in random order.

(1) C# natural minor

C# harmonic minor

C# melodic minor

(2) F natural minor

F harmonic minor

F melodic minor

(3) B natural minor

B harmonic minor

B melodic minor

(4) G# natural minor

G# harmonic minor

G# melodic minor

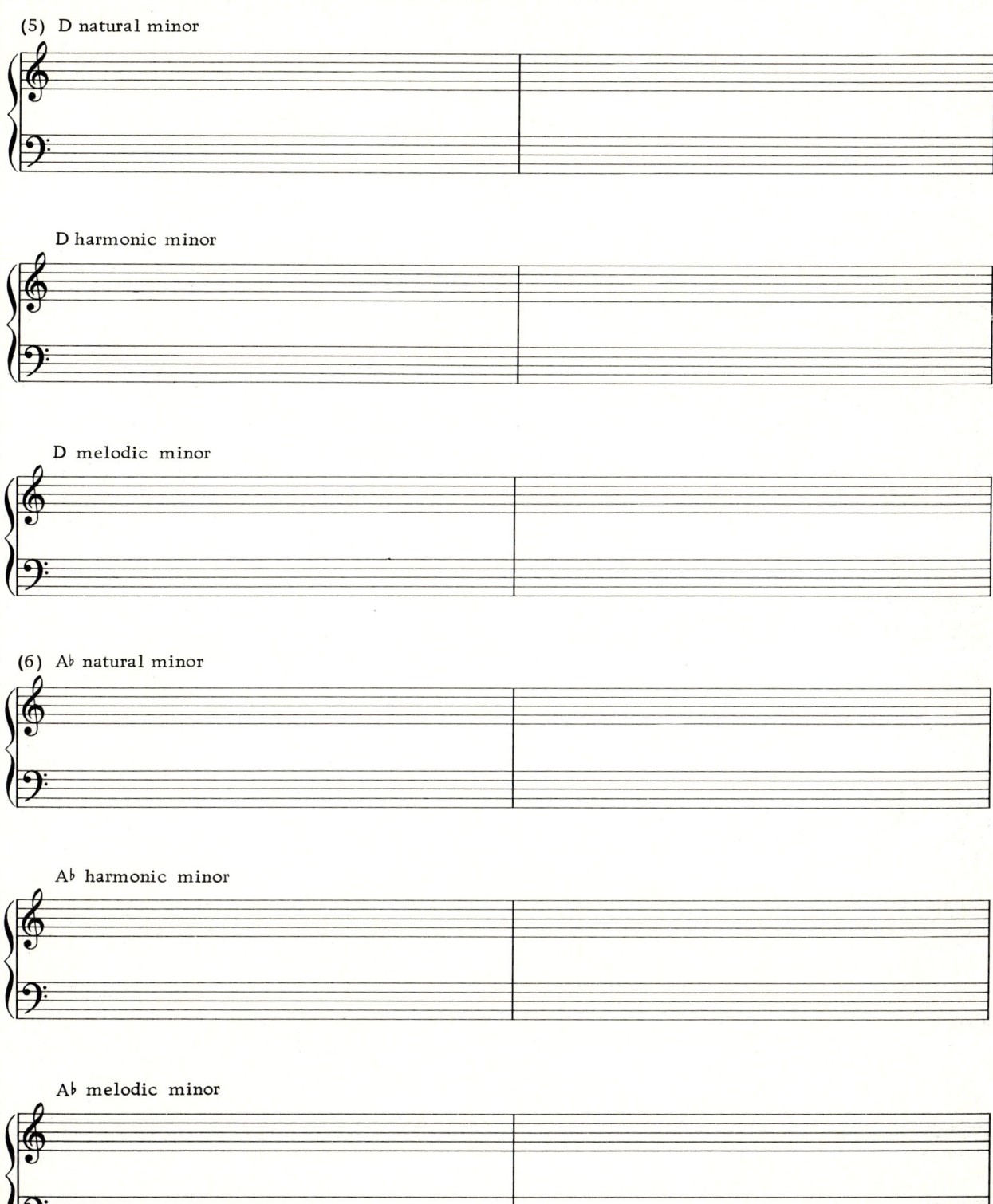

_____ NAME

EXERCISE 16.3
Spelling Minor Scales

Write minor scales using letter names with accidentals where needed. Indicate half-steps in the natural minor and the additional accidentals needed in the harmonic and melodic forms.

Example: C minor (spell the three forms of the C minor scale)

Answer: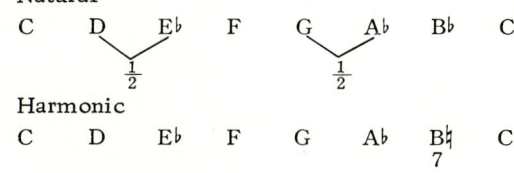

Harmonic
C   D   E♭   F   G   A♭   B♮   C
                              7

Melodic (ascending) | (descending)
C D E♭ F G A♮ B♮ C | C   B♭ A♭ G   F   E♭ D   C
                6   7 | 7   6

(a) F♯ minor

   Natural

   Harmonic

   Melodic

(b) B♭ minor

   Natural

   Harmonic

   Melodic

209

(c) A♯ minor

    Natural

    Harmonic

    Melodic

(d) G minor

    Natural

    Harmonic

    Melodic

(e) E minor

    Natural

    Harmonic

    Melodic

_____ NAME

(f) E♭ minor

　　Natural

　　Harmonic

　　Melodic

(g) D♯ minor

　　Natural

　　Harmonic

　　Melodic

CHAPTER SEVENTEEN

MINOR SCALES
(continued)

Names of Scale Degrees in Minor

Scale degrees in minor utilize the same names as those for the major scale (Chapter Twelve), but because of the alteration of the 6th and 7th steps, additional terminology is required for *names of scale degrees in minor*.

Names of Scale Degrees in Minor

The term *leading tone* in minor refers to the tone one half-step below the tonic, just as in major. Therefore, in minor, the leading tone is the raised seventh scale degree. When the seventh scale degree is not raised, it is known as the *subtonic*.

FIGURE 17.1. *The Leading Tone and Subtonic in the Minor Scale.*

Submediant in minor refers to the natural sixth scale step. When the sixth scale step is raised, it is called *raised submediant*.

FIGURE 17.2. *The Submediant and Raised Submediant in the Minor Scale.*

The ascending and descending melodic minor scale displays all possible scale degree names.

FIGURE 17.3. *Names of the Scale Degrees in Melodic Minor.*

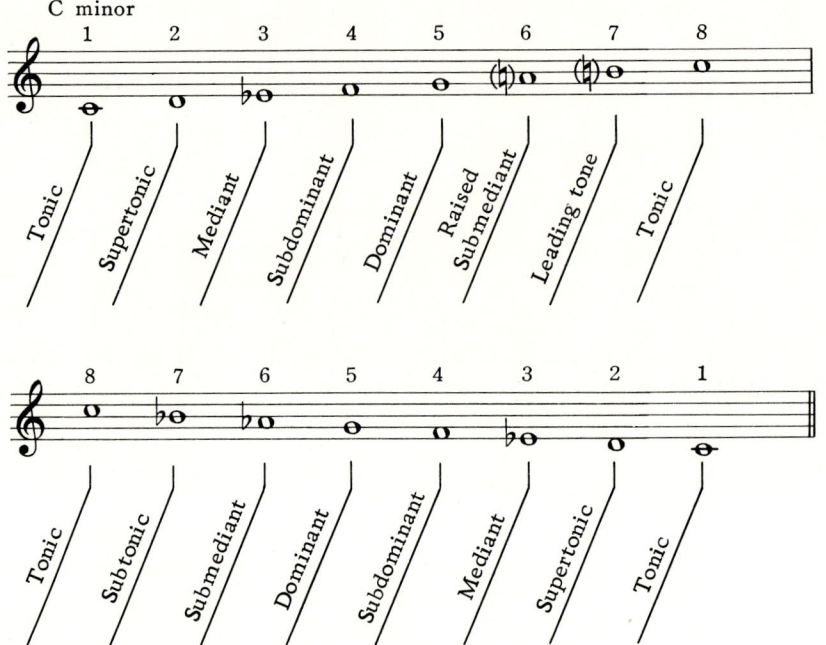

EXERCISE 17.1
Identifying Scale Degrees in Minor

Write the name of the scale degree below each note on the staff. Each example includes both varieties of the sixth and seventh scale degrees. The first note on each staff is the tonic note of the scale.

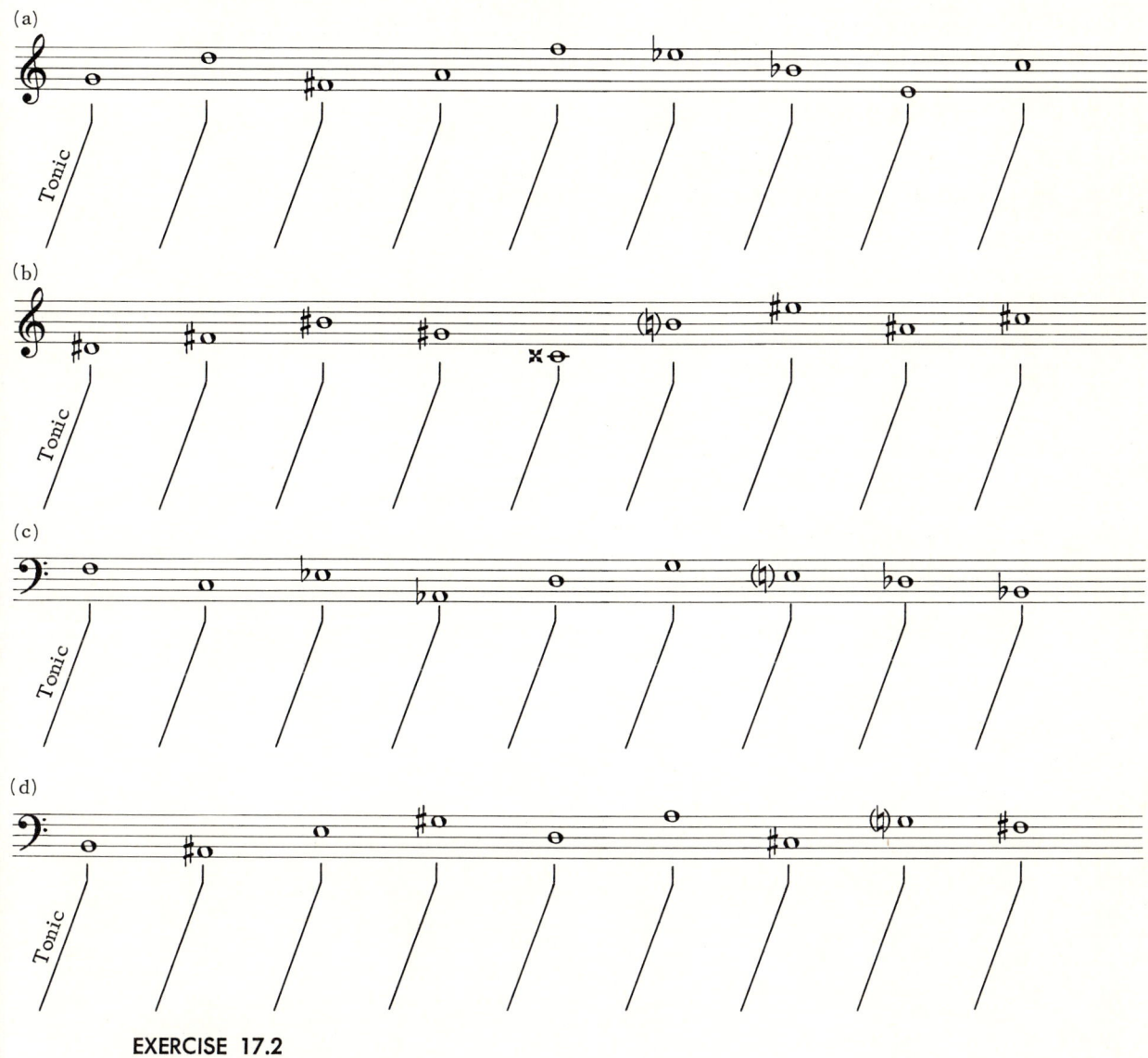

EXERCISE 17.2
Identifying Scale Degrees in Minor

Give the pitch name for each scale degree listed when the tonic is identified.

Example:		Answer:	
Tonic	C	Tonic	C
Mediant	_____	Mediant	E♭

215

	Subtonic	___		Subtonic	B♭
	Raised submediant	___		Raised submediant	A
	etc.				
(a)	Tonic	E	(c)	Tonic	D
	Leading tone	___		Mediant	___
	Dominant	___		Subtonic	___
	Supertonic	___		Submediant	___
	Subtonic	___		Leading tone	___
	Submediant	___		Supertonic	___
	Subdominant	___		Raised submediant	___
	Mediant	___		Dominant	___
	Raised submediant	___		Subdominant	___
(b)	Tonic	G♯	(d)	Tonic	B♭
	Subdominant	___		Submediant	___
	Subtonic	___		Supertonic	___
	Mediant	___		Subtonic	___
	Raised submediant	___		Leading tone	___
	Submediant	___		Subdominant	___
	Supertonic	___		Mediant	___
	Dominant	___		Raised submediant	___
	Leading tone	___		Dominant	___

EXERCISE 17.3

Identifying Scale Degrees in Minor
Name the tonic pitch when the scale degree is identified by pitch name.

Example: G is dominant: C   is tonic.

(a) E is subdominant: B   is tonic.

(b) F♯ is raised submediant: A   is tonic.

(c) F𝄪 is leading tone: G♯   is tonic.

(d) A is supertonic: G   is tonic.

(e) F is dominant: B♭   is tonic.

(f) D♭ is subtonic: E♭   is tonic.

(g) D is submediant: F♯   is tonic.

(h) E is mediant: C♯   is tonic.

(i) C♯ is leading tone: D   is tonic.

(j) F is subdominant: C   is tonic.

(k) B♯ is raised submediant: D♯   is tonic.

(l) E♭ is subtonic: F   is tonic.

(m) C is submediant: E   is tonic.

(n) C♭ is mediant: A♭   is tonic.

CHAPTER EIGHTEEN

MINOR SCALES
(continued)

Playing Minor Scales at the Keyboard

The playing of minor scales follows the same procedures outlined for playing major scales in Chapter Thirteen.

PLAYING MINOR SCALES AT THE KEYBOARD [1]

(a) The A Minor Scale

By playing the white key *a* and the next seven white keys above it, an *a* minor scale (natural form) will be produced. Playing only white keys from this given pitch *a* automatically places the half-steps in their correct scale locations, between 2 and 3 and between 5 and 6, as shown in Figure 18.1.

FIGURE 18.1.   *Playing the A Minor Scale, Natural Form.*

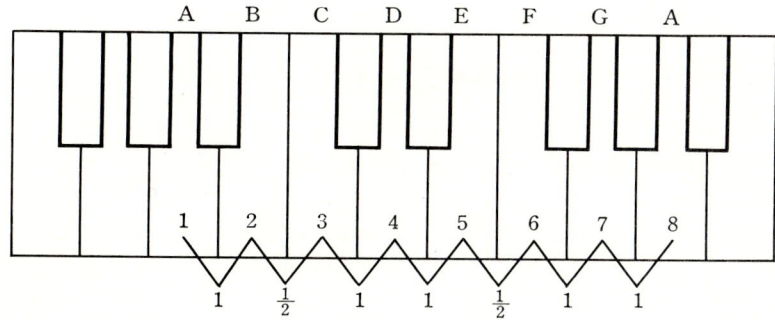

To play the harmonic form of the *a* minor scale, raise the seventh scale step *g* to *g♯*.

---

[1] See Appendix, page 300 for fingering of minor scales.

FIGURE 18.2. *Playing the A Minor Scale, Harmonic Form.*

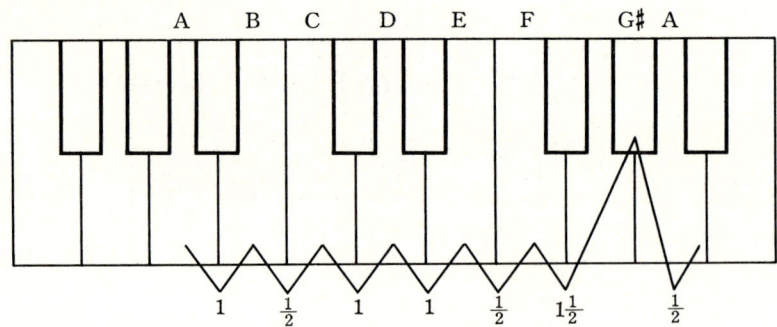

To play the melodic form of the *a* minor scale, raise the sixth scale step *f* to *f♯* and the seventh scale step *g* to *g♯* when ascending.

FIGURE 18.3. *Playing the A Minor Scale, Melodic Form.*

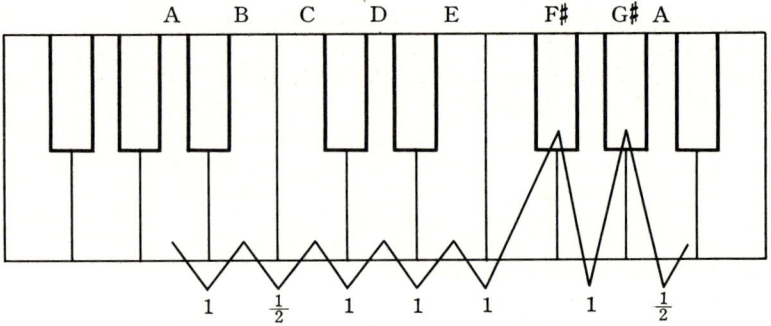

When descending, play the natural form of the scale as shown in Figure 18.1.

(b) All Other Minor Scales Except Those on G♯, D♯ and A♯

These scales (with *a* minor) include all those written in Exercise 16.1 except *g♯*, *d♯* and *a♯*, which will be considered in section (c). Playing minor scales other than *a* involves the use of black keys. Practice in playing these scales should be done in each of these three ways:

1. Play the scales listed in this section, reading from the scales you wrote in Exercise 16.1. Spell the scale orally as you play it.
2. Without the music, choose one of the starting pitches except *g♯*, *d♯*, or *a♯*. Play each note in succession by determining if the next note will be a half-step or whole-step. For example, choose B♭. Figure 18.4 shows the whole-steps and half-steps necessary to play these intervals in each of the three forms of the scale. Spell each scale orally as you play it.

FIGURE 18.4. *Playing the B♭ Minor Scale.*

Natural form

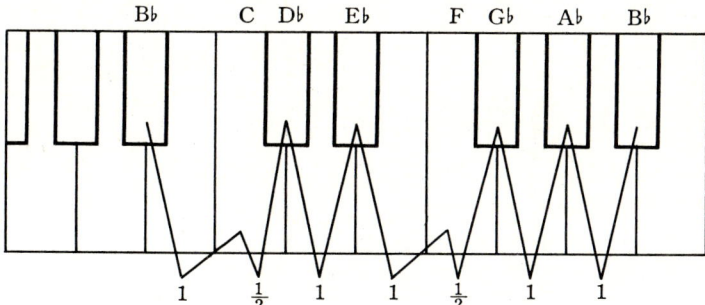

Harmonic form

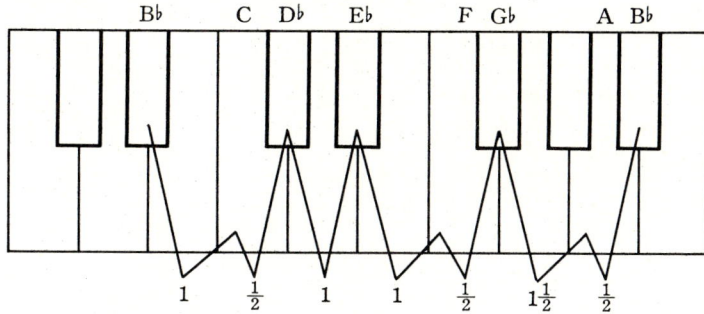

Melodic form

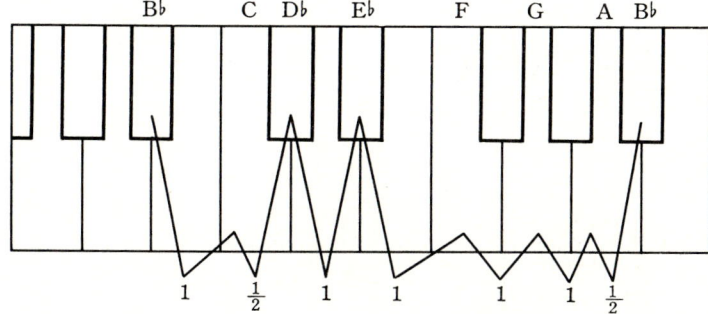

To play this scale descending, use the natural form

3. Choose a note as tonic. Spell the scale orally and play each key as you spell it.

(c) Minor Scales on G♯, D♯ and A♯

These scales require the use of double sharps.
These specific double sharps are used:

G♯ minor	raised 7th scale step	F ✖
D♯ minor	raised 7th scale step	C ✖
A♯ minor	raised 6th scale step	F ✖
	raised 7th scale step	G ✖

Here is how these doubly sharped notes appear on the keyboard.

221

FIGURE 18.5. *Locating C✕, F✕ and G✕ on the Keyboard.*

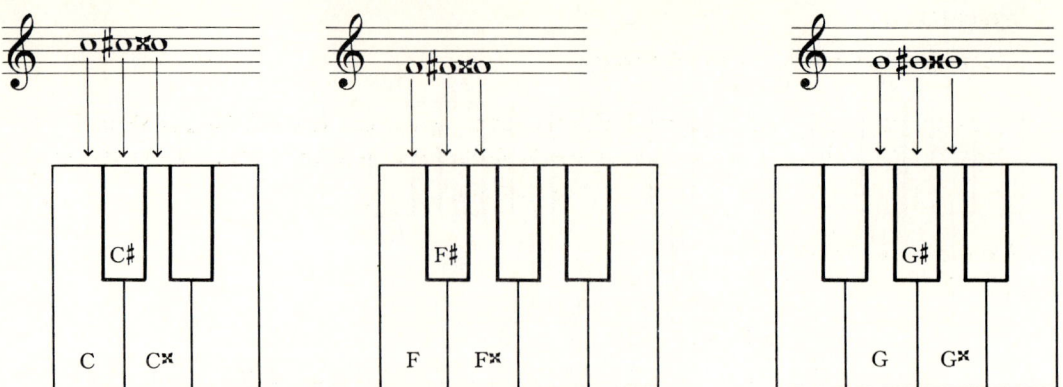

In the g♯ minor scale shown below the ✕ is used to raise the seventh scale degree (f♯) one half-step up to f✕.

FIGURE 18.6. *Playing the G♯ Minor Scale.*

Natural form

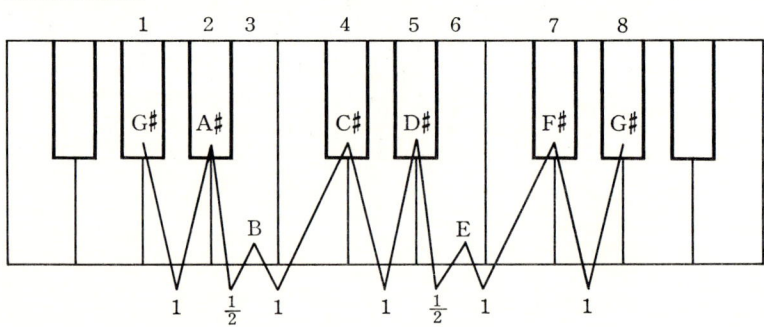

Harmonic form

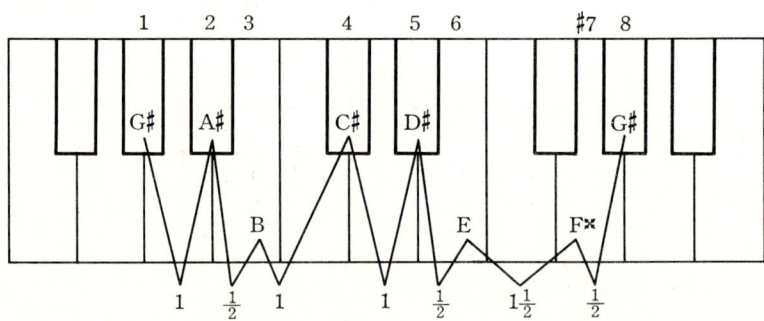

Melodic form

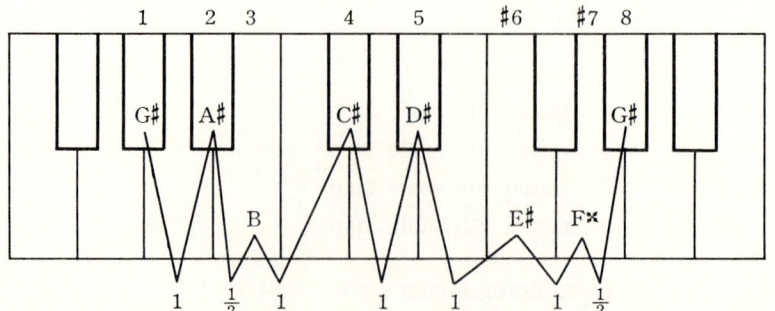

descending same as the natural form

222

_____ NAME

EXERCISE 18.1

Locating Minor Scales on the Keyboard

Using the example as a guide, write the given scale on the staff, then indicate by arrows and number, 1–8, the keys on the keyboard required to produce the sound of this scale. Also indicate whole-steps and half-steps.

Example: B♭ Minor.

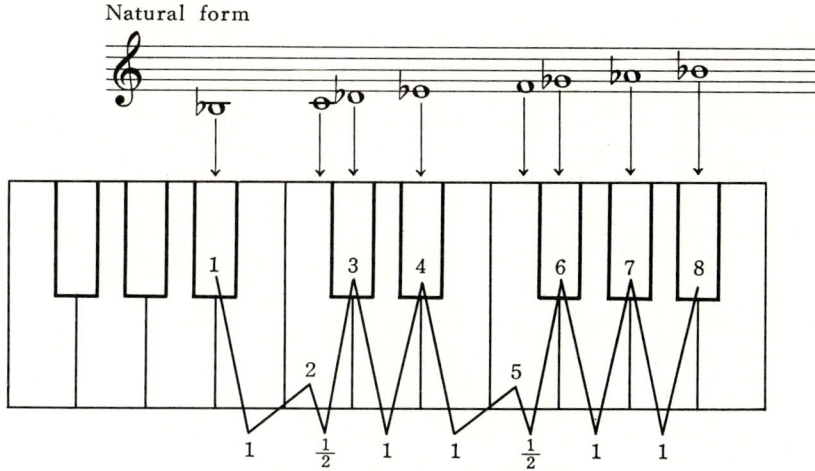

Natural form

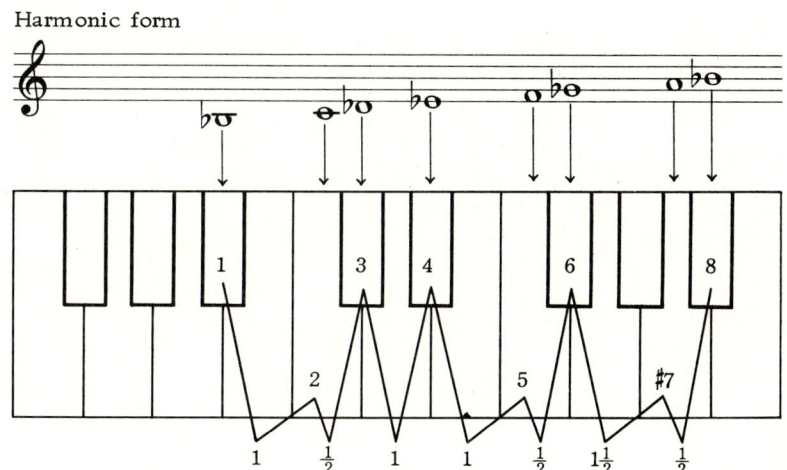

Harmonic form

223

Melodic form (When descending, use natural form)

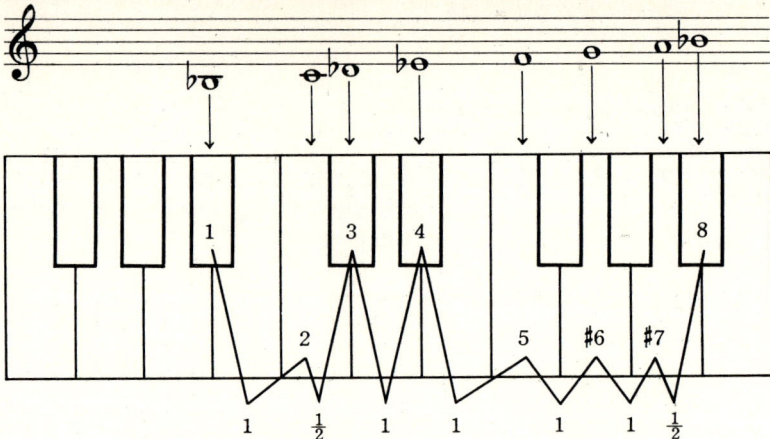

224

NAME

(a) G Minor
Natural form

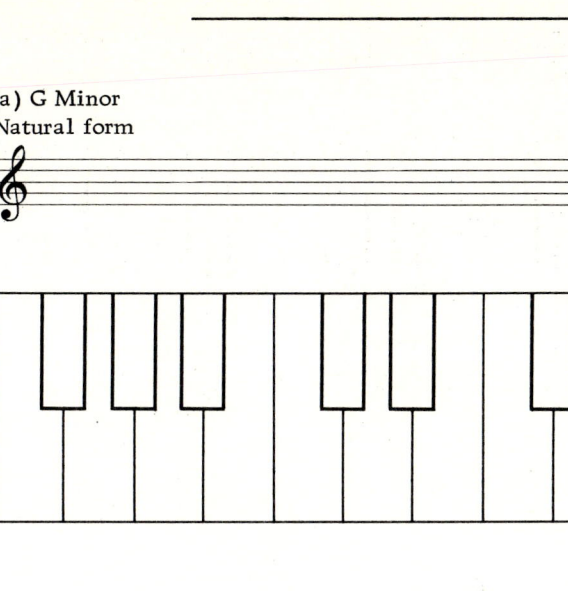

Harmonic form

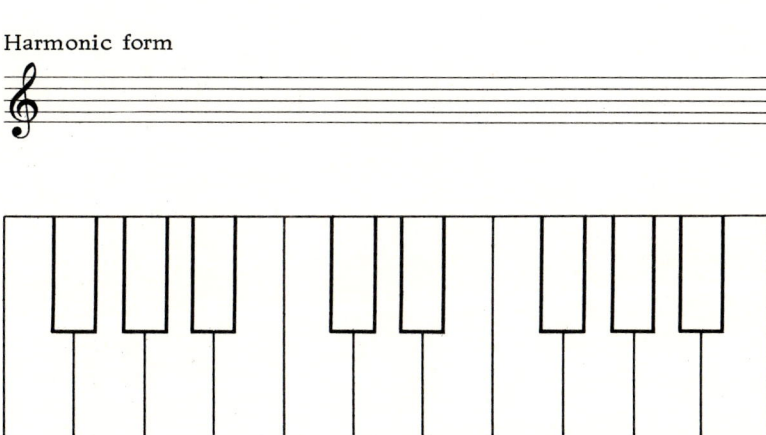

Melodic form, ascending

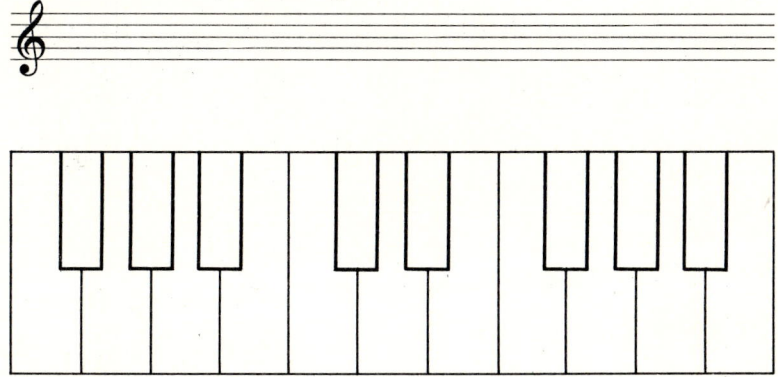

225

(b) F Minor, natural form (only)

(c) C# Minor, harmonic form

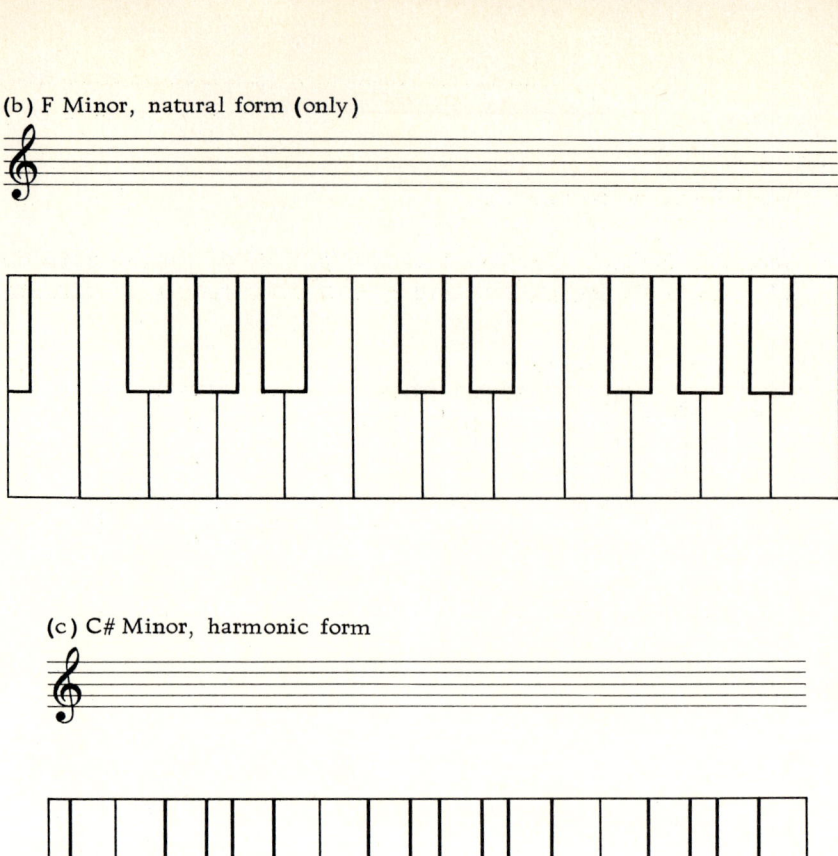

(d) D# Minor, melodic form, ascending

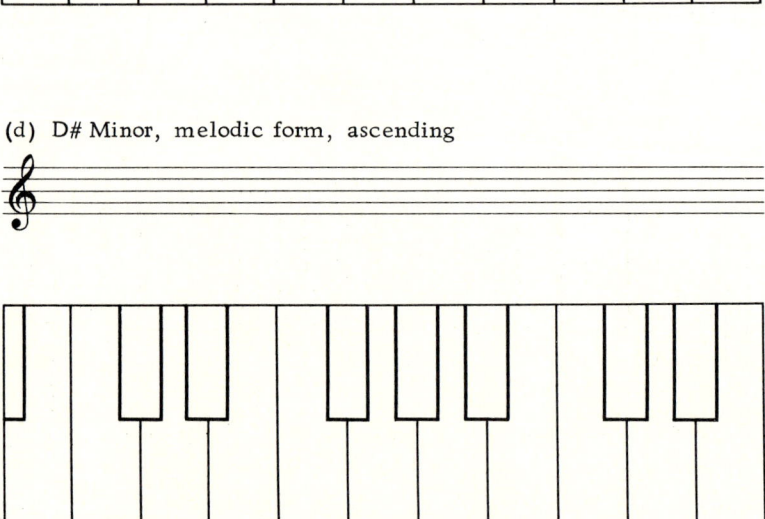

EXERCISE 18.2

Locating Minor Scales at the Keyboard

This exercise is similar to Exercise 18.1, except that you will not write the scale on the staff, but will number the keys and indicate whole-steps and half-steps.

(a) E Minor, natural form

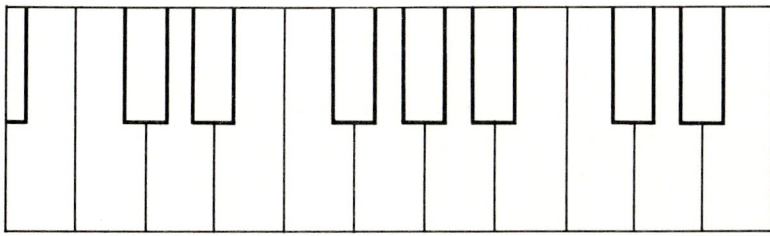

(b) D Minor, harmonic form

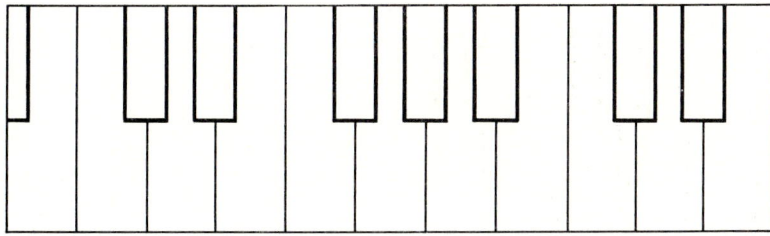

(c) C Minor, melodic form, ascending

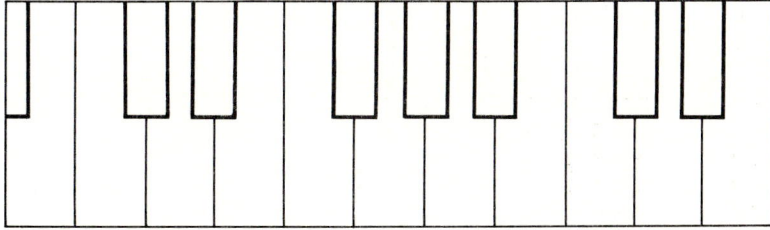

(d) F# Minor, natural form

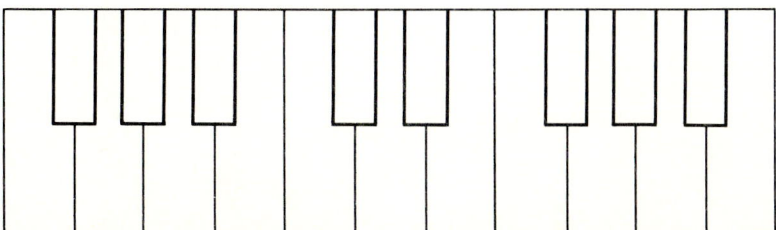

(e) B Minor, harmonic form

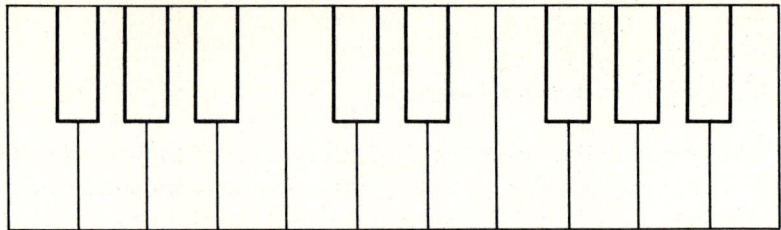

(f) G# Minor, melodic form, ascending

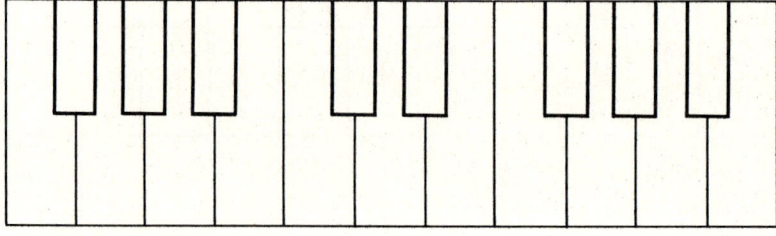

(g) E♭ Minor natural form

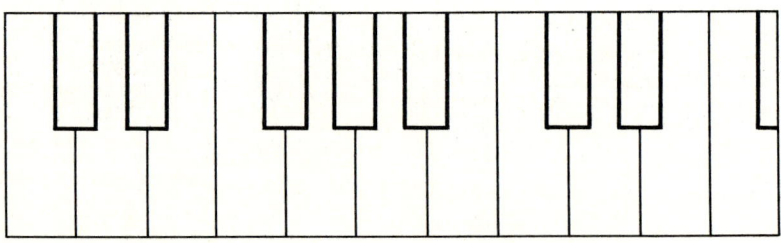

(h) A# Minor, harmonic form

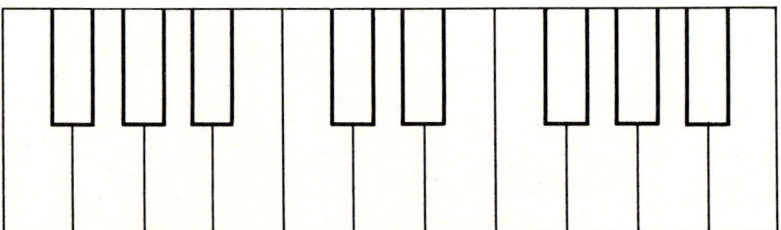

(i) A♭ Minor, melodic form, ascending

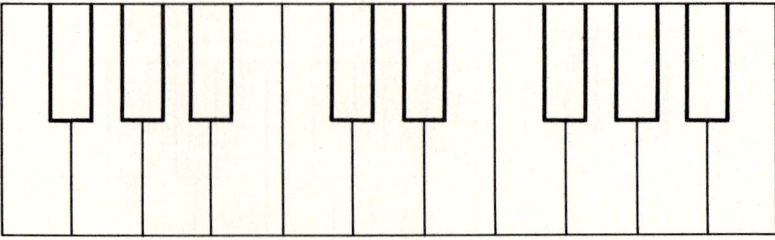

EXERCISE 18.3
Playing the A Minor Scale at the Keyboard

Play at the keyboard the three forms of the *a* minor scale as shown in Exercise 16.1, page 197. Play each scale shown in the treble clef using only the right hand, or play each scale shown in the bass clef using only the left hand. It is not intended that you play both hands together. Spell the scale orally as you play, and make sure that the half-steps indicated on the staff coincide with the white-key half-steps on the keyboard.

EXERCISE 18.4
Playing the Minor Scales E, B, F♯ and C♯ at the Keyboard

These scales were written as part of your work for Exercise 16.1. Play each of them in each of the three forms as described in Exercise 18.3. When these four scales are played in the order given, each scale starts a perfect fifth higher than the previous one, with the result that each new scale in its natural form has one additional sharp, located on the second scale degree.

EXERCISE 18.5
Playing the Minor Scales D, G, C, F, B♭, E♭ and A♭

Play the three forms of each of these scales, following procedures outlined in Exercises 18.3 and 18.4. When these seven scales are played in the order given, each scale starts a perfect fifth lower than the previous one, with the result that each new scale in its natural form has one additional flat located on the sixth scale degree.

EXERCISE 18.6
Playing the Minor Scales G♯, D♯ and A♯

Follow directions given in Exercises 18.3–18.5, but note particularly the use of double sharps as described on page 187 and 192.

EXERCISE 18.7
Playing All Minor Scales at the Keyboard

Play any minor scale without looking at the music. Spell each scale as you play it. Be sure that each interval on the keyboard is the correct half-step or whole-step, and, in the harmonic form of the scale, that the step-and-a-half (augmented second) is correctly placed.

CHAPTER NINETEEN

MINOR SCALES
(continued)

Singing Minor Scales

Singing Minor Scales

Minor scales can be sung using the three methods practiced in singing major scales: by numbers, by letter names and by syllables. In public schools, the most widespread practice for applying syllables to the minor scale is to call the tonic *la*.[1] Figure 19.1 shows application of the three methods for singing all forms of minor scales.

FIGURE 19.1. *Singing the Three Forms of the Minor Scale on Numbers, Letter Names and Syllables, in C Minor.*

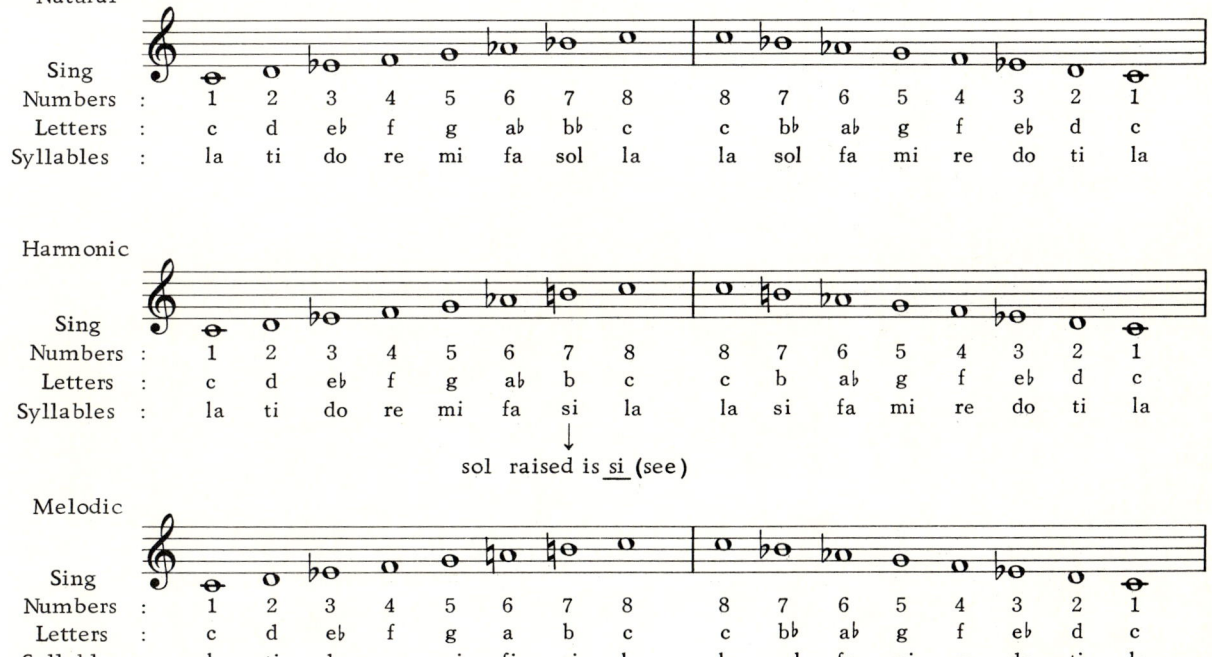

[1] The relationship of syllables in major and minor will be shown in Chapter 21.

EXERCISE 19.1
Singing Minor Scales

Choose any single pitch name which can be used as the tonic of a minor scale. Sing the three forms of the scale in each of three ways: (1) with numbers, (2) with letter names, and (3) with syllables, as shown in Figure 19.1. Sing each of the fifteen scales in this manner. You may sing from the scales you wrote in Exercise 16.1. If necessary, play the scale as you sing until you feel able to sing without the piano. Use the piano at any time to check your accuracy.

EXERCISE 19.2T
Singing the Melodic Minor Scale from a Beginning Note Other Than One or La [2]

You will hear a pitch with its identification as a number other than "1" or a syllable other than "la." By using your knowledge of the construction of the melodic minor scale and your ability to sing whole-steps and half-steps, sing up or down the melodic form of the minor scale as directed, ending on the tonic.

Example: The instructor calls the given pitch "6" with directions to sing down the scale.

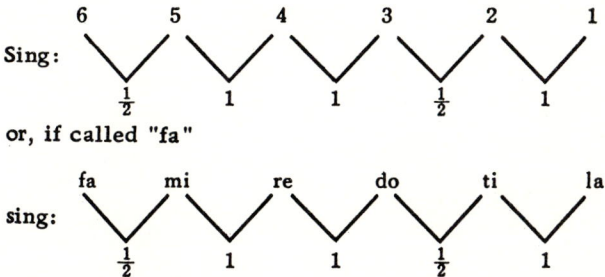

When practicing this exercise at the piano, check your response by playing the necessary portion of the scale. For example, with *c* given as "6" or "fa,"

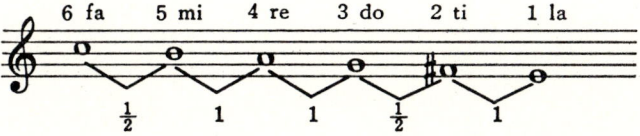

For practice, use these pitches, or choose your own combinations.

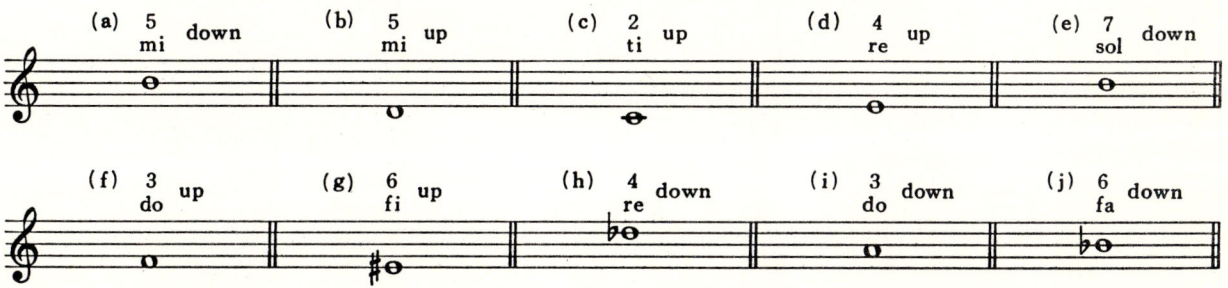

[2] Melodic lines with adjacent 6th and 7th scale steps ordinarily use the melodic form of the scale. Examples in this exercise should be thought of as excerpts from melodic lines.

CHAPTER TWENTY

MINOR KEY SIGNATURES

Circle of Fifths for Minor Keys
Minor Key Signatures on the Staff

The function of the key signature is the same in minor as it is in major (Chapter Fifteen). The key signature in minor uses the accidentals found in the natural (pure) form of the scale, which, you will remember, is the same as the Aeolian mode, the predecessor of the modern minor scale. If the accidentals found in the natural form of the minor scale are extracted and grouped together they will form the particular minor key signature. Including A minor, no sharps or flats, there are fifteen minor key signatures.

FIGURE 20.1. *Number and Names of Accidentals for Minor Key Signatures.*

Name of minor key	Number of #'s or ♭'s in key signature	Names of #'s or ♭'s						
A minor	none							
E minor	1#	f#						
B minor	2#	f#,	c#					
F# minor	3#	f#,	c#,	g#				
C# minor	4#	f#,	c#,	g#,	d#			
G# minor	5#	f#,	c#,	g#,	d#,	a#		
D# minor	6#	f#,	c#,	g#,	d#,	a#,	e#	
A# minor	7#	f#,	c#,	g#,	d#,	a#,	e#,	b#
(A minor)	(none)							
D minor	1♭	b♭						
G minor	2♭	b♭	e♭					
C minor	3♭	b♭	e♭	a♭				
F minor	4♭	b♭	e♭	a♭	d♭			
B♭ minor	5♭	b♭	e♭	a♭	d♭	g♭		
E♭ minor	6♭	b♭	e♭	a♭	d♭	g♭	c♭	
A♭ minor	7♭	b♭	e♭	a♭	d♭	g♭	c♭	f♭

You will notice in Figure 20.1 that, starting with A minor, we progressed up a perfect fifth to each new sharp key, and down a perfect fifth to each new flat key. This order is shown on the *circle of fifths for minor keys*.

Circle of Fifths for Minor Keys

The *circle of fifths for minor keys* is built exactly as its counterpart for major keys (p. 175). The key name for the key with no sharps or flats, A minor, is placed at the top of the circle. Sharp keys proceed clockwise and flat keys counterclockwise as shown in Figure 20.2. Notice the enharmonic keys of 5, 6, and 7 accidentals at the bottom of the circle, just as in major.

FIGURE 20.2. *The Circle of Fifths for Minor [1] Keys.*

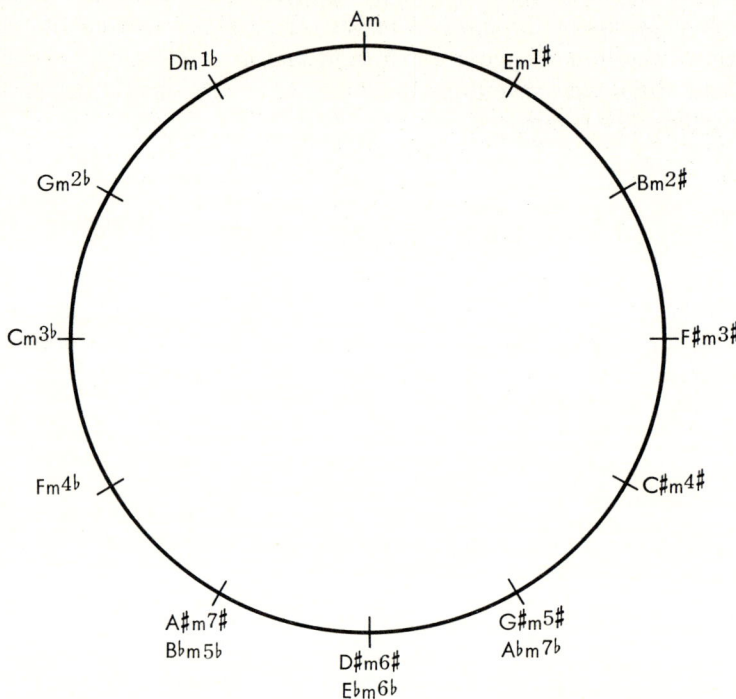

The accidentals of the minor key signatures are placed on the staff in the same order of appearance as in the circle of fifths.

Minor Key Signatures on the Staff

The order of accidentals of the key signature on the staff is the same for minor as for major.

---

[1] The small letter *m* is used as an abbreviation for *minor*.

FIGURE 20.3. *Minor Key Signatures.*

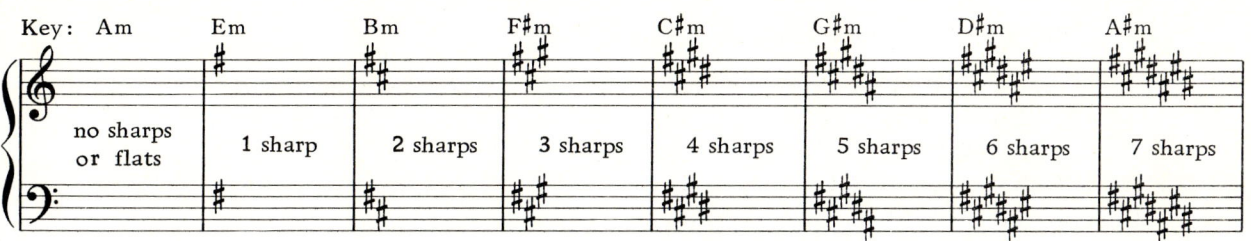

The key signatures may now be used to identify the key. When it is known that the music is in a minor key, the number of sharps or flats in the signature will indicate the name of that minor key as shown in Figure 20.3. For example, when the key is minor, four sharps always indicate the key of C♯ minor.

EXERCISE 20.1
Identifying Minor Key Signatures from the Circle of Fifths

On the circle of fifths below, the minor key names are given. Beside each key name write the correct number of sharps or flats. The answer for E minor is given.

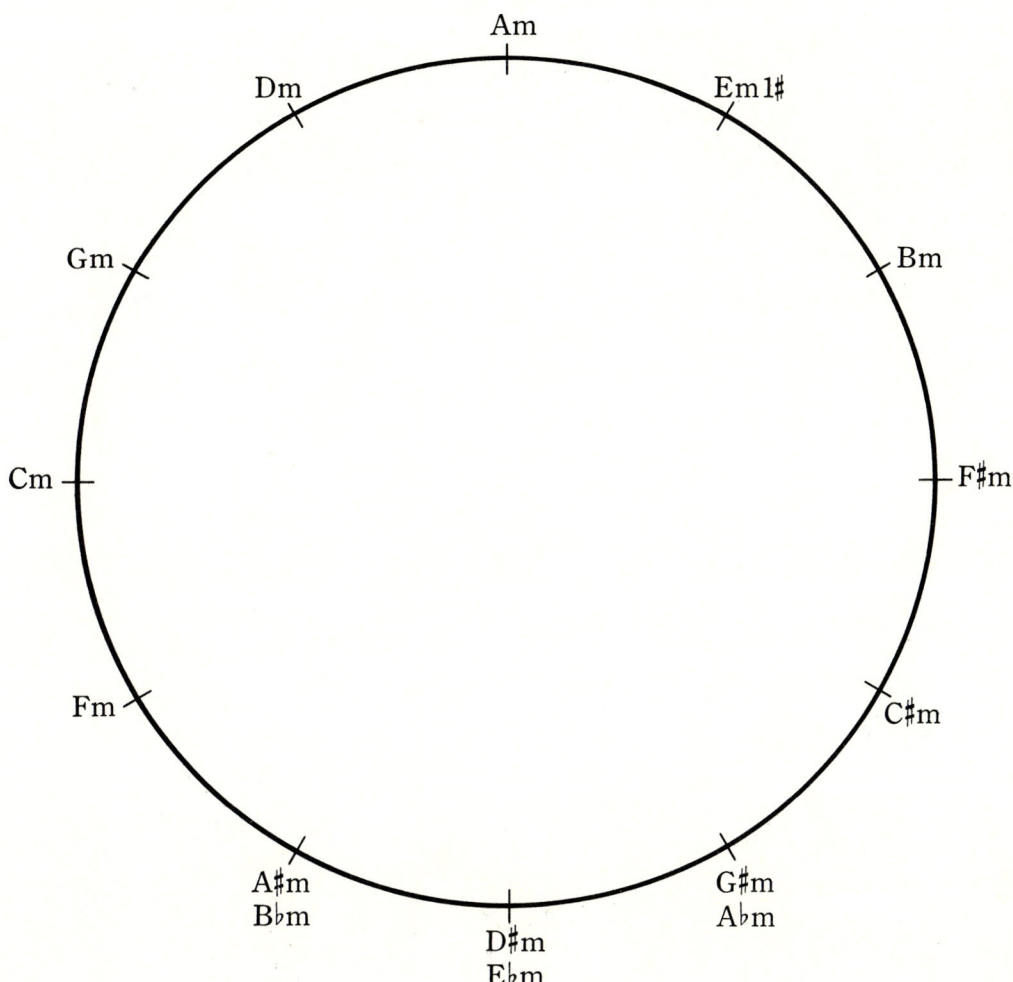

EXERCISE 20.2

Identifying the Name of the Minor Key from the Circle of Fifths

On the circle below, the minor key signatures are given. Beside each, give the name of the minor key. The answer for one flat is given.

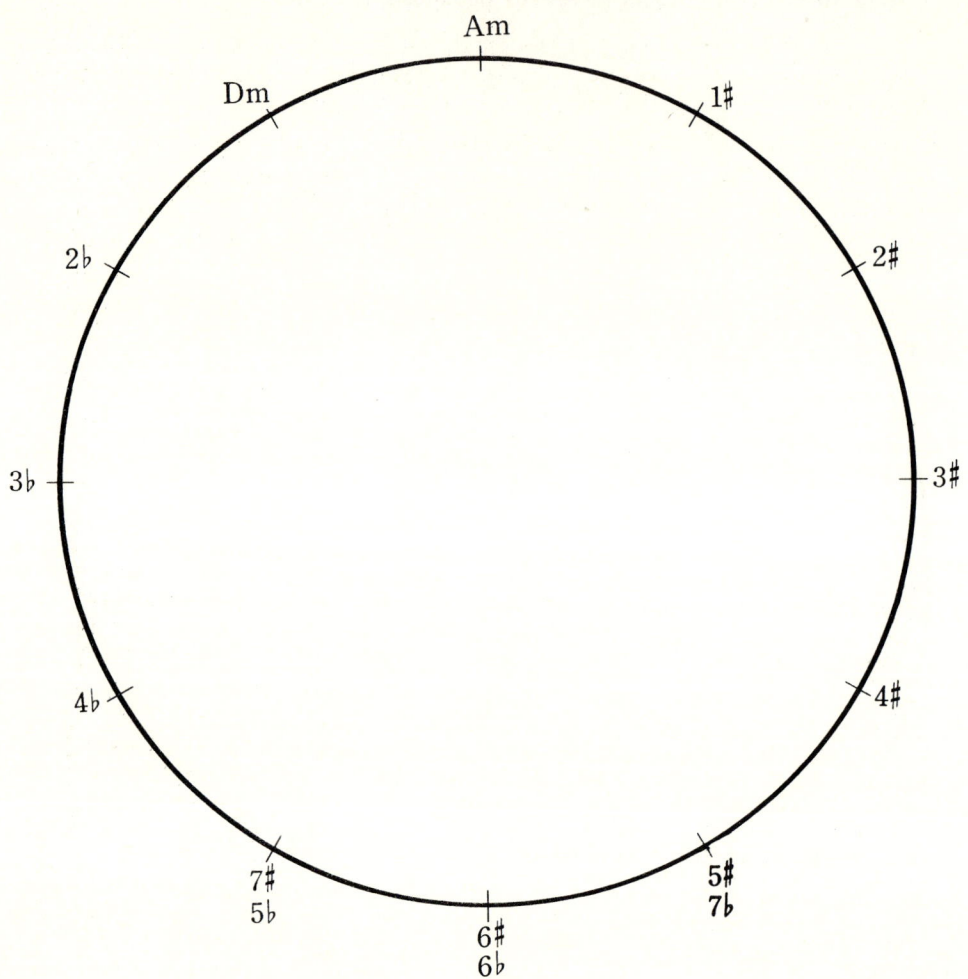

_____ NAME

EXERCISE 20.3

Procedure for Constructing the Circle of Fifths for Minor Keys

1. On the circle below, mark twelve points like the face of a clock. This provides places for all fifteen minor keys including three enharmonic keys.
2. At 12 o'clock place A minor (no sharps or flats).
3. Proceeding clockwise, at 1 o'clock place the letter name of the minor key a fifth above A minor, which is E minor (1 sharp); continue clockwise in fifths and add sharps through the key of A♯ minor (7 sharps).
4. Proceeding counterclockwise, at 11 o'clock place the letter name of the minor key a fifth below A minor, which is D minor (1♭); continue counterclockwise in fifths and add flats through the key of A♭ minor (7 flats).

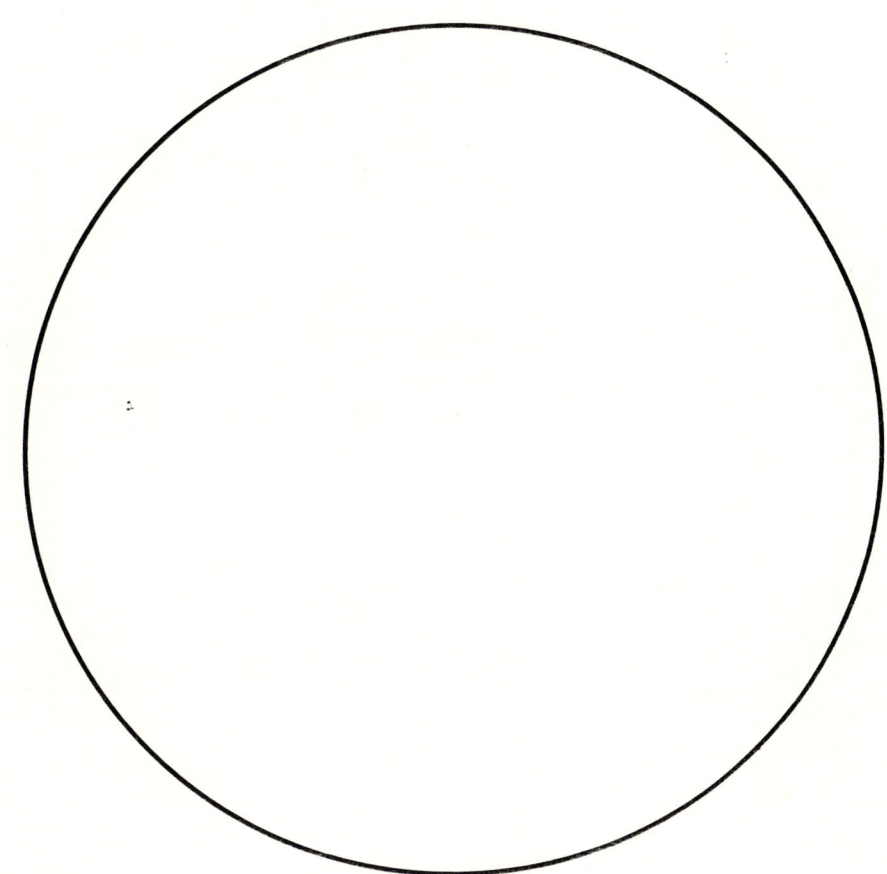

_____ NAME

EXERCISE 20.4
Constructing the Circle of Fifths for Minor Keys

Construct from memory the circle of fifths for minor keys. You should be able to demonstrate the circle on paper or at the board in *one minute*. To check your work, see Figure 20.2.

_____ NAME

EXERCISE 20.5

Identifying Minor Key Names from Number of Accidentals

In each blank space, write the correct minor key name according to the number of sharps or flats given.

(a) 2 sharps _____   (h) 7 sharps _____

(b) 4 flats _____   (i) 6 flats _____

(c) 3 flats _____   (j) 5 flats _____

(d) 5 sharps _____   (k) 4 sharps _____

(e) 1 sharp _____   (l) 1 flat _____

(f) 7 flats _____   (m) 6 sharps _____

(g) 3 sharps _____   (n) 2 flats _____

EXERCISE 20.6

Naming the Number of Sharps or Flats When the Minor Key Is Given

In each blank space, write the correct number of sharps or flats for the given minor key.

(a) B flat minor _____   (h) G minor _____

(b) C sharp minor _____   (i) E minor _____

(c) A flat minor _____   (j) F sharp minor _____

(d) G sharp minor _____   (k) F minor _____

(e) C minor _____   (l) B minor _____

(f) E flat minor _____   (m) D sharp minor _____

(g) D minor _____   (n) A sharp minor _____

EXERCISE 20.7

Identifying Name of Minor Key When Key Signature Is Given

For each key signature (1) write the name of the minor key below the staff, and (2) write the tonic note of the key on the staff, using a whole-note.

EXERCISE 20.8
Writing Minor Key Signatures

Write the correct number of sharps or flats on the correct lines and spaces of the great staff for each given minor key.

Example: given D minor

Answer:

1. E minor 2. C minor 3. A# minor 4. E♭ minor

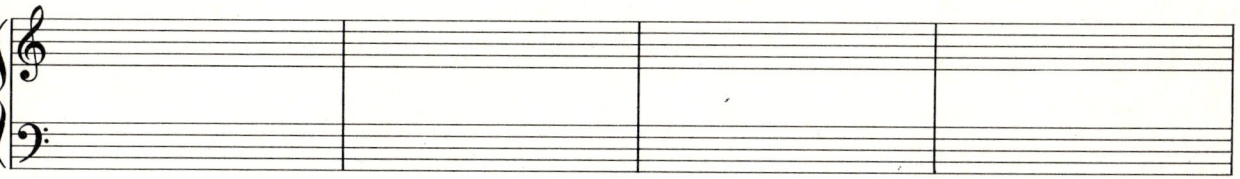

5. F# minor 6. D# minor 7. B minor 8. A♭ minor

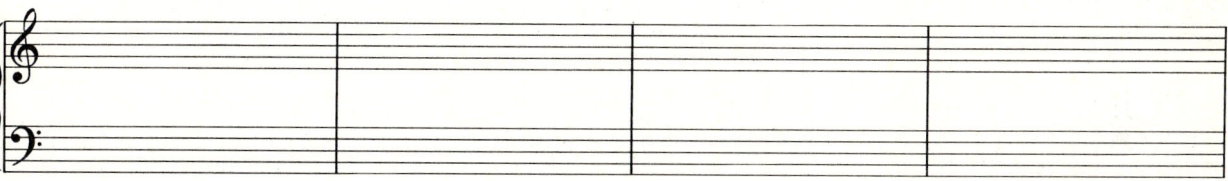

9. C# minor 10. B♭ minor 11. G# minor 12. G minor 13. F minor

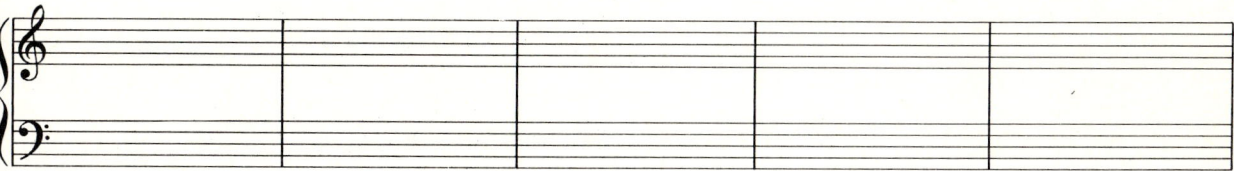

To check your work, see Figure 20.3.

247

EXERCISE 20.9

Identifying Minor Key Signatures

Write the minor key name for each of the following numbers located in *Music for Sight Singing*.

Melody Number	Name of Key	Melody Number	Name of Key
45		124	
46		125	
47		130	
48		133	
49		136	
51		263	
52		316	
53		344	
55		389	
57		398	
78		452	
104		488	

CHAPTER TWENTY-ONE

MAJOR AND MINOR KEY RELATIONSHIPS

The Circle of Fifths for Major and Minor Keys Together
Relative Keys
Parallel Keys
Solmization in Relative Major and Minor Keys

Although major and minor keys have been covered in two separate presentations, certain relationships exist between the two systems. The fact that there are seven sharp keys, seven flat keys, and one key without accidentals in each of major and minor is evidence that such relationship exists. This evidence can be demonstrated graphically through further study of the circles of fifths.

The Circle of Fifths for Major and Minor Keys Together

We have already built one circle of fifths for major keys and another circle of fifths for minor keys. In common, each started with the key signature of no sharps or flats at the top of the circle, and each progressed clockwise by fifths up (sharp keys) and counterclockwise by fifths down (flat keys). This being so, we should be able to place major and minor keys in the same circle. Figure 21.1 shows such a circle, with the major keys outside the circle and minor keys inside the circle.

At each point in the circle are two keys, or two pairs of enharmonic keys. These are known as *relative keys*.

Relative Keys

A pair of keys, one major and one minor, located at the same point in the circle of fifths will each have the same accidentals and are known as *relative keys*. Each of these two relative keys will have identical signatures when placed on the staff. (Figure 21.2.) Notice that the tonic of a minor key is *three half-steps* [1] below the tonic of its relative major key. For example, the tonic note of A minor is three half-steps below C. The tonic note of E minor is three half-steps below G; the tonic note of D minor is three half-steps below F. (Figure 21.3.)

---

[1] These three half-steps equal the interval of a *minor third,* so-called because the interval encompasses three letter names, for example, *c* down to *a* in Figure 21.2, first example, and Figure 21.3, first measure. The interval identified on page 195 as an augmented second also contains three half-steps, but encompasses only two letter names, for example *a♭* up to *b* as in Figure 16.16. Intervals will be studied in Chapter 22.

FIGURE 21.1. *The Circle of Fifths for Major and Minor Keys Together.*

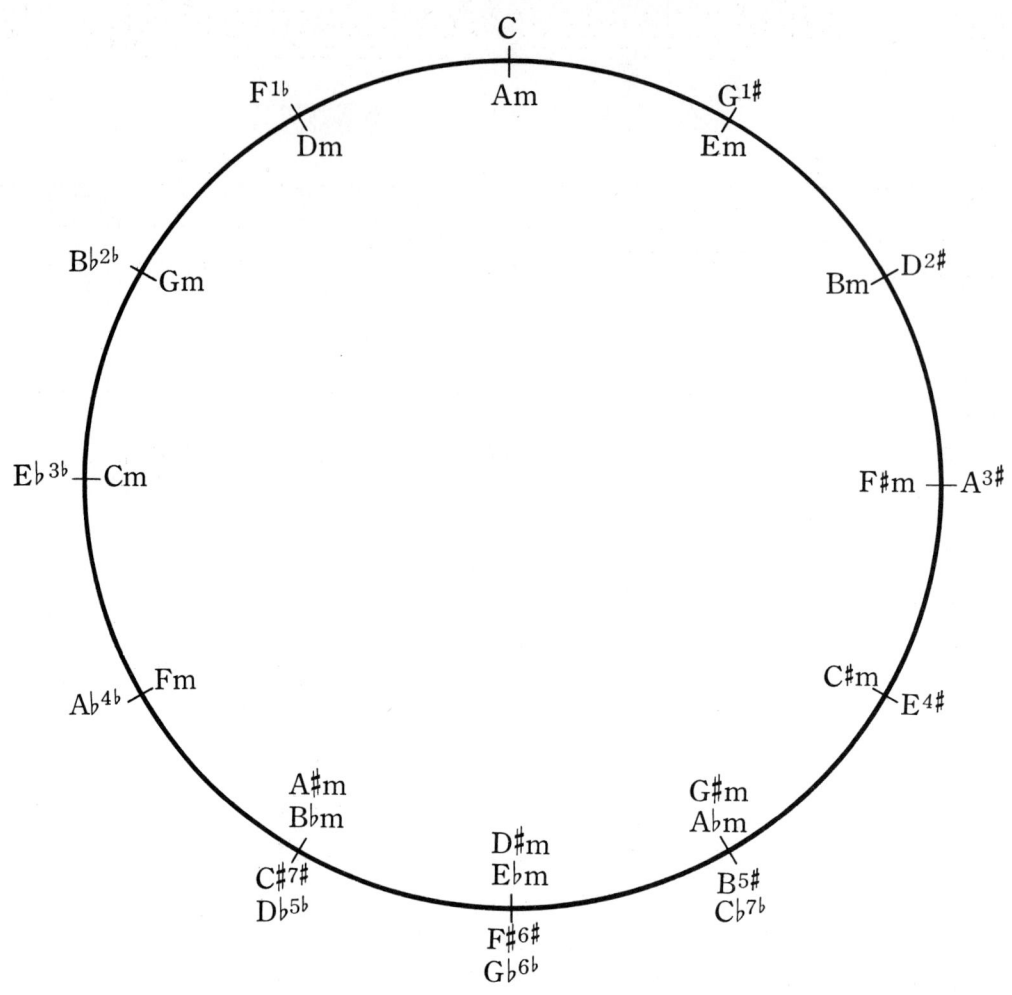

FIGURE 21.2. *Identical Signatures for Relative Major and Minor Keys.*

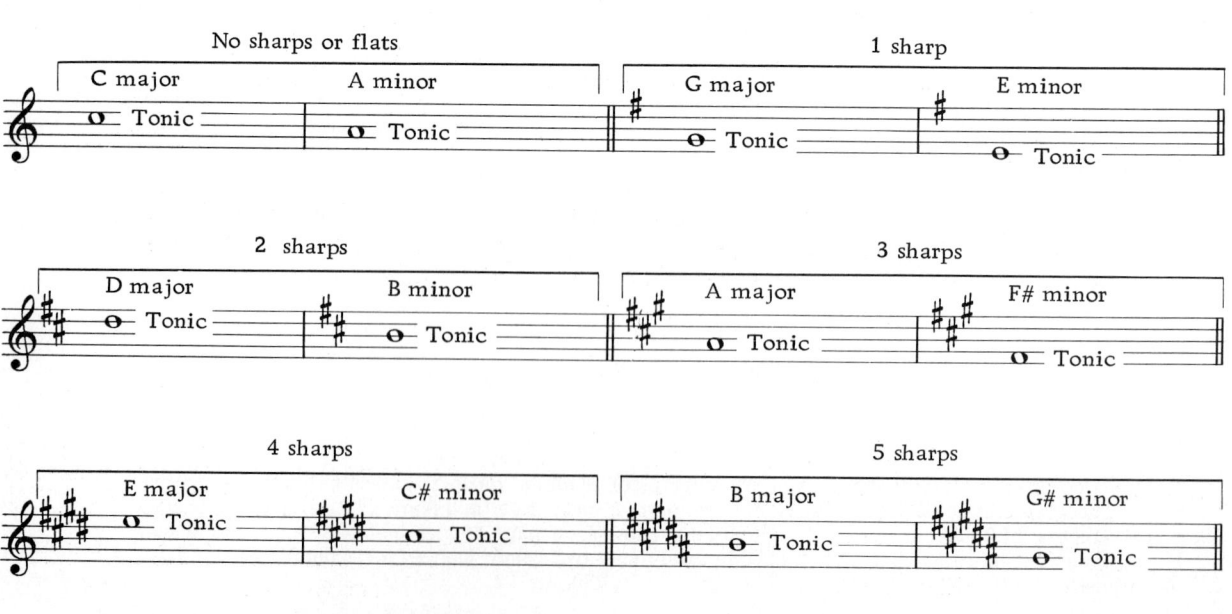

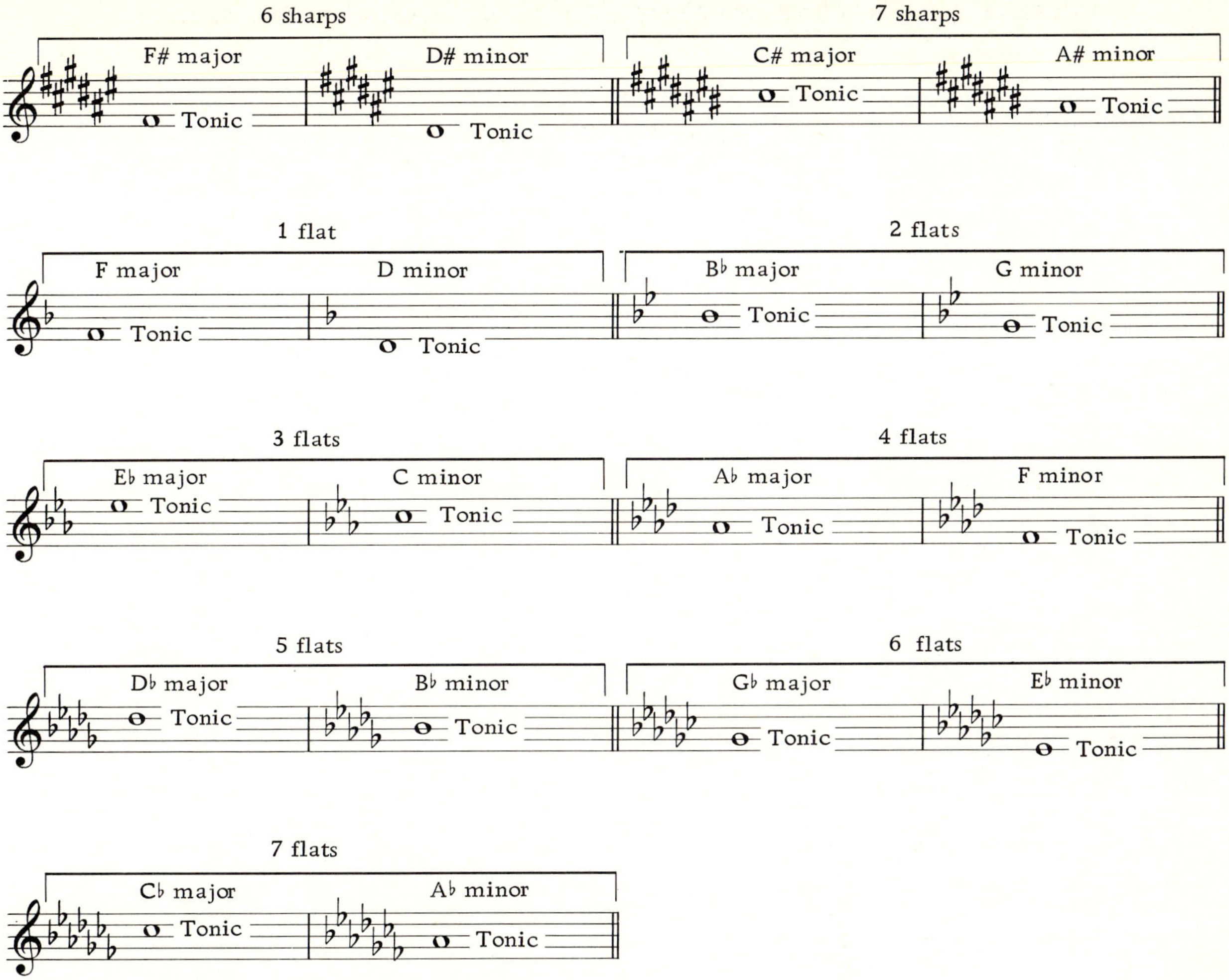

FIGURE 21.3. *Locating Tonic Notes of Relative Keys.*

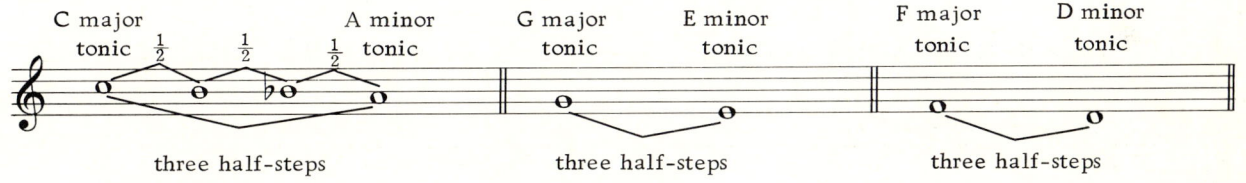

Parallel Keys

Parallel keys are keys with the same tonic note, but with completely different key signatures. For example, C major and C minor are parallel keys, each with *c* as tonic, but with two different key signatures. Here are two other examples:

FIGURE 21.4. *Parallel Keys.*

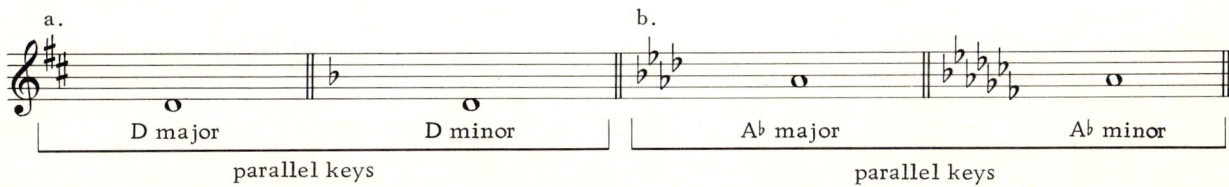

Solmization in Relative Major and Minor Keys

Relationship between major and minor keys is further revealed in the application of syllables to the scales. In formulating the system of the seven basic syllables, it was the intent that, whether the scale formation be major or minor, *mi-fa* and *ti-do* always represent half-steps, and that any other pair of adjacent syllables represent whole steps. In order that these pairs of syllables coincide with their corresponding half-steps and whole-steps, the minor scale of necessity starts on *la,* as shown in Figure 21.5. Observe also, that the first degree *do* of the major scale is identical to the third degree *do* of the relative minor scale, or that the first degree *la* of the minor scale is identical to the sixth degree *la* of the relative major scale.

FIGURE 21.5. *The Syllabic Relationship Between Major and Minor Scales.*

C Major and Its Relative Key, A Minor.

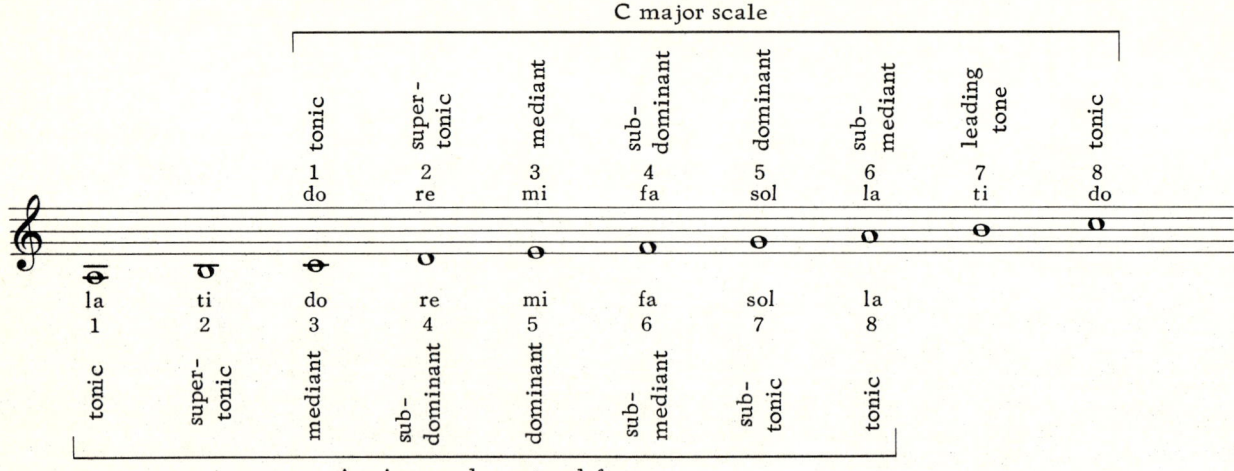

For minor scales containing accidentals, the necessary syllables *fi* for raised 6 and *si* for raised 7 would be added.

_____ NAME

EXERCISE 21.1
Constructing the Circle of Fifths for Major and Minor Keys Together

On the circle given, place the major keys on the outside of the circle, and the minor keys on the inside of the circle.

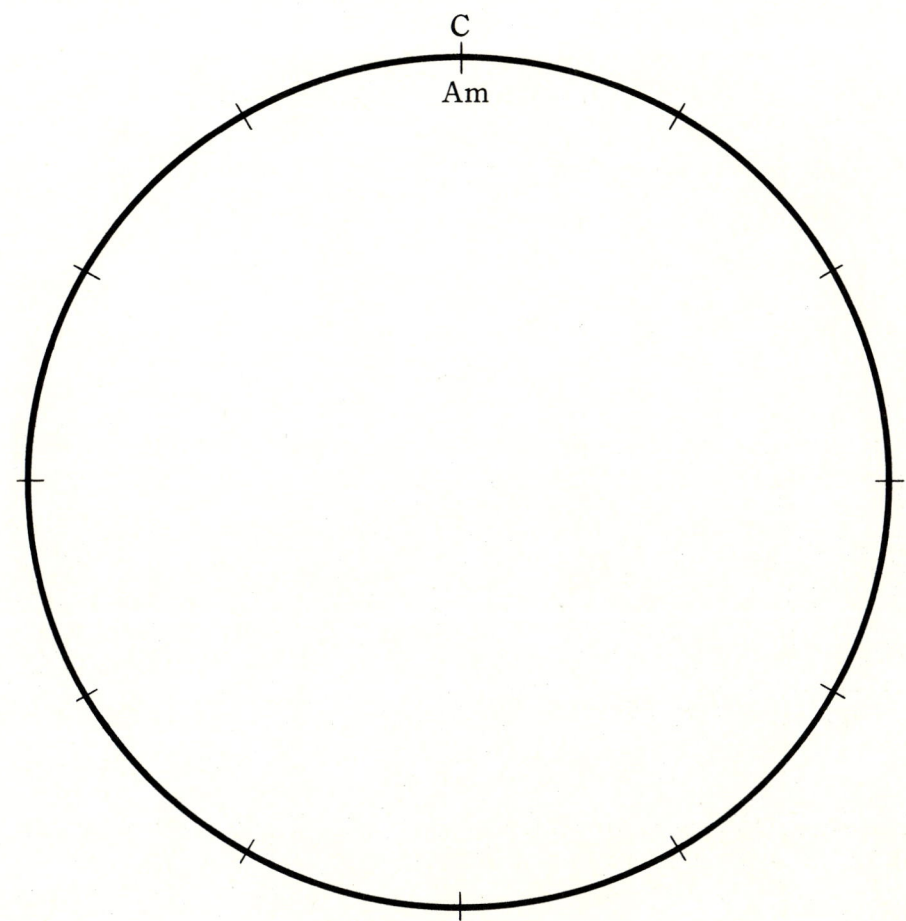

253

_____ NAME

EXERCISE 21.2

Identifying Relative Keys

To determine the name of a key which is relative to a given key, either of two procedures may be used, the first of which is recommended because it is easier.

(a) The relative key has the same key signature as the given key. Knowing the key name for the given signature will provide the correct answer.

(b) The relative minor key can be found by counting *down* three half-steps (to a pitch name three letter names down) from the tonic of a major key. The relative major key can be found by counting *up* three half-steps (to a pitch name three letter names up) from the tonic of the minor key.

Using either procedure, name the key relative to each of the following.

Example: given, E♭ major; answer,   C minor

(1) C Major   _____

(2) D Minor   _____

(3) B Minor   _____

(4) B♭ Major   _____

(5) C♯ Minor   _____

(6) F♯ Major   _____

(7) G Minor   _____

(8) A♭ Major   _____

(9) A♭ Minor   _____

(10) D Major   _____

(11) F Major   _____

(12) F♯ Minor   _____

(13) A♯ Minor   _____

(14) E Major   _____

(15) D♯ Minor   _____

(16) A Minor   _____

(17) D♭ Major   _____

(18) G♯ Minor   _____

(19) E♭ Minor   _____

(20) G Major   _____

(21) G♭ Major   _____

(22) B♭ Minor   _____

(23) B Major   _____

(24) C Minor   _____

(25) C♭ Major   _____

(26) E Minor   _____

(27) C♯ Major   _____

(28) F Minor   _____

(29) A Major   _____

_____ NAME

EXERCISE 21.3
Naming Relative Keys

Name the two keys, one major and one minor, indicated by the given key signature.

	Major Key	*Minor Key*
(1) 1 sharp	G Major	E Minor
(2) 4 flats	_____	_____
(3) 3 sharps	_____	_____
(4) none	_____	_____
(5) 2 flats	_____	_____
(6) 6 flats	_____	_____
(7) 5 sharps	_____	_____
(8) 2 sharps	_____	_____
(9) 1 flat	_____	_____
(10) 7 flats	_____	_____
(11) 3 flats	_____	_____
(12) 4 sharps	_____	_____
(13) 6 sharps	_____	_____
(14) 7 sharps	_____	_____
(15) 5 flats	_____	_____

EXERCISE 21.4
Naming Key Signatures of Parallel Keys

State the key signatures for both the major and minor keys for which the given pitch is the tonic.

	Major	Minor
(1) A♭	4♭	7♭
(2) E	___	___
(3) F♯	___	___
(4) G	___	___
(5) C	___	___
(6) E♭	___	___
(7) C♯	___	___
(8) B	___	___
(9) D	___	___
(10) A	___	___
(11) F	___	___
(12) B♭	___	___

EXERCISE 21.5

Solmization of Major and Minor Scales

(a) Starting on any pitch as *do,* sing a major scale ascending and descending. Then sing down from *do* to *la* and sing the natural form of the relative minor scale.

(b) Starting on any pitch as *la,* sing the natural minor scale. Then, sing up from *la* to *do,* and sing the relative major scale.

CHAPTER TWENTY-TWO

INTERVALS: MAJOR AND PERFECT

Interval
Major and Perfect Intervals in the Major Scale
Naming the Interval
Simple and Compound Intervals
Analysis of Major and Perfect Intervals in the Major Scale

At various times in the preceding chapters we have had occasion to refer to *intervals;* the term itself was defined as early as Chapter Two, page 21. We have used intervals of the half-step and whole-step to help us in constructing the scale, and we have used the interval of the perfect fifth to help us understand the circle of fifths. We will now make a more complete study beginning with a review of the definition of the term *interval*.

Interval

An *interval* is the distance or difference between two pitches. A *harmonic interval* is the sounding of two pitches simultaneously; a *melodic interval* is the sounding of two pitches consecutively.

FIGURE 22.1. *Harmonic and Melodic Intervals.*

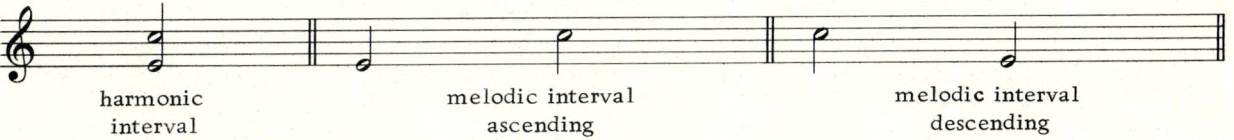

harmonic interval   melodic interval ascending   melodic interval descending

There are two different approaches to the study of intervals. One approach deals with intervals as found above the tonic of the major scale—the approach commonly used in public school music. A second approach deals with intervals as found in chords.[1] The second approach is the more mature and meaningful one because it considers the interval in a truly musical situation, for example, in an actual composition. Nevertheless, in order to expedite our mastery of fundamentals, it is necessary that we thoroughly understand the first approach: intervals found above the tonic of the major scale.

[1] A *chord* is the simultaneous sounding of more than two notes. Detailed description of chords and the intervals included in them is usually studied under the subject heading, *Harmony*.

261

Major and Perfect Intervals in the Major Scale

In a major scale, distance from the tonic note up to each of the other scale tones provides seven different intervals. These, with their interval names, are:

from scale degree	up to scale degree	the interval name is	abbreviated
1	2	Major Second or whole-step	M 2
1	3	Major Third	M 3
1	4	Perfect Fourth	P 4
1	5	Perfect Fifth	P 5
1	6	Major Sixth	M 6
1	7	Major Seventh	M 7
1	8	Perfect Octave	P 8
1	1	Perfect Prime or Unison [2]	P 1 (P P)

FIGURE 22.2. *Intervals in the C Major Scale.*

These intervals are found in the same order in any major scale, for example, D major.

FIGURE 22.3. *Intervals in the D Major Scale.*

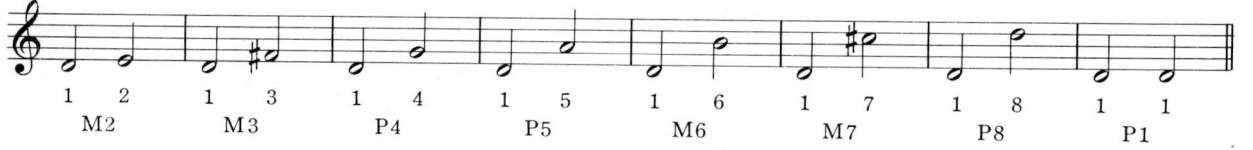

Naming the Interval

The name of the interval always consists of two parts: (1) an adjective expressing *quality,* and (2) a noun representing *quantity.* In notation, most obvious is the *quantity* of the interval which is seen by the number of staff degrees, including both notes, spanned by the interval. In Figure 22.4 c^1 up to e^1 is a third because three staff degrees, *c, d,* and *e,* are spanned; c^1 up to a^1, a span of six staff degrees, is a sixth.

---

[2] The perfect prime, while not an interval by previous definition, is the name given to two notes of the same pitch; it is commonly known by the name, *unison.*

FIGURE 22.4. *Determining the Quantity (Number) of the Interval.*

Observe that for even-numbered intervals, 2, 4, 6 and 8, one note of a particular interval will occupy a line and the other a space:

For odd-numbered intervals, 3, 5 and 7, both notes of a particular interval will occupy lines or both will occupy spaces:

Quality of intervals found between tonic and other degrees of the major scale is expressed by the adjectives *major* or *perfect*.[3] *Major* modifies or specifies 2, 3, 6 and 7; *perfect* modifies or specifies 4, 5 and 8 (or 1). There are no interval names such as major fourth or perfect third.

FIGURE 22.5. *Specific Major and Perfect Intervals in the Major Scale.*

Major Intervals		Perfect Intervals	
Name	Scale Steps	Name	Scale Steps
M2	1 — 2	P4	1 — 4
M3	1 — 3	P5	1 — 5
M6	1 — 6	P8	1 — 8
M7	1 — 7		

Other intervals which will be studied later use the adjectives *minor, diminished* and *augmented*. However, in the major scale only major and perfect intervals occur above the tonic note.

Simple and Compound Intervals

Intervals encompassing a perfect octave or less are known as *simple* intervals. Intervals larger than a perfect octave are called *compound* intervals, meaning an

---

[3] Perfect intervals are so named for acoustical reasons (see *Groves Dictionary of Music and Musicians*, fifth edition, 1960, "Intervals," Vol. IV, p. 519). The terms *major* (this chapter) and *minor* (next chapter) when applied to intervals mean simply larger (greater) or smaller (lesser).

octave plus a *simple* interval already named. Like simple intervals, compound intervals are designated by the number of scale degrees spanned.

FIGURE 22.6. *Simple and Compound Intervals in the C Major Scale.*

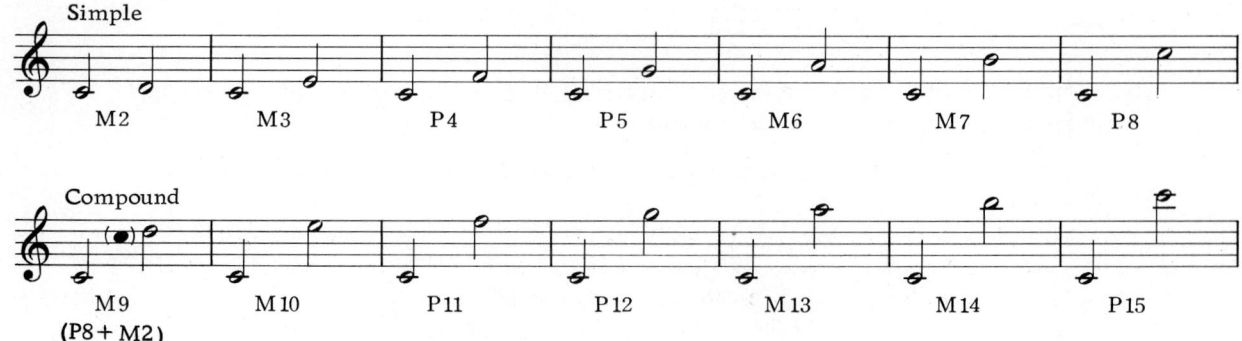

When adding two intervals together, as shown for the major ninth, the intervallic sum is always one number less than the arithmetical sum:

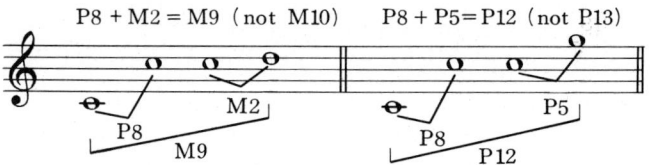

In musical analysis, compound intervals are frequently reduced to simple terminology. For example, although the interval c^1 to g^2 is a perfect twelfth, it may be called a perfect fifth.

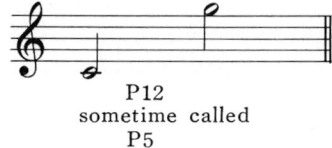

For the immediate needs of our study, we shall deal only with simple intervals.

Analysis of Major and Perfect Intervals in the Major Scale

In analyzing an interval, assume the lower note to be 1 (tonic) and count the scale degrees to the upper note. The number of scale degrees will determine the name of the interval. For example, *d* up to *a*:

a appears as the fifth degree in the D major scale; therefore, *d* up to *a* is a perfect fifth.

Also, *b*♭ up to *G*:

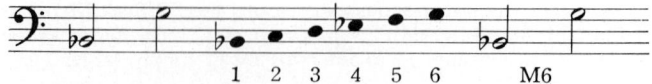

g appears as the sixth degree in the B♭ major scale; therefore *b♭* up to *g* is a major sixth.

This procedure for analysis, assuming the lower note to be 1, is the same for harmonic intervals. For example *g* and *b*:

b appears as the third degree in the G major scale; therefore, the interval is a major third.

The procedure is the same for descending melodic intervals. Calculate from the lower note of the interval. For example, while the interval appears *a* down to *e*, calculate from *e*, the lower note, up to *a*.

A appears as the fourth degree in the E major scale and *e* up to *a* is a perfect fourth. *A* down to *e* is, of course, the same interval as *e* up to *a*, therefore, *a* down to *e* is a perfect fourth.

Gary East

EXERCISE 22.1

Naming Intervals Found Above the Tonic in the Major Scale

The first note or lower note of each measure is the tonic of the scale. In parts (a) and (b) the intervals are found in ascending order. In parts (c), (d) and (e) the intervals are ascending in random order. In part (f) the intervals are descending; the lower note is the tonic of the scale.

267

EXERCISE 22.2
Analyzing Major and Perfect Intervals

Identify interval by name. Write abbreviation below each interval given.

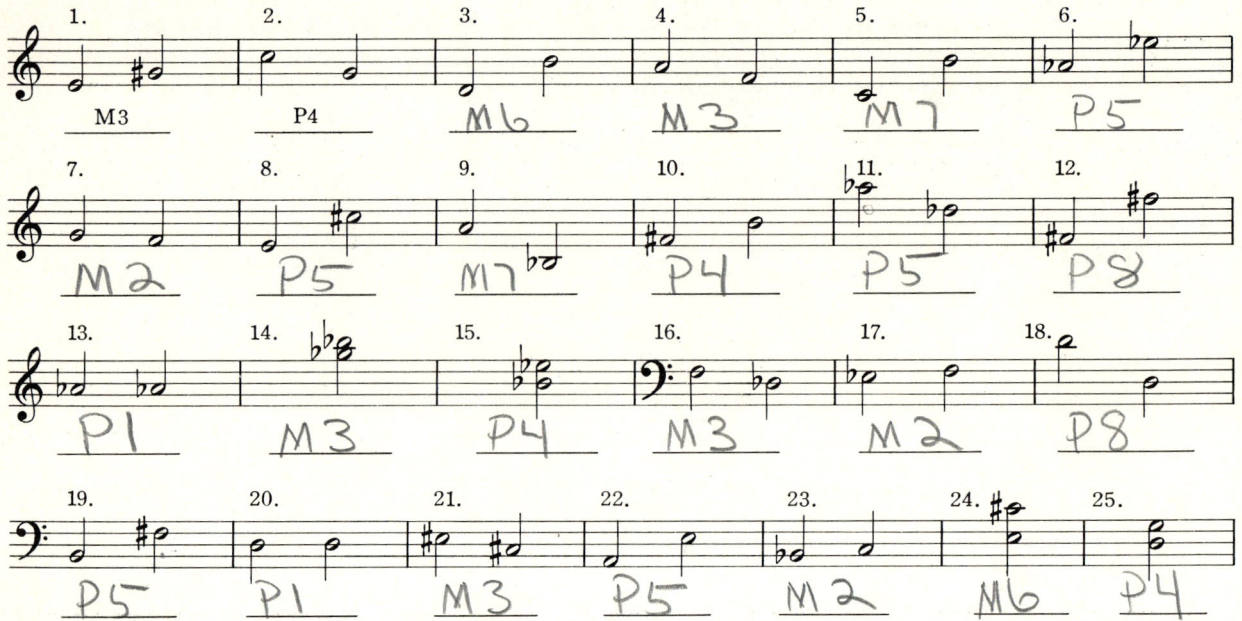

EXERCISE 22.3

Writing Major and Perfect Intervals

Write on the staff the second note of each interval. The answer for number 1 is given. Use half-notes and be sure each stem is placed correctly (review page 63).

EXERCISE 22.4
Spelling Major and Perfect Intervals

Write the letter name of the second note of each interval given.

Example: M3 down from E is   C

(a) M2 up from C is   D

(b) P5 down from A is   D

(c) M6 up from F♯ is   _____

(d) M3 up from F is   _____

(e) M7 up from E♭ is   _____

(f) P4 down from A♭ is   _____

(g) P8 down from C♯ is   _____

(h) P4 up from D♭ is   _____

(i) M2 down from B is   _____

(j) M7 down from D♯ is   _____

(k) M3 up from G♭ is   _____

(l) P5 up from F♯ is   _____

(m) M6 down from C is   _____

(n) P8 up from F is   _____

(o) M6 down from A♯ is   _____

(p) P5 up from B is   _____

(q) M2 down from E♭ is   _____

(r) M3 down from G♯ is _____

(s) M7 up from B♭ is _____

(t) P4 down from B is _____

(u) M6 down from B♭ is _____

EXERCISE 22.5

Playing Intervals Above Tonic in the Major Scale

Using Figure 22.2 or Exercise 22.1a or b as a guide, play on the keyboard each interval above the tonic note in ascending order. Play in this manner from each tonic note in the *circle of fifths* for major keys. Name each interval as you play it.

EXERCISE 22.6

Playing Major and Perfect Intervals

The first note and the name of an interval are given. Play both notes of the interval at the keyboard.

CHAPTER TWENTY-THREE

INTERVALS
(continued)

**Minor Intervals
Diminished Intervals
Augmented Intervals
Modification of Intervals
Intervals Above Tonic Notes Other Than C
Intervals Above Notes Which Cannot Be Tonics of Major Scales
Analysis of All Types of Intervals**

In the previous chapter, we measured the distance of each note of the major scale from the tonic and obtained either major or perfect intervals. Three other types of intervals also exist in music; none of these is found as an interval above the tonic of the major scale. To measure these new intervals, each will be compared to the major and perfect intervals already studied. These new intervals are:

> minor (abbr. *m.* or *min.*)
> diminished (abbr. *dim.* or sometimes °)
> augmented (abbr. *aug.* or sometimes +)

Minor Intervals

A *minor* interval is one half-step smaller than a major interval. To emphasize this distinction, the word *small* is sometimes used in place of *minor* and the word *large* in place of *major*. For example, a *small* third is a *minor* third; a *large* third is a *major* third. Figure 23.1, column 3, shows that minor intervals are one half-step smaller than the major intervals of column 1.

Diminished Intervals

A *diminished* interval is one half-step smaller than a perfect or minor interval. See Figure 23.1 and compare column 4 with columns 2 and 3.

If a diminished interval is compared to a major interval, it is two half-steps (one whole-step) smaller. A major interval smaller by one half-step is minor; the minor interval smaller by one half-step is diminished. See Figure 23.1 and compare column 4 with column 1.

Augmented Intervals

An *augmented* interval is one half-step larger than a major or perfect interval. See Figure 23.1 and compare column 5 with columns 1 and 2.

In all, there are five adjectives employed in describing intervals: (1) *major,* (2) *perfect,* (3) *minor,* (4) *diminished,* and (5) *augmented.*

FIGURE 23.1. *Intervals Above C.*

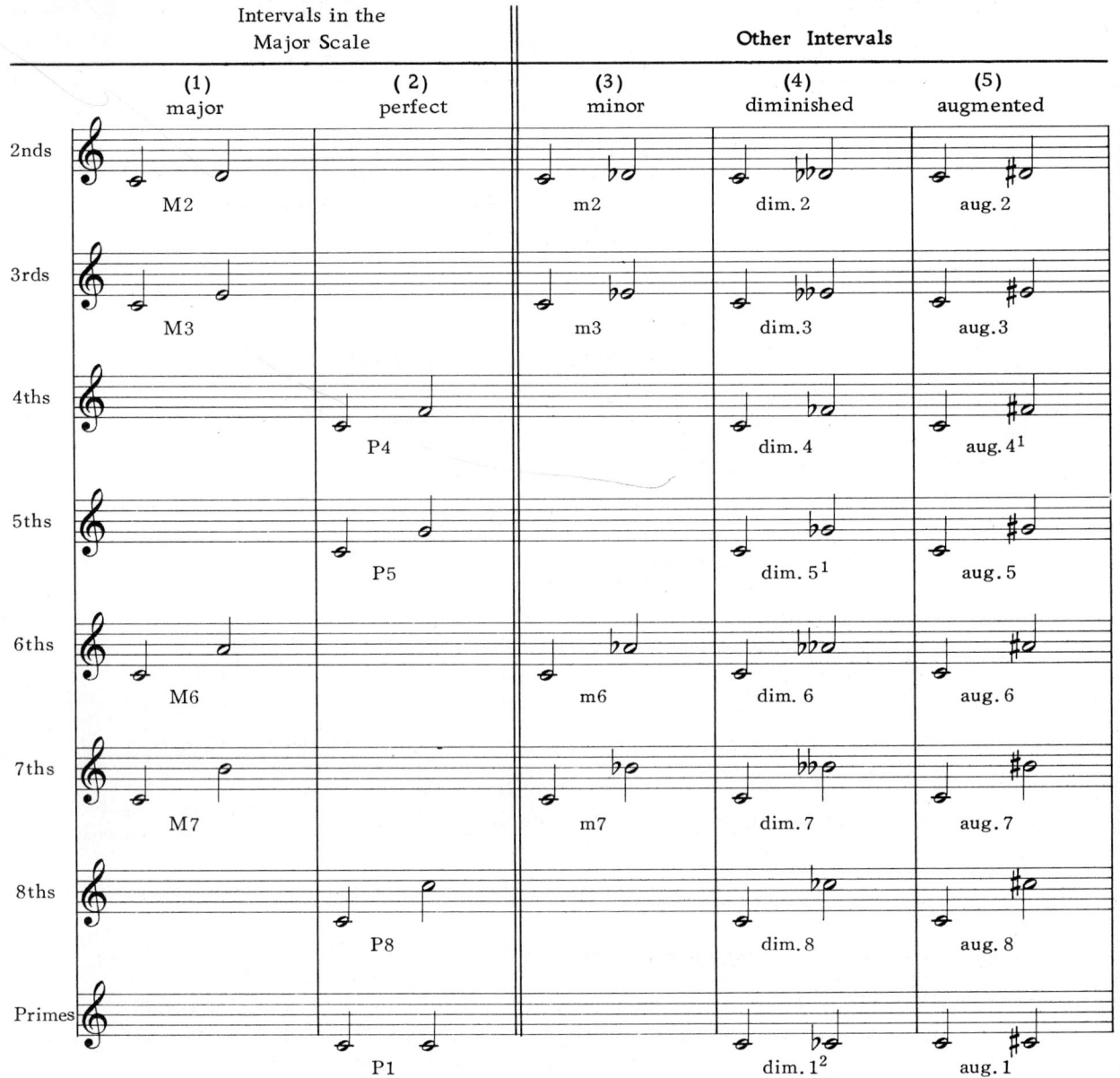

Modification of Intervals

In Figure 23.1, it can be seen that any type of interval (M, m, P, dim. or aug.) is a modification by one half-step of some other type of interval. This is shown in Figure 23.2.

---

[1] Also called *tritone*. The dim. 5 and aug. 4 each encompass three whole-steps and thus are enharmonic with each other.
[2] The second note of a dim. prime is lower than the first note.

FIGURE 23.2. *Modification of Intervals.*

Type of Interval Before	Modification		Type of Interval After
M	− ½ step	=	m
m	− ½ step	=	dim.
P	− ½ step	=	dim.
dim.	− ½ step	=	(doubly dim.³)
aug.	− ½ step	=	P or M
M	+ ½ step	=	aug.
m	+ ½ step	=	M
P	+ ½ step	=	aug.
dim.	+ ½ step	=	P or m
aug.	+ ½ step	=	(doubly aug.³)

An interval can be modified by applying the alteration to *either* the upper or lower note. For example, a P5 becomes a dim.5 by either lowering the upper note one half-step, *or* raising the lower note one half-step. In either case the distance between the two pitches is decreased.

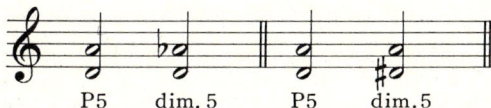

A P5 becomes an aug.5 by either raising the upper note one half-step or lowering the lower note one half-step.

Intervals Above Tonic Notes Other Than C

In Figure 23.1, using *c* as tonic and as the lower note of the interval, the higher note of every interval is natural (not sharp or flat); therefore, to create a minor or diminished interval above *c,* we used a flat-sign to lower the upper note, or, to create an augmented interval above *c,* we used a sharp-sign to raise the upper note. Scales other than *c* can be used as the basis of a table similar to Figure 23.1. In so doing, use of other notes as tonic will make necessary the use of other accidentals in columns 3, 4 and 5. The following procedures will be helpful:

(1) When the second note of the major or perfect interval carries a sharp, it is lowered by using the natural (♮) sign.

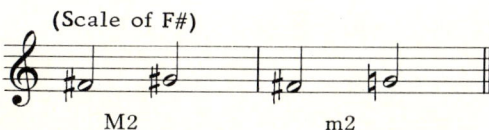

---

[3] Doubly diminished and doubly augmented intervals are uncommon in musical practice and will not be considered further in this text.

277

(2) When the second note of the major or perfect interval carries a flat, it is lowered by using the double flat (b♭).

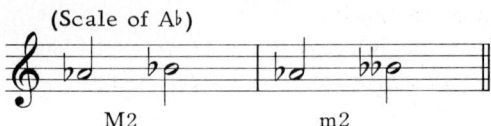

(3) When using scales with a key signature of four or more flats as tonic, some of the intervals in colum 4 (diminished) would require a "triple flat" (bbb), e.g., gb up to b bbb. This type of notation is impractical. If such an interval were needed in actual music (and this would be rare), it would be spelled enharmonically.

Intervals Above Notes Which Cannot Be Tonics of Major Scales

The fifteen major scales supply a total of fifteen tonic notes which can be used as a basis for locating intervals, as in Figure 23.1. Other notes, always preceded by ♯ or ♭, can also be used as the lower note of an interval. To find the second note of such a given interval,

1. temporarily substitute a natural sign (♮) for the given accidental,
2. find the interval above the natural note,
3. and replace the original accidental on the lower note, at the same time altering the upper note one half-step in the same direction.

Analysis of All Types of Intervals

To analyze, describe, or name any interval, procedures just learned will suffice. (1) *When the lower note is tonic of a major scale.* As established in Chapter Twenty-Two, assume the lower note to be 1 (tonic) and count the scale degrees to the upper note. If the upper note appears in the major scale it is either a *major* or *perfect* interval. If the upper note does not belong to the major scale, then it is a *minor*, a *diminished*, or an *augmented* interval according to its alteration (see Fig. 23.2. Modification of Intervals).

For example, consider the interval c up to e♭: c up to e would be a M3, therefore, c up to e♭, a decrease by a half-step, is a m3.

Analyze the interval c up to g♯: c up to g would be a P5; therefore, c up to g♯, an increase of a half-step, is an aug.5.

(2) *When the lower note is not the tonic of a major scale.* By changing the ♯ or ♭ of the lower note to natural ♮, we can easily find an interval based on the lower note as tonic of a major scale. By replacing the ♯ or ♭ and observing the increase or decrease in the size of the interval, according to Figure 23.2, the name of the original interval will become apparent. Consider the interval d♯ up to a: d natural up to a would be a P5; therefore, d♯ up to a, a decrease by a half-step, is a dim.5.

Consider f♭ up to b♭: since there is no scale of f♭, calculate the interval from f natural up to b♭, a P4; therefore, f♭ up to b♭, an increase by a half-step, is an aug.4.

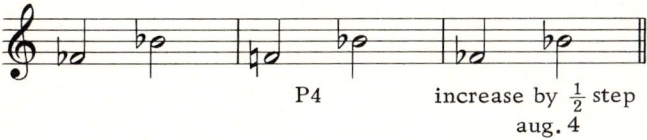

A few intervals may be more complex in their analysis:

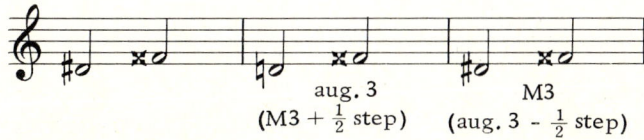

279

The student's power of reasoning, however, might supply a simpler solution: since *d* to *f♯* is a M3, then *d♯* to *f*𝄪, with both notes raised a half-step, is the same type of interval, a M3.

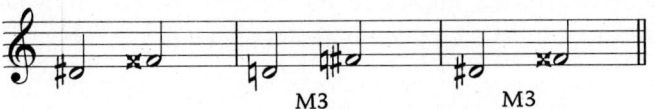

Enharmonic intervals are frequently obvious, especially when related to the keyboard. In fact, any diminished or augmented interval is enharmonic with some perfect, major, or minor interval, except the diminished fifth and the augmented fourth (tritone) which are enharmonic with each other. For example, *c* up to *g♯* is an aug.5 and *c* up to *a♭* is a m6; *g♯* and *a♭* are enharmonic and are the same key on the keyboard. Caution is due in this respect: proper spellings must be maintained according to the designation of the interval. It is wrong to say that *c* up to *g♯* is a m6 or that *c* up to *a♭* is an aug.5 even though the intervals are enharmonic.

FIGURE 23.3. *Enharmonic Intervals.*

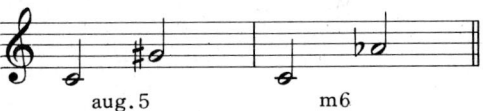

Calculation of specific intervals above certain pitches according to explanations and directions just supplied may seem to be unnecessarily complex both in theory and in application. In your subsequent study of harmony, you will find another approach to interval study based on the context of intervals in chords. Knowing their harmonic context will greatly simplify the writing or analysis of the more complex intervals.

Rapid identification and comprehension of intervals is one of the most important accomplishments in guaranteeing success in future work in theory and its application to performance practices. Therefore you will find that time spent in learning intervals by whatever method is time well spent.

NAME: Gary East

EXERCISE 23.1

Modification of Intervals

(a) Major to minor. Supply the second note of the minor interval as indicated. For this exercise, use a natural-sign ♮ if the second note is natural. Use half-notes.

(b) Minor to diminished. Supply the second note of each diminished interval as directed. Use half-notes.

NAME

(c) Perfect to diminished. Supply the second note of each diminished interval. Use half-notes.

(d) Major to augmented. Supply the second note of each augmented interval. Use half-notes.

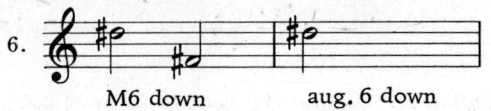
6. M6 down   aug. 6 down

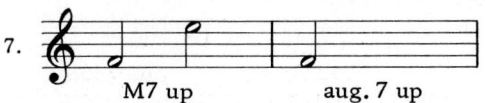
7. M7 up   aug. 7 up

8. M7 down   aug. 7 down

(e) Perfect to augmented. Supply the second note of each augmented interval. Use half-notes.

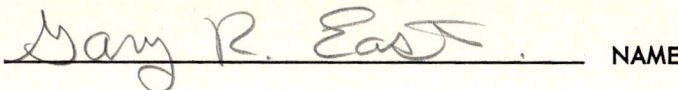
NAME

EXERCISE 23.2
Writing Minor, Diminished and Augmented Intervals Above C

Write on the staff the second note of each interval above *c*. Use half-notes.

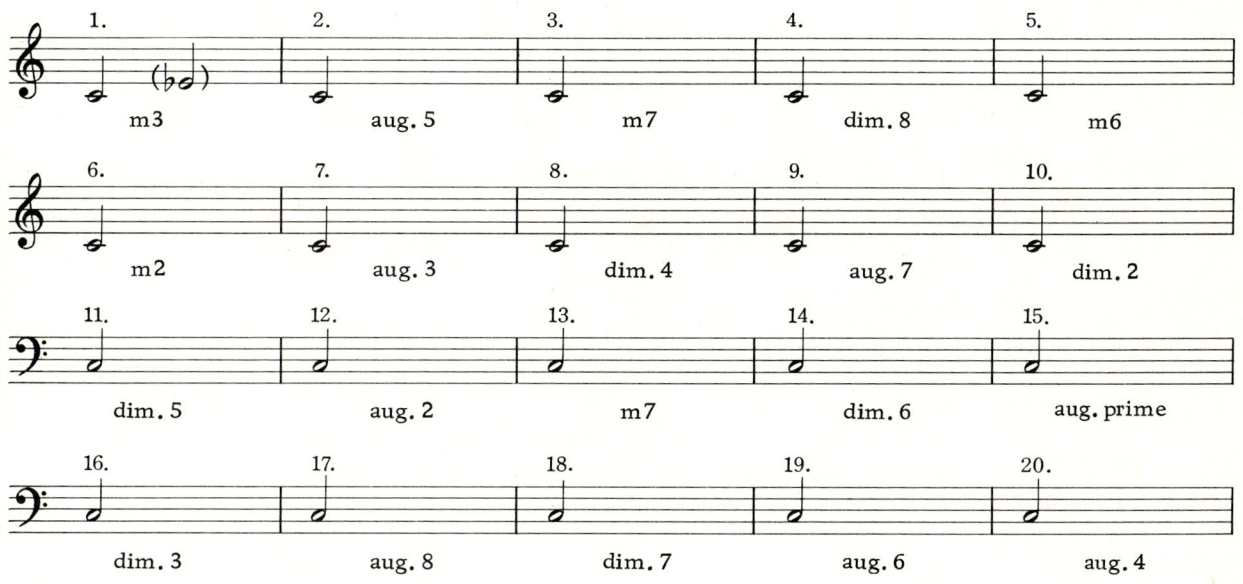

EXERCISE 23.3
Writing Minor, Diminished and Augmented Intervals Above Tonic Notes Other Than C

Write on the staff the second note of the ascending intervals. Use half-notes.

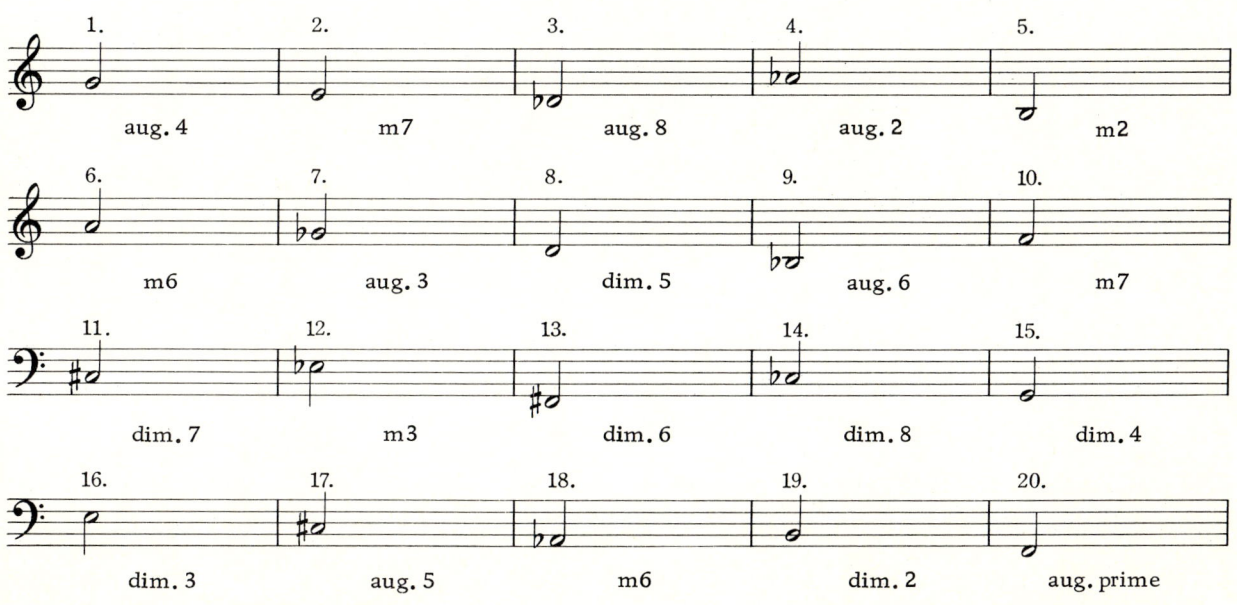

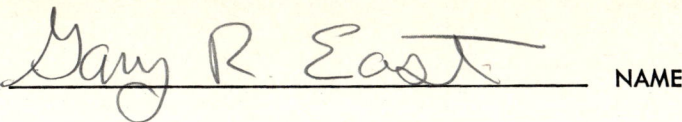

EXERCISE 23.4

Writing Intervals Above Notes Which Cannot Be Tonics of Major Scales

Write on the staff the second note of the ascending intervals. Use half-notes.

EXERCISE 23.5

Writing All Types of Intervals, Ascending and Descending

Write on the staff the second note of each interval. Use half-notes.

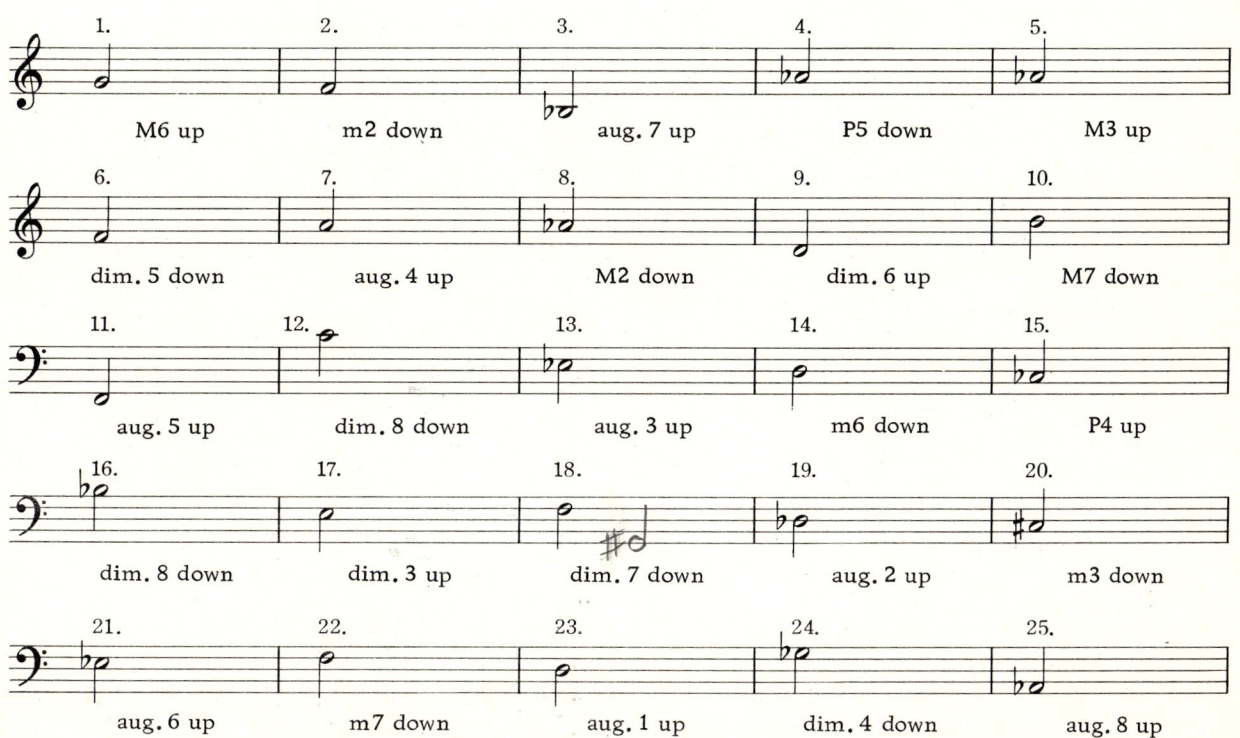

EXERCISE 23.6
Analyzing All Types of Intervals

Identify interval by name. Write abbreviation below each interval given.

EXERCISE 23.7

Spelling All Types of Intervals

Write the letter name of the second note of each interval given.

Example: m3 below E♭ is   C

(a) M3 above B is   _____

(b) Dim.5 below A♭ is   _____

(c) P8 above E♯ is   E♯

(d) m7 below G is   _____

(e) Aug.3 above G is   _____

(f) P4 below F♯ is   _____

(g) Dim.7 above F♯ is   _____

(h) P5 below D♯ is   _____

(i) M2 above G♭ is   _____

(j) M6 below C♯ is   _____

(k) Aug.8 above F♯ is   F𝄪

(l) M7 below E is   _____

(m) Aug.6 above B♭ is   _____

(n) m2 below C♯ is   _____

(o) m6 above D♯ is   _____

(p) Aug.5 below E is   _____

(q) Aug.1 above D♭ is   _____

(r) M3 below G is   _____

(s) Aug.4 above F is _____

(t) m6 below F♭ is _____

(u) Dim.4 above E♭ is _____

(v) m3 below A is _____

(w) Aug.2 above E is _____

(x) P5 below F♯ is _____

(y) Dim.3 above B is _____

EXERCISE 23.8
Playing All Types of Intervals

Play the intervals shown in Exercise 23.6. Name each interval as you play it.

EXERCISE 23.9
Playing All Types of Intervals

The first note and the name of an interval are given. Play both notes of the interval at the keyboard.

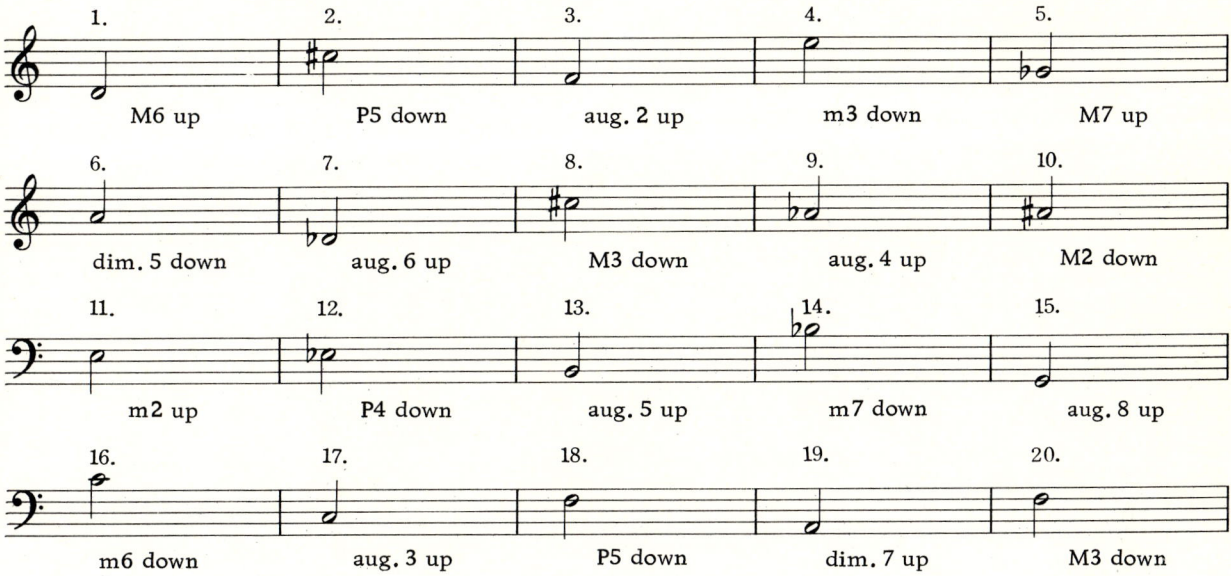

APPENDIX 2

THE CHROMATIC SCALE AND SYLLABLES

The chromatic scale is comprised entirely of half-steps. Between one note and its octave, there are twelve half-steps in the chromatic scale.

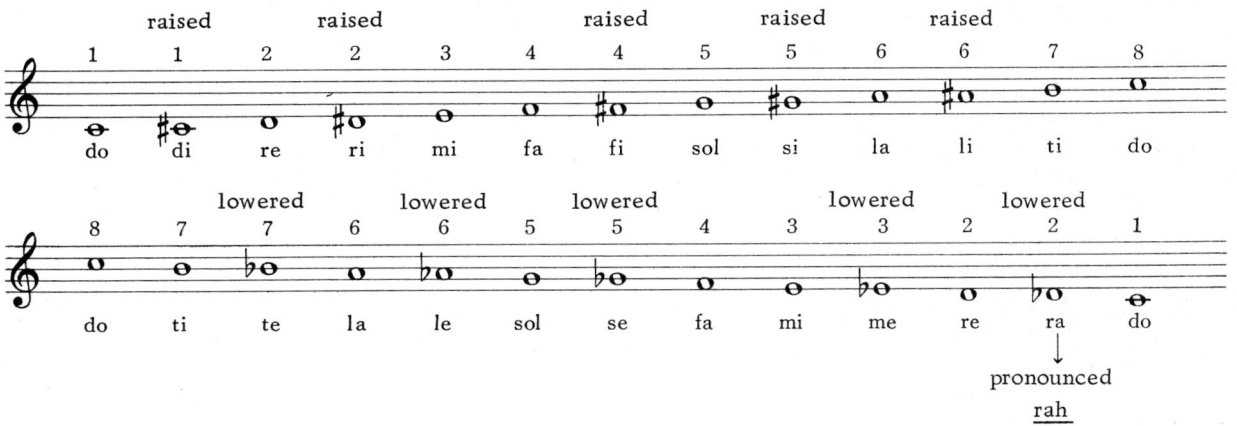

APPENDIX 3

FOREIGN WORDS AND MUSICAL TERMS

Most music commonly performed at the present time contains directions for performance, particularly in reference to tempo and dynamics. These directions are often found in the Italian language, a custom dating back to the seventeenth century. It was at that time that such markings were first added to the music score, and because of the prevalence of Italian music, these markings became standard in all languages.

In the late nineteenth century, composers began using directions from their native languages, such as French, German, and English, though the older Italian terms continue to be commonly used.

This list presents a selection of terms most frequently encountered in music, including all terms found in *Music for Sight Singing* (suggested in this text for supplementary exercises). Unless indicated otherwise, the language is Italian. Fr = French, Gr = German, L = Latin.

A

a, à (Fr) — by
accelerando — getting faster
adagietto — slightly faster than adagio
adagio — slow, leisurely
ad libitum (L) — at will (abbr. *ad lib.*)
agitato — agitated
al — to
all', alla — to the, at the, in the, in the style of
all' ottava — play an octave higher (when above the notes); play an octave lower (when below the notes)
all' unisono — play in unison
allargando — growing broader, slowing down with fuller tone (abbr. *allarg.*)
allegretto — moderately fast; slower than allegro
allegro — lively, fast
andante — moderately slow
andantino — slower than andante
animato — animated
animé (Fr) — animated
a piacere — freely
appassionato — with passion
assai — very
assez (Fr) — enough, rather
a tempo — return to original tempo after a change
attacca — begin next section at once
aussi (Fr) — as

B

ben — well
bien (Fr) — well, very
brio — vivacity, spirit, fire

C

cantabile — in a singing style
coda — end of piece
col, coll', colla, colle — with
comodo, commodo — comfortable tempo
con — with
crescendo — increasing in volume (abbr. *cresc.*)

D

da capo — from the beginning (abbr. *D.C.*)
dal segno — from the sign (abbr. *D.S.*)
declamato — in declamatory style
decrescendo — decreasing in volume (abbr. *decresc.*)
diminuendo — decreasing in volume (abbr. *dim.*)
dolce — soft
doppio — double
douce, doux (Fr.) — soft, sweet

E

einfach (G) — simple, plain
ernst (G) — earnest, serious
espressivo — expressive
et (Fr.) — and
etwas (G) — somewhat

F

feierlich (G) — solemn
fine — end
forte — loud (abbr. *f*)
forte-piano — loud, then immediately soft (abbr. *fp*)
fortissimo — very loud (abbr. *ff*)
forzando — with force (abbr. *fz*)
frisch (G) — brisk, lively
fröhlich (G) — glad, joyous
fuoco — fire

G

gai (Fr) — gay, brisk
gesangvoll (G) — in a singing style
giocoso — playful

giusto — correct
gracieusement (Fr) — graciously
gracieux (Fr) — gracious
grandioso — grand, pompous
grave — slow, ponderous
grazia — grace, elegance
grazioso — graceful
gut (G) — good, well

H

heimlich (G) — mysterious
herzlich (G) — heartily, affectionate

I

immer (G) — always
innig (G) — heartfelt, fervent
innigkeit (G) — deep emotion
istesso — same
istesso tempo — after a change of time signature, the value of either the measure or the beat note remains the same

J

joyeuse, joyeux (Fr) — joyous

K

klagend (G) — mourning
kurz (G) — short, crisp

L

langoureuse, langoureux (Fr) — languorous
langsam (G) — slow
langsamer (G) — slower
largamente — broadly
larghetto — not as slow as largo
largo — slow and broad, stately
lebhaft (G) — lively, animated
legato — smoothly connected
leger (Fr) — light
leggiero — light (abbr. *legg.*)
leicht (G) — light
leise (G) — soft
lent (Fr) — slow
lenteur (Fr) — slowness
lento — slow
liberamente — freely
lieblich (G) — with charm
l'istesso tempo — same as istesso tempo
lustig (G) — merry, gay

M

ma — but
mächtig (G) — powerful
maestoso — with majesty or dignity
malinconico — in a melancholy style
marcato — marked, emphatic
marcia — march
marziale — martial
mässig (G) — moderate
même (Fr) — same
meno — less
mesto — sad
mezzo — half (mezzo forte, *mf;* mezzo piano, *mp*)
misterioso — mysteriously
mit (G) — with
moderato — moderately
modéré (Fr) — moderately
molto — much, very
morendo — dying away
mosso — "moved"; (*meno mosso* — less rapid; *più mosso* — more rapid)
moto — motion
munter (G) — lively, animated

N

nicht (G) — not
non — not
non tanto — not so much
non troppo — not too much
nobilmente — with nobility

O

ossia — or
ottava — octave

P

parlando — singing in a speaking style
pas (Fr) — not
pas trop lent (Fr) — not too slow
pesante — heavy
peu (Fr) — little
peu à peu (Fr) — little by little
piano — soft (abbr. *p*)
pianissimo — very soft (abbr. *pp*)
più — more
plus (Fr) — more
poco — little
presto — fast, rapid
prima, primo — first

Q

quasi — as if, nearly (*andante quasi allegretto*)

R

rallentando — slowing down (abbr. *rall.*)
rasch (G) — quick
rinforzando — reinforcing; sudden increase in loudness for single tone, chord or passage. (abbr. *rfz*)
ritardando — slowing down (abbr. *rit.*)
rubato — perform freely
ruhig (G) — quiet

S

sanft (G) — soft
scherzando — playfully
sans (Fr) — without
schnell (G) — fast
secco — dry
segue — follows; next section follows immediately, or, continue in a similar manner
sehr (G) — very
semplice — simple
semplicemente — simply
sempre — always
senza — without
senza misure — without measure
sforzando — forcing; perform a single note or chord with sudden emphasis (abbr. *sfz*)
simile — similarly; continue in the same manner (abbr. *sim.*)
sostenuto — sustained
sotto — under
sotto voce — in an undertone, subdued volume
spirito — spirit
staccato — detached, separate
stark (G) — strong
stringendo — pressing onward
subito — suddenly

T

tant (Fr) — as much
tanto — so much
tempo giusto — correct tempo
tendrement (Fr) — tenderly
teneramente — tenderly
tenuto — held
tranquillo — tranquil
traurig (G) — sad
très (Fr) — very
triste (It., Fr.) — sad
trop (Fr) — too much
troppo — too much

U

un, uno — one, an, a
una corde — one string; on the piano, *use soft pedal* (abbr. *u.c.*)
unisono — unison
un peu (*Fr*) — a little

V

vif (*Fr*) — lively
vite (*Fr*) — quick
vivace — very fast
vivo — lively

Z

zart (*G*) — tender, delicate
ziemlich (*G*) — somewhat, rather

INDEX

A

Accidental, 22
  use of, 188
Aeolian mode, 193
All' ottava, 40
Anacrusis, 101
Augmented intervals, 276
Augmented second, 195, 249, 276

B

Background of beats, 54
Bar-lines, 82
Bass clef, 2
Beam, 64, 113
Beat, 47
  compound, 53
  conductor's, 93
  division, 53
  downbeat, 94
  groupings, 49
  notation, 75
  simple, 53
  upbeat, 94
Beethoven, Ludwig van, 49
Bind, 105
Black keys, 23

C

Chord, 261
Circle of fifths, 173
  major keys, 175
  minor keys, 236
Clef, 2
  bass, 2
  F clef, 2
  G clef, 2
  transposing treble, 3
  treble, 2
Common time, 77

Compound beat, 54
  background, 54
  division, 54
  notation, 79
Compound intervals, 263
Compound meter signature, 79
Conductor's beat, 93
Cut time, 77 fn

D

Da capo (D.C.), 103
Dal segno (D.S.), 103
D.C., 103
Dictation, rhythmic, 113, 115
Diminished intervals, 276
Division of beats, 53
  compound, 54
  notation, 75
  simple, 54
Dominant, 149, 214
Dorian mode, 193
Dot, 79
Dotted note, 79
Dotted rest, 114
Double bar, 102
Double flat, 22, 187
Double sharp, 22, 187
Doubly augmented intervals, 277
Doubly diminished intervals, 277
Downbeat, 94
D.S., 103
Duration, 47

E

Eleven-line staff, 4
Ending, 103
Enharmonic, 24
  interval, 280
  key, 175, 236

309

F

F clef, 2
Fifth, perfect, 173, 262
Fine, 103
First ending, 103
Flag, 3, 64
Flat, 22
Fourth, perfect, 262

G

G clef, 2
Grand staff, 4
Great staff, 4
Grouping of beats, 49

H

Half-step, 21
Handel, George F., 171
Harmonic minor scale, 190, 195
Haydn, Franz Joseph, 67
Hook, 64

I

Interval, 21
  augmented, 275
  compound, 263
  definition, 21, 261
  diminished, 275
  doubly augmented, 277
  doubly diminished, 277
  enharmonic, 280
  fifth, perfect, 173, 262
  fourth, perfect, 262
  half-step, 21
  harmonic, 261
  melodic, 261
  minor, 275
  octave, 3, 39
    perfect, 262
  prime, perfect, 262
  quality, 262
  quantity, 262
  second, augmented, 195, 249, 276
  second, major, 262
  second, minor, 276
  seventh, major, 262
  seventh, minor, 276
  simple, 263
  sixth, major, 262
  sixth, minor, 276
  third, major, 262
  third, minor, 249, 276

Interval (Cont.):
  tritone, 276
  unison, 262
  whole-step, 21, 22
Ionian mode, 193

K

K., 5
Key, 172
Keyboard, 19
Keynote, 172
Keys:
  enharmonic, 175, 236
  parallel, 251
  relative, 249
Key signature:
  major, 171
  minor, 235
Köchel, Ludwig von, 5

L

Leading tone, 150, 214
Ledger (leger) lines, 2
Ligature, 64
Locrian mode, 193
Lydian mode, 193

M

Major scale, 137
Major second, 262
Major seventh, 262
Major sixth, 262
Major third, 262
Mälzel, Johann N., 49
Measure, 82
Mediant, 150, 214
Melodic minor scale, 191, 195
Meter, 54, 101
Meter signature, 76
  compound, 79
  simple, 76
Metronome, 49
Middle C, 4, 20
Minor scales, 189
Minor third, 249, 276
Mixolydian mode, 193
M.M., 49
Mode, 193
Mozart, Wolfgang Amadeus, 5
Musica ficta, 193
Musical alphabet, 1

N

Natural minor scale, 189
Natural sign, 22, 188
Note, 3, 63
   construction, 63
   dotted, 79
Note-head, 3 fn, 63

O

Octave, 3, 39
   perfect, 262
Octave registers, 39
Opus, 5

P

Parallel keys, 251
Perfect fifth, 173, 262
Perfect fourth, 262
Perfect octave, 262
Perfect prime, 262
Phrygian mode, 193
Piano keyboard, 19
   names of black keys, 23
   names of white keys, 20
Piano staff, 4
Pitch, 1
Prime, perfect, 262
Pulsation, 47
Pure minor scale, 189

Q

Quality of interval, 262
Quantity of interval, 262

R

Raised submediant, 213
Relative keys, 249
Repeat sign, 102
Rest, 66
   dotted, 114
   notation, 114
Rhythm, 101
Rhythmic dictation, 113
Rhythmic reading, 104
Rhythmic transcription, 117

S

Scale:
   keyboard fingerings, 299
   major, 137
   minor, harmonic, 190, 195
   minor, melodic, 191, 195
   minor, natural, 189
   minor, pure, 189
Scale degree, 149
   names, major, 149
   names, minor, 214
Scales, history, 192
Scale step, 149
Scale tone, 149
Scherchen, Herman, 93
Second, augmented, 195, 249, 276
Second, major, 262
Second ending, 103
Seventh, major, 262
Seventh, minor, 276
Sharp, 22
Signature:
   key, major, 172
   key, minor, 235
   meter, 76
   time, 76
Simple beat, 53
   background, 54
   division, 54
   notation, 75
Simple intervals, 263
Simple meter signature, 76
Sixth, major, 262
Sixth, minor, 276
Solfeggio, 168
Solmization, 168
Staff, staves, 1
   eleven-line, 4
   grand, 4
   great, 4
   piano, 4
Staves, 1
Stem, 3, 63
Subdominant, 149, 214
Submediant, 150, 214
Subtonic, 150, 213, 214
Supertonic, 150, 214
Syllables:
   major scale, 168
   minor scale, 231

T

Tempo, tempi, 49
Third, major, 262
Third, minor, 249, 276

Tie, 105
Time signature (*see also* Meter signature), 76
Tonic, 149, 214
Tonic sol-fa, 168
Transcription, rhythmic, 117
Transposing treble clef, 3
Treble clef, 2
Tremolo, 67
Tritone, 276

U

Unison, 262
Upbeat, 94

W

White keys, 20
Whole-step, 21, 22